What Works in Therapeutic Prisons

M000105052

Also by Jennifer Brown

THE FUTURE OF POLICING (*ed.*)

HANDBOOK OF SEXUAL VIOLENCE (*co-edited with S.L. Walklate*)

CAMBRIDGE HANDBOOK OF FORENSIC PSYCHOLOGY (*co-edited with E.A. Campbell*)

RAPE: Challenging Contemporary Thinking (*co-edited with M.A.H. Horvath*)

What Works in Therapeutic Prisons

Evaluating Psychological Change in Dovegate Therapeutic Community

Jennifer Brown
London School of Economics, UK

Sarah Miller
Bond University, Australia

Sara Northey
Sussex Partnerships Secure and Forensic Services, UK

Darragh O'Neill
University College London, UK

© Jennifer Brown, Sarah Miller, Sara Northey and Darragh O'Neill 2014
Foreword © Roland Woodward 2014

All rights reserved. No reproduction, copy or transmission of this
publication may be made without written permission.

No portion of this publication may be reproduced, copied or transmitted
save with written permission or in accordance with the provisions of the
Copyright, Designs and Patents Act 1988, or under the terms of any licence
permitting limited copying issued by the Copyright Licensing Agency,
Saffron House, 6–10 Kirby Street, London EC1N 8TS.

Any person who does any unauthorized act in relation to this publication
may be liable to criminal prosecution and civil claims for damages.

The authors have asserted their rights to be identified as the authors of this
work in accordance with the Copyright, Designs and Patents Act 1988.

First published 2014 by
PALGRAVE MACMILLAN

Palgrave Macmillan in the UK is an imprint of Macmillan Publishers Limited,
registered in England, company number 785998, of Houndmills, Basingstoke,
Hampshire RG21 6XS.

Palgrave Macmillan in the US is a division of St Martin's Press LLC,
175 Fifth Avenue, New York, NY 10010.

Palgrave Macmillan is the global academic imprint of the above companies
and has companies and representatives throughout the world.

Palgrave® and Macmillan® are registered trademarks in the United States,
the United Kingdom, Europe and other countries.

ISBN 978–1–137–30619–7 hardback
ISBN 978–1–137–30620–3 paperback

This book is printed on paper suitable for recycling and made from fully
managed and sustained forest sources. Logging, pulping and manufacturing
processes are expected to conform to the environmental regulations of the
country of origin.

A catalogue record for this book is available from the British Library.

A catalog record for this book is available from the Library of Congress.

Contents

Figures, Tables and Boxes

Figures

Tables

Chapter Appendices

Boxes

Foreword

Roland Woodward

Is research the observation that kills or saves Schrödinger's cat?

The seven-year research contract that was undertaken at HMP Dovegate Therapeutic Community (TC) by Jennifer Brown and her team from Surrey University is a landmark undertaking in the British prison system. The nature and the variety of approaches, coupled with the integration of the work into the fabric of the new TC, afforded a real opportunity to explore the nature of change within this unique form of therapy. Jennifer and her team have provided everyone interested in this work with new ideas and evidence about how men change in prison.

Within this book the authors are rigorous in their description and review of the research related to adult democratic TCs in the English prison system. The major reviews and descriptions of TCs and the research related to them are reviewed and referenced so that the reader is easily directed to the wealth of information that the researchers considered.

They paint a clear picture of the nature and intentions of prison-based TCs that is easily accessible to those who have not previously experienced them.

Alongside the reviews of previous literature, the researchers have woven into their account the way in which the changing landscape of Dovegate TC brought different views about what the research was dealing with. The change of Director of Therapy brought different perceptions and constructions of what the TC was about and what it should aspire to be. This was also true for the changing management of the prison of which the TC was part. Like most things, this research was a journey for all concerned, and this book reflects that process.

This foreword is a description of the way in which the research came into being and how the questions that should be asked came to be asked within the context of the time that HMP Dovegate TC was being planned and opened.

It is a strange and somewhat disconcerting experience to read within the chapters of this book the content of interviews given many years ago and to be reminded of the aspirations, anxieties and motivations that were held as Dovegate TC started out. Reading how those elements were received and interpreted in the thought behind the research was a strange experience, and reminded me that each of us is a construction in others' minds. What people choose to do with you in their own heads, and how that affects their own actions, is a process that most of the time is beyond knowing or control. It is also true that people's constructions are written into histories. There are now accounts of the development of HMP Dovegate and its TC, along with commentary on the people involved, which are exemplars of how this constructive process works. Only if time is taken to check out the perceptions and carry out the process of receiving and giving feedback, can a clear picture emerge of who you are inside someone else's head. In many ways this process is a description of intimacy, but, more importantly, it is a description of how we construct our own universe, people it and then relate to it. In essence, this is what a TC does for its residents and staff. They are engaged in the search for meaning in their constructed universe and the way that their universe allows them to live alongside others in the world. Underpinning this, of course, is the constant search for meaning: both why they have constructed a universe and what it is for.

The TC provides a psychological environment designed to enable people to ask these questions. It is a psychosocial search engine for meaning in which people are actively looking to change. In prison the task goes beyond the intellectual. It is not about just constructing a new understanding and an adapted personal universe; it is about changing the way the person relates and behaves in the world in order to avoid conflict with the criminal justice system. The most important translation of this used by the staff and residents of the TC was: to live a life that does not create any more victims.

The question for the researchers is: "What questions best unlock this process for the people in it?"

I think most people are familiar with the problem posed by Schrödinger's cat: the possibility that a cat in a box in a certain set of circumstances can be thought of as being both dead and alive until observation confirms that it is either one or the other. People in therapy may be thought of as being both changed and unchanged at the same time. It is not until some form of observation is made that it is possible to state whether they have changed or not. However, as noted earlier, people construct their universe and the people in it, and for this reason it seems to me that the relational interpretation makes sense.

In the case of the cat in the box, if you make no fundamental distinction between the human experimenter, the cat and the apparatus, or between animate and inanimate systems, all are quantum systems governed by the same rules, and all may be considered "observers". The relational interpretation allows that different observers can give different accounts of the same series of events, depending on the information they have about the system. The cat can be considered an observer of the apparatus; meanwhile, the experimenter can be considered another observer of the system in the box (the cat plus the apparatus). Before the box is opened, the cat, by nature of its being alive or dead, has information about the state of the apparatus (things in the box have either changed or not changed); but the experimenter does not have information about the state of the box contents. In this way, the two observers simultaneously have different accounts of the situation. To the cat, the state of the apparatus may have appeared to "collapse"; to the experimenter, the contents of the box appear to be in superposition (the cat possibly being and not being alive at the same time). Not until the box is opened, and both observers have the same information about what happened, do both system states appear to "collapse" into the same definite result, a cat that is either alive or dead.

Not until the people who constitute the TC and the researchers have the same information will it be possible to establish whether change has taken place and what the possible mechanisms for that change might be.

The challenge was, therefore, to conduct research that enabled all the people involved in the TC and the research team access to the same information and for them to be able to recognise change and, if possible, the mechanisms of change.

As the first Director of Therapy for Dovegate TC, it fell to me to draw up the tender documents for the research project that had been written into the contract under which Premier Prisons had won the right to design, construct, manage and finance the new 600-bed prison in Staffordshire. It had been agreed at the very early stages of the Prison Service deciding to include a TC in the new prison that an independent research project should be imbedded in the contract. This had been influenced by the publication of the study of HMP Grendon by Genders and Player in 1995, and the fact that one of the authors had been an advisor to the Prison Service in drawing up the tender specification for the contract. There was also a growing body of research from prison TCs, mostly HMP Grendon, that was showing a reduction in reconviction rates for those men who had completed therapy in a TC. There had been early indications in 1971 and 1973, when George and Newton had reported reductions; however, Cullen's findings in 1993 started a fresh interest in reconviction, with papers by Newton and Thornton in 1994, Cullen in 1994, Marshall in 1997 and Jones in 1988, all indicating reduction in reconviction for TC residents. Against this background, it had been argued that continuing research was required and that a new purpose-built TC would provide an ideal opportunity to test the model and any modifications that were to be made.

TCs had become a focus for some of the wider discussions about research methods for psychosocial interventions, in particular the relevance of randomised controlled trials (RCTs). In 2005, in his Maxwell Jones Memorial Lecture, Nick Manning noted the continuing difficulties that the methodological debates created for TCs and also demonstrated that the social and political context into which evidence is put affects whether or not evidence is accepted. In part, this echoes Tom Main's classic paper of 1966 ("Knowledge, learning and freedom from thought"), republished as Main (1990), in which he argues that as knowledge becomes integrated into our personal universe it acquires emotional attachment. The acceptance of new knowledge can, therefore, be problematic, or, as Main puts it, "The reception of new knowledge thus often involves loving or aggressive impulses, feelings as well as intellect."

So, in making the decision to include an independent research contract as part of the creation of Dovegate TC, what had been opened were the research agendas of those involved and the processes by which they might conflict.

The initial view was that there was a good opportunity to replicate the Grendon study, in part to confirm the previous studies and in part to look for similar social processes. My own inclination was to avoid this and to think anew about what opportunities a new TC with all its innovations and published rationale could offer. This was also a golden moment when research could become truly integrated into the living system that was to be the TC.

Prisons, historically, were not good at tolerating the intrusion of researchers and the questions they asked. Researchers were apt to be seen as liabilities that would cause problems operationally and were likely to come up with uncomfortable conclusions. The disappearance of one or some of the research population due to a whole range of prison-related issues did not only make it difficult for researchers to plan and complete data collection; it often raised more interesting questions about the culture and the norms of prison life. There is a cultural paranoia and distrust in prisons of almost anyone who comes into the prison with a research brief. This, I would suggest, has diminished over the years due to the influence of modernising the Prison Service and the changing cultural and legal environment that has evolved from the mid-1970s. Reading through various publications, such as Cohen and Taylor's *Prison Secrets* (1976), Fitzgerald and Sim's *British Prisons* (1979), Liebling and Price's *The Prison Officer* (2001) and Crawley's *Doing Prison Work* (2004), it is clear that prison work has become more accessible during this time and more carefully considered. This is especially true of the emotional components of prison life for both staff and residents, as more emphasis is placed on the nature of the containment relationship than the punishment and maintenance of power.

There is, though, still a wariness of research, as it implies access to areas that were either physically or emotionally out of bounds to anyone other than staff.

The task, as I saw it, was to integrate the research into the life of the TC, and that this should be done as early as possible. The key word had to be "openness". In order for the researchers to do their work properly and to apply their skills to maximum effect, it was going to be necessary to allow them open access and ensure that everything that we did in the TC should be transparent and open to question. If we were confident that we had designed a TC based on the best evidence that we had at the time, and had written a detailed theory and practice manual, then we should be confident enough and eager for people to examine our work and help us understand and illuminate the things that worked well and those that did not. Like the men who came to Dovegate willing to change, we too had the obligation to learn and grow.

So, like many things about the start of Dovegate, it was relatively easy to establish the principles of the research. The researchers, whoever they were, would have a central office with the resources they needed and they would have keys like other staff. They would have access to the communities and they would have access to staff and residents. The research team would have the opportunity to have input into the assessment process of new residents to enable them to track people through the whole process, and they would have the opportunity to suggest amendments to our procedures once they started to gather data.

What was also clear was that, by the nature of the TC, the research team would recognise the need to do the work collaboratively with the men. In modern parlance, the service users needed to be involved in the process of design and delivery of the research project. These men were to become experts by experience and had a lot to offer the process. This also reflects the TC ethos that things happen by consensus and democratic process, not by enforcement of a rigid set of rules.

In thinking about these issues whilst drafting the tender documents, we began to get an idea of what criteria we might look for in the research proposals that would be submitted. We would certainly be looking for teams that were proposing high levels of resident participation and collaboration.

This still left us with the issue of what the questions should be.

The Grendon study by Genders and Player (1995) had concentrated on the social processes of the TC and the outcomes as reflected by the psychometric testing that had been part of the Grendon process for some time. The use of participant observation was a major method used, amongst others, to draw data from the day-to-day functioning of the community. What was achieved was a detailed description of the social processes of the community and the construction of a model of change based on the research observations. There were also some indications of what psychometric measures appeared to change as a result of time being spent in the TC. All of the outcomes and the suggested processes were useful in focusing attention on the development model of cognition and the phases of engagement with the TC.

I was confident that the Dovegate TC would contain the same, or very similar, social processes, as the core components of the therapy would be the same as Grendon's and other TCs before them. It seemed to me that, as the same underlying rationale and framework of the group therapy would also be using Yalom's (1995) model of group therapy, there was a need to look beyond a social explanation. As a psychologist, I was interested in how each of the men came to the point where they understood what it meant to change and how that could occur.

It had been a common observation amongst TC workers that people appeared to suddenly "get it". There were times when there appeared to be dramatic shifts in people's comprehension of the process that they were in and their understanding of the world. In essence, the universe that they had built, lived in and related to changed, and changed dramatically. It was also a common observation that this "getting it" was unpredictable, in that it could occur at almost any time in a person's stay in a TC. Furthermore, it appeared to happen in response to a bewildering number of events, interactions or stimuli, such that it seemed to take the person and those around them by surprise. This shift in the way in which the person changed their construction of the world seemed to be a crucial element of change. It is true that not everyone in a TC had this experience as a sudden revelation; many people changed gradually as they assimilated more and more information about possible alternative explanations for why things happened the way they did. However, there appeared to be a point at which there was a distinctive shift, almost like a Kuhnian paradigm shift. It seemed to me that this observed phenomenon needed to be investigated, first to confirm that it actually happened and was not a psychological urban myth, and second, assuming it did exist, to understand what was actually happening.

Focusing on this element of experience brought the individual's experience to the forefront of the research and meant that what was important for the individual to change became a primary focus.

It is true that the work by Cullen (1993) and others on the reconviction rates at HMP Grendon had added weight to the argument to build a new purpose-built TC prison. It is also my belief that one of the first questions to be asked would be "What difference to the reconviction rate will it make?" If sending people to prison is meant to stop them reoffending, then what effect will going to a TC have? Tax-payers are entitled to ask whether their money is being spent well, and in the case of prison that means less crime by those who are released from prison. The effect of the TC on reconviction had to be in the research contract. There are real problems with the concept of reconviction as an outcome measure for TCs in prison. There is the argument that reconviction is a crude all-or-nothing measure and takes little or no account of the severity of any new convictions. Nor can it take into account crimes committed that are not detected. It is also difficult to determine how much of an effect being in a TC may have alongside all the other experiences that a person may have during a prison sentence, including other offender courses. Despite these difficulties, there is evidence that reconviction rates can be ascertained and that variables such as the time spent in therapy can be shown to affect reconviction. Lawrence Jones's work demonstrating the relationship between therapy time and reconviction rates is a good example of how this work can be done. The challenge, therefore, was for whoever won the contract to explore this element and be able to follow people up once they left Dovegate TC.

Genders, in her 2002 paper "Legitimacy, accountability and private prisons", examines the issues around outcome measures as accountability measures, but also notes in passing that, due to the contractual nature of the private prison, money ring-fenced for research cannot be hived off for other things, which meant that the Dovegate research was likely to be more secure and therefore have time to overcome some of the problems inherent in this type of research.

Finally, I was clear that I wanted to leave space for innovation. In designing the TC we had departed from the Grendon model and the traditional prison model that split clinicians and discipline staff into two distinct groups. At Dovegate TC we all wore uniform and we all trained as prison custody officers. There was no resident "work" beyond maintaining the environment, but there was work-related education. Clinical staff had operational responsibility and discipline staff had equal therapy roles. These kinds of differences would throw up unexpected dynamics, and I wanted a research team that could pick these up and be able to incorporate them into their research programme. Any team that was going to come in to the TC was going to be creative and flexible.

The tender process was something new to me, and I was very grateful for the expert assistance that Ron Blackburn provided throughout the whole process. The rigours of receiving and reviewing non-identifiable bids were a long and demanding task. As always, there were some really good and exciting ideas mixed in with other notions that seemed not to be relevant. Eventually we invited a number of the bidders to present their proposals.

It is a strange experience to be presented to by previous colleagues and to try and keep an objective focus on the content of what is being proposed. At the end of the process, Jennifer Brown and her team were awarded the contract. For my part, I was thrilled at the board's choice, as it seemed to me that there was a real commitment to involving the residents and staff. The fact that they had thought about how they could integrate into the community process and were open to the residents and staff generating ideas gave a strong message that they had a clear idea of what it meant to work transparently and co-operatively.

The team came in and gently but assuredly built close and productive relationships with the staff team and the residents, recruiting them into the process of research and feeding back to them the results as they became available. Each quarter the team provided me with a report so that I could update the company's managers. It took very little time for the research team to become part of the community, accepted across the board and respected for their work.

I left before the research came to a conclusion, so this book provides for me a view of something that I helped create and that I could never have had without them. It is for me a valuable source of information with which to adjust my own construction of Dovegate TC and the work that it did.

Did observation kill or save Schrödinger's cat? It would appear, as in so many situations with humans trying to understand and change, that some did, some did not and for some it is difficult to tell.

For those interested in how individuals' constructions of the world and people affect the work they do and the stances they take, I offer this as my view, according to which I worked in creating Dovegate TC and the research programme that was undertaken.

"Man simply is. Not that he is simply what he conceives himself to be but he is what he wills, and as he conceives himself after already existing – as he wills to be after that leap into existence. Man is nothing else but that which he makes of himself"

Jean-Paul Sartre

References

Cohen, S., & Taylor, L. (1976). *Prison Secrets*. London: Pluto Press.

Crawley, E. (2004). *Doing Prison Work*. Cullompton: Willan Publishing.

Cullen, E. (1993). The Grendon reconviction study, part 1. *Prison Service Journal*, 90, 35–37.

Cullen, E. (1994). Grendon: the therapeutic prison that works. *Journal of Therapeutic Communities*, 15, 307–311.

Fitzgerald, M., & Sim, J. (1979). *British Prisons*. Oxford: Blackwell.

Genders, E., & Player, E. (1995). *Grendon: A Study of a Therapeutic Prison*. Oxford: Clarendon Press.

Genders, E. (2002). Legitimacy, accountability and private prisons. *Punishment and Society*, 4, 285–303.

George, R. (1971). *Grendon Follow Up 1967–68*. Grendon: Psychology Unit Series. Report No. 47.

Jones, L. (1988). *The Hospital Annexe. A Preliminary Evaluation*. London: Directorate of Psychological Services Series II Report. Prison Service, Home Office.

Kuhn, T.S. (1962). *The Structure of Scientific Revolutions*. Chicago: University of Chicago Press.

Leibling, A., & Price, D. (2001). *The Prison Officer*. Hook, Hants: Waterside Press.

Main, T. (1990). Knowledge, learning, and freedom from thought. *Psychoanalytic Psychotherapy*, 5, 59–78.

Manning, N. (2005). Does the therapeutic community work? The politics of knowledge. *Therapeutic Communities*, 26, 385–396.

Marshall, P. (1996). The Grendon Reconviction Study. Part II. Unpublished report from the Home Office Research &Statistics Directorate.

Newton, M. (1973). *Reconviction after Treatment at Grendon*. CP Report Series B, No.1. London: Prison Service, Home Office.

Newton, M. & Thornton, D. (1994). *Grendon Reconviction Study, Part 1 update*. Unpublished internal communication.

Sartre, J.P. (1948). *Existentialism and Humanism*. London: Methuen.

Yalom, I. (1995). *The Theory and Practice of Group Psychotherapy*. Fourth edition. New York: Basic Books.

Acknowledgements

We wish to acknowledge our appreciation to Premier Prisons for providing the funding for this research. We were totally reliant on the participation and co-operation of the resident members both staff and inmates, and the graduates of HMP Dovegate Therapeutic Community. We wish to thank you all for sharing your experiences and contributing to a greater understanding of how therapeutic communities in prison work.

We are extremely grateful to Roland Woodward, who was the first director of therapy and instrumental in shaping the research as well as creating the ethos of the Dovegate Therapeutic Community. We are also grateful to Roland's successors, David Lynes and Ray Duckworth, and to all the staff members at HMP Dovegate. Very special thanks go to "Jewels" Cooper for her unfailing generosity and good humour in facilitating our many requests for help.

There have been numerous researchers associated with the project. The original team comprised Jennifer Brown, Kate Fritzon, Sarah Miller and Carly Sees. Other research staff associated with the project include Lorna Christoforo, Caroline Di Franco, Louise Harsent, Darren Hollett, Sara Houston, Lisa Lewis, Cassie Philpin, Gerda Speller and Rosemary Simmonds as well as Surrey University master's and doctoral students Amelie Bobsien, Krystian Burchnell, Sarah Burdett, Emily Cahalane, Sarah Frith, Paul Lackman, Lucy Neville, Sara Northey, Darragh O'Neill, Alex Scott, Peter Thompson and Nicola Vallice. Their combined efforts greatly contributed to the thinking, data collection and analysis. All are appreciated for their ideas, energy and enthusiasm. We particularly thank Rosemary Simmonds who undertook most of the post-TC interviews, which involved many miles of travel to visit ex-TC residents in the various prison establishments around the country, a task which she tackled with dedication and guardianship of the integrity of the data.

Our external advisors, Derek Perkins, Sean Hammond, Yvonne Shell, Adrian Needs and Fiona Warren, were generous with their advice and offered us a sounding board and technical assistance for which we are extremely grateful.

We are also grateful to the anonymous referees who gave us constructive feedback which has helped us to streamline the narrative and hopefully make the book more accessible.

The responsibility for the contents of the book and any of its shortcomings remains with us, the authors.

About the Authors

Jennifer Brown is currently a visiting professor and co-director of the Mannheim Centre for Criminology at the London School of Economics. She co-directed the early stages of the Dovegate project with Katarina Fritzon until Katarina moved to Bond University, Australia, when Jennifer took overall control. She is a chartered forensic and a chartered occupational psychologist. Her research interests include aspects of occupational culture and stress within the criminal justice system, and she has a particular interest in mixed research methods. She has edited a number of books in the area of forensic psychology, including the *Handbook on Sexual Violence* (with Sandra Walklate) and the *Cambridge Handbook of Forensic Psychology* (with the late Elizabeth Campbell).

Sarah Miller is a chartered psychologist and registered forensic psychologist. She is currently living and working in Australia, and has recently commenced a PhD at Bond University in Queensland, examining risk and protective factors for deliberate fire-setting, under the supervision of Katarina Fritzon and Rebekah Doley. Aside from fire-setting, her research interests include domestic violence and offender treatment and its evaluation.

Sara Northey is a chartered psychologist, currently working for Sussex Partnerships Secure and Forensic Services at the Hellingly Centre medium secure unit. She is a trained DBT therapist and has experience of working with males and females in secure settings, in addition to working with Child and Adolescent Mental Health Services at The Priory – Ticehurst House. Her research focuses on the treatment of personality disorder, and she was awarded her PhD from the University of Surrey in 2012.

Darragh O'Neill is currently undertaking audit research into the National Health Service and is based in the School of Life and Medical Sciences at University College London. He completed his doctorate in psychology at the University of Surrey in 2011, examining behavioural change in therapeutic community residents through the lens of interpersonal theory. He has previously conducted research into a number of domains of forensic psychology, and has a strong interest in quantitative methodologies.

1
Aims and Overview

Introduction

> If I was in mainstream prison I'd be in a workshop but here basically I'm
> doing an NVQ in catering, so I'm working towards being a chef and this
> was something different to try, but I got the bug, it makes me wish I was 25
> year younger, but I'm not, but at the end of the day I've got to congratulate
> them because they've come here, they haven't gone "Oh my god, prisoners",
> they've treated me as equals they've coached me when I've been struggling.
> They've given me encouragement; they are a nice set of people to work with.

Primarily this book is about the residents of the Therapeutic Community (TC)
in Her Majesty's Prison (HMP) Dovegate. We wanted the first, and last, words
to be those of a TC resident. There are several reasons for this. First, politi-
cally, it rather pins our colours to the mast by privileging the residents as the
most important people in both the therapeutic enterprise and the research that
we are reporting. Second, it highlights the importance of our attentiveness to
what the TC residents had to say and the insights they had to offer about their
own experiences of therapy. Third, embedded within the extract is a clue about
the difference between mainstream prison and a therapeutic community, and
it offers some tantalising hints about the TC Dovegate ethos, which will be
explained in full later. It is also suggestive about the outcomes for this resident.
Ultimately interventions within prisons, particularly TCs, are about changing
lives. A strong theme of this book is "change" and the role that the TC played in
bringing about changes, what they are, whether they are sustainable and what
they mean to individual residents.

In this Introduction we provide some background to what we, as researchers,
set out to do. We thought it useful to look briefly at the work of HMP Grendon,
in terms of both its TC and also some of its associated research activity, not
only to show how the Dovegate TC and its research evaluation learnt from

1

these but also to explain some similarities to and differences from the Grendon experience. As Roland Woodward, the first director of therapy at Dovegate, was very keen that the Dovegate TC "was not a replica of Grendon" (Woodward chapter in Cullen and MacKenzie, 2011, p. 129), it seemed helpful to provide some comparison.

As part of the context, we set out some of the dilemmas and tensions inherent in undertaking a complicated piece of research in a complex setting. This includes some discussion of the competing demands and sometimes conflicting aims of conducting therapy in a private prison and the challenges in undertaking research. We also describe the philosophy underpinning the research and sketch out the key theoretical constructs. A recently published joint inspection by HMI Prison and HMI Probation Services not only provides a timely reminder of why working therapeutically with prisoners is so important but also strengthens the rationale for evaluating the gains to be had from such an intervention (Criminal Justice Joint Inspection, 2013). The inspection team noted (p. 7):

> prisoners were able to drift through their sentence without being challenged ... Offending behaviour work done in closed prisons was not always consolidated on arrival in open conditions. Transfer from closed to open conditions was a key transitional phase of the life sentence, but prisoners were often poorly prepared for this move; as a result, many suffered a "culture shock" on their arrival in open prison .... The quality of assessments and plans completed in prison to manage risk of harm to others was insufficient, with many lacking thorough analysis of the motivation and triggers for the original offending.

This assessment indicates the continuing difficulties in getting assessments and interventions right and supporting the rehabilitative ideals of incarceration. TCs within prisons challenge and address motivation for offending in order to reduce risk of harm to others. We will be describing how this was done within the Dovegate TC and what it achieved. We found evidence of culture shock on re-entry into mainstream prison, and we discuss how ex-TC residents attempted to consolidate the progress they had made when transferring.

From the outset we want to record that we were fully supported in conducting the research by the management of Dovegate and the TC staff. The research that the four of us are reporting was a collaborative effort of many hands, and we endeavour to indicate where a particular set of findings was the work of one of our collaborators. But, above all, we were not only heartened by the generosity of our TC resident research participants but also struck by their insights, and hope that, in the pages that follow, we do these justice.

In the beginning

Setting up Dovegate

Dovegate Therapeutic Community Prison opened in November 2001. Premier Prison won the competitive bid to build a modern purpose-built prison with a TC (Cullen and Miller, 2010). There were four communities, A, B, C and D, later renamed Avalon, Camelot, Genesis and Endeavour, holding up to 60 residents in each within an 800-bedded category B mainstream prison. The TC complex was built around a "market square" which had a decorative fountain and garden with no inner boundary fences. Roland Woodward, the original first director of therapy, was anxious to create a physical environment that supported the TC lifestyle that he and Eric Cullen (who was the lead consultant in the successful bid to operate the Dovegate TC) were to design (Woodward chapter in Cullen and MacKenzie, 2011). The space was important in several regards. It had to accommodate the activities that were to take place and also needed to reflect the openness of the therapeutic model that Roland Woodward wished to create. Part of that openness involved work that Roland did with the local communities living near Uttoxeter, where the prison was to be built, by finding out what it might mean for residents of the two nearby villages to have a prison close by.

There were several other distinctive features that reflected Roland's inimitable imprint on the genesis of Dovegate. One was his approach to the training of people who were to staff the TCs, and the other was his organising principles for his management team, which became known as the Senate, and its informal shadow, "the fluffy" (more of which shortly). In order to reflect his egalitarian principles, he insisted on a round table to seat the 15 or so members of the Senate, even though this meant building the table in the room that was to house it. His logic was clear. If TC residents were to sit in circles for group therapy, so too were the members of the Senate. This was one tangible attempt to break down the "us and them" barriers. From the outset, both discipline staff and therapy staff wore uniform as a symbolic way to fuse the therapeutic and security functions and also to inhibit some informal hierarchy of professional staff vs. "screws" building up. This fusing was consolidated by the therapy managers being responsible for both functions.

The invention of "the fluffy" was a Roland inspiration, coined after a Harry Potter character (Fluffy was the name of a three-headed dog guarding the "Philosopher's Stone"). Roland describes the origin of the naming as follows: "It was obvious that our sensitivity meeting that was meant to deal with our unconscious material could only be called one thing. What could be more obvious than the three-headed monster that guards the lower level of our being? Hence, Fluffy" (Woodward chapter in Cullen and MacKenzie, 2011, p. 141).

"The fluffy" was really what members of the Senate wanted it to be – a place to express irritations and frustrations, work through rivalries and jealousies – essentially, Roland created an environment for his staff to allow them to do for themselves what the residents were being asked to do.

"Educom" was a creative mixture of education and commerce designed for the TC residents. Roland was keen that the Dovegate TC was not going to have the light industrial processes of other prisons; rather, he wanted to widen the learning skills and possibilities made available to TC residents through peer tutors as an operationalisation of the "learning from others" principle.

Staff were drawn from newly recruited prison custody officers, many of whom had no prior prison experience, and professionals from psychology, psychiatry and counselling backgrounds. Roland and Eric Cullen prepared a training programme for the new staff. In Chapter 2 we chart the historical origins of the TC movement, and in Chapter 3 we describe in more detail the founding principles and the structuring of the Dovegate TC regime.

Some context

Our research at Dovegate began a decade or so after Elaine Genders and Elaine Player published their ground-breaking study of HMP Grendon TC (Genders and Player, 1995). The background to that study was the climate of despair within the prison system in general, and the therapy community in particular, because of the demise of the rehabilitative ideals of the early 1970s. What came to be labelled "nothing works", emanating from the Martinson (1974) research, was a critical appraisal of the apparent ineffectualness of prison interventions which painted a bleak picture of the intractability of offending behaviour. In the next chapter, we present an overview of the "nothing works" debate and the development of a rather more optimistic "what works" approach. We also show where the TCs fit, as well as providing an account of TC policies and practices.

The sense of crisis was also being played out through the industrial action taken by prison officers in the 1990s. Prison buildings were in a sad state of neglect, and in 1990 prisoners at HMP Strangeways rioted for 25 days, during which the prison was virtually destroyed, one prisoner died and almost 200 officers and prisoners were injured. The subsequent Woolf report (25 February 1991) was a high water mark of pessimism, noting that the prison system itself, impoverished regimes and poor staff–inmate relationships had contributed to the rioting.

Lord Woolf found a sorry picture when he conducted his review of the prison system. In the ten-year anniversary debate of Lord Woolf's report in the House of Commons (Hansard, 2001) it was noted that "[i]n 1989–90, the 40-odd local prisons and remand centres were overcrowded by an average of 37 per cent. Some were overcrowded 100 per cent, holding double the number of prisoners that should have been held." The effects of the overcrowding meant that often there were three prisoners held in a cell without sanitation or washing facilities and there was a lack of "purposeful activity for prisoners". The rising prison population exacerbated an already pressurised system.

Genders and Player suggest that, in the aftermath of Woolf, Grendon, which had opened in 1962 to provide treatment for offenders whose mental disorders were insufficient to warrant transfer to hospital, was recognised as an antidote to the dreadful conditions and punitive regimes that were the precursor to the prison riots of 1991. As they indicate, the main aim of therapy at Grendon, when they were undertaking their research, was to facilitate and promote the welfare and well-being of each individual inmate; it was not seen as the apparatus of crime control. Whilst they observed that prevention of crime was an ambition of the Grendon regime, it was not the primary one.

There were other indicators that attention to the rehabilitative aims of prison was restirring. Just when we were beginning our research at Dovegate, The House of Commons Home Affairs Committee, in its investigation into the rehabilitation of offenders, offered a strikingly upbeat note:

> We endorse the view of the Prison Service that HMP Grendon is a model of good prison practice and a leader in the treatment of severe personality-disordered offenders. Although by its nature this model of treatment will only be suitable for a minority of offenders, we consider it important that the work done at Grendon should continue. We recommend that the Government should commit itself to maintain and if possible increase the present level of resourcing of Grendon and other therapeutic units.
> (House of Commons, Home Affairs Committee, 2004, para. 240)

Government reports such as Corston in 2007 and Bradley in 2009 were more sympathetic to the rehabilitative ideals of prison. The Carter review of prisons seemed, however, to counterbalance this by recommending large-scale, state-of-the-art Titan prisons and focused on the modernisation of the prison estate and better strategic management as the means to manage the ever-increasing prison population (Carter, 2007).

A resurgence of academic interest was also evident. Since the late 1980s, a movement that came to be known as therapeutic jurisprudence (Petrucci et al., 2003) had been evolving. The aim was to bring mental health insights into the legal arena and counter anti-therapeutic outcomes by improving the emotional well-being of prisoners. Work by Prochaska and DiClemente (1983) on smoking cessation had developed a model of change which, during the intervening years, had progressively evolved and been adapted to measuring change in a range of treatment contexts. Change was said to be a process and took place as a series of stages: precontemplation, when the person is unaware of or unconcerned about problem behaviour; contemplation, when there is an acknowledgement of but ambivalence about changing; action, when there is an attempt to change; and maintenance, during which change is consolidated. These ideas about readiness to change and the role of affective as well as cognitive elements, together with the means to measure these, were increasingly being used to assess progress in treatment and demonstrate changes in behaviours. Egan (2010) discusses a renewed interest in the concept of personality and an integration into models of offending, notably the work on cognitive schemas and their role in antisocial behaviour and maladaptive responses to challenging life events. Concurrently, psychometric measures were being devised and published, for example, the Psychological Inventory of Critical Thinking Styles (PICTS, Walters, 2002), which tried to capture aspects of thoughtlessness and callousness. As Egan describes, thoughtlessness is implicated in impulsivity, which is a core feature observed in offenders, and increasingly intervention programmes tried to inculcate greater self-insight and self-control and thus less inclination to offend. This is an area we address in our research, and we spend Chapter 5 discussing personality disorder (PD), its implications for offending and propensity for change within the TC, and problems in measuring it.

By the 1990s there was a growing response to the "nothing works" critique. Better statistical techniques and new conceptual thinking drew attention to models of change (McMurran, 2010). Andrews and Bonta (1990) developed the risk-need-responsivity (RNR) model. The risk principle states that criminal behaviour can be reliably predicted and that treatment should focus on high-risk offenders. The need principle argues that treatment interventions should focus on issues that relate to criminal behaviour, that is, criminogenic needs. The responsivity principle looks to maximise the offender's motivation and ability to engage in treatment and behaviour change. We incorporated these principles within our research design. We describe our approaches to measuring change in Chapter 4 and present our results in chapters 6–10, dividing these according to the primary research method, which to some extent also corresponds to the chronological sequence of the prisoners' progression through Dovegate, back into mainstream prison and into the outside world.

Countering the "nothing works" argument was an impetus to develop more and better evaluations of prison-based treatment interventions. Another was the drive to have accredited interventions, and a third was to demonstrate value for money, spawned in the wake of the New Public Sector Management initiatives (Wakeling and Travers, 2010). The government wanted to ensure that interventions were reducing recidivism and warranted the investment of public money in programmes, and defined reduction in reoffending as one of its main objectives. In 2002, the Home Office had set a Public Service Agreement Target of reducing the predicted rate of reoffending by 5% by April 2004, and again by 5% by April 2006. The Prison Service stated that "reducing re-offending by released prisoners is central to reducing crime and is therefore part of the Prison Service's core business of protecting the public" (House of Commons Home Affairs Committee, 2005). A further identifiable trend has been the recognition that the service users' perspective should be incorporated into programme evaluations (Glasby et al., 2003).

The implications from these trends are twofold. First, they confront the question of what constitutes outcomes, and, second, they provoke the issue of how to measure these, or, more broadly, what research methods to employ. We describe more fully the way we went about conducting the research and its more technical aspects in Chapter 4. Here we wanted to lay out our approach and present some of the conundrums and our solutions to these before we explain the detail.

Evolving our approach to the research

As mentioned above, Genders and Player (1995) alluded to the goals of the Grendon TC being wider than the crime control and desistence from offending desired by the authorities, and this had an impact on their research questions and methods. So it was with our research. The research brief set by Roland Woodward encouraged those bidding for the research contract to consider (a) the extent and process of psychological and behavioural change within Dovegate TC; (b) TC residents' behaviour and experiences after transfer to another prison; and (c) TC residents' behaviour and experiences after release into the community. Roland Woodward did not want just a replication of a study of TC social processes that had characterised the Grendon research at that time. As well as having a post-Dovegate element to the research design, he was keen to explore the therapeutic process "as it related to individuals reaching a point of psychological change readiness" (Woodward's chapter in Cullen and MacKenzie, 2011, p. 148). Roland described his notion of change and the centrality of meaning in his conception of the Dovegate TC in a study undertaken by a Counselling and Psychotherapy doctoral student, Amelie Bobsien, in 2004. In answer to Amelie's question of what the Dovegate TC was all about, Roland said:

> It's about making meaning. It's about how each individual makes a new meaning of their lives and how they make sense of their universe and their place in it ... so it's really about enabling people to change their basic schema and acquire the skills to be able to live that new understanding and that new meaning.

Amelie then asked: "if you had to describe the TC what words or image comes to mind?" Roland's answer was:

> A moving garden. A place in which people have the opportunity to grow and develop with the recognition that some people don't actually grow or develop, some grow and blossom and move on and some actually don't grow and just wither. But that garden in itself is actually moving and changing all the time, providing different environments in which people sort of grow.

He went on to explain that his fundamental interest was in how people change. This was very much the steer in his demand for the research, and responded to his intellectual curiosity and the culture of enquiry that infused the Dovegate TC.

We were extremely fortunate in having two clinical consultants, Sean Hammond and Yvonne Shell, and three external advisors, Derek Perkins, Adrian Needs and Fiona Warren, to assist the research team. Their experience incorporated treatment of offenders in special hospitals (Yvonne and Derek) and prisons (Adrian). Fiona, with colleagues (Warren et al., 2003), had undertaken a systematic review of treatment modalities that had included TCs, and Sean was highly proficient in statistical analyses. It was Sean who pointed us in the direction of idiographic approaches. He explains these as follows:

> [T]here are situations in psychological research where focus is upon the individual respondent...where the researcher wishes to follow a patient over a course of psychotherapy and attempt to measure change in their psychological state. In this case the respondent may be asked to complete some form of questionnaire on a number of occasions and the changes over time serve as the focus of interest. This approach is known as idiographic since it focuses on the individual respondent in isolation... [and is] of great value when the focus of interest is upon the dynamic processes within individuals.
>
> (Hammond, 2000, p. 181)

Sean and Yvonne between them suggested a number of psychometric tests that would chart, for example, TC residents' self-esteem, thinking styles, impulsivity and sense of alienation, which could be repeated at set time intervals. Some of the measures were part of the battery of Dovegate TC's assessment inventory (in keeping with other democratic prison TCs) and others were chosen for specific research purposes.

Often these types of questionnaires are collectively analysed and presented by way of group-level changes between various points in time. This shows general trends, but could not achieve the more detailed levels of analysis we were striving for; hence we used the reliable change index (RCI). Using inferential statistics and comparing group average scores ignores variability in treatment. For example, some people may actually be deteriorating after completing the treatment (Ogles et al., 2001). Furthermore, there may be a statistically significant improvement following treatment, but this does not necessarily help us to assess whether change is clinically significant. Jacobson and Traux (1991) developed the RCI to generate three percentages, of people who have improved, deteriorated or stayed the same against a yardstick of normal functioning.

Thus, part of our research strategy was to track TC residents through time both within and beyond Dovegate by building up a composite picture of their cognitive functioning and affective states and being able to demonstrate clinically significant improvement, deterioration or no progression. Chapter 6 presents analyses of our psychometric data.

Our statistical advisor Sean had suggested that the repertory grid arising from Kelly's Personal Construct Theory was another appropriate idiographic method. However, this is a rather laborious method and we wondered whether residents would enjoy taking part. We elected instead to use a card-sorting procedure which represented a simplified version of the more elaborate repertory grid (Canter et al., 1985). This allows individuals to "map out" the ways in which they thought or felt about significant people, places or events, and we drew on attachment theory to try to demonstrate changes over time. The story of this means of gathering responses and the insights it revealed are fully described in Chapter 8.

We also wanted personal accounts that would truly give voice to the residents, and opted for semi-structured interviews and focus groups. We conducted a series of focus groups with TC residents to gain a sense of their progress and also to gauge the climate and atmosphere of various stages in the therapy. This was particularly helpful when we wanted to follow our Dovegate residents into their next destination after their residency, and our account of this part of our study can be found in Chapter 9.

So now we had a mixture of "hard-nosed" quantitative measurement in the form of psychometric questionnaires and "softer" data generated through our focus groups, card sorts and interviews. In addition, we decided to use Blackburn's CIRCLE, which is an assessment of residents behaviour undertaken by staff, enabling us to monitor changes over time.

This range of methods raised some uncomfortable issues about epistemology. Stated simply, this has to do with ways of knowing, that is, the kind of assumptions researchers make when setting out on a research inquiry (Creswell, 2003). Qualitative and quantitative methods tend to have different starting positions. The latter are often associated with the "scientific" method, whereby knowledge has some objective reality and the researcher's task is simply to find it. The former assume that knowledge about the world and how it works is rather more subjective, and understanding is found through some negotiation between the person experiencing the events of interest and the researcher.

Evaluations that emerged from the what works debate increasingly used has been argued to be the "gold standard" of scientific rigour, the Randomised Control Trial (RCT). This commonly allocates people randomly to a "treatment" group and constructs an equivalent "control" in order to compare the results of those having the treatment with those who do not. The assumption is that, if all other possible influences are tightly controlled, any changes must be due to the treatment. Often quantitative measurement is used to assess changes. Research that hails from an alternative tradition, which might be, in shorthand, labelled the desistence approach, focuses on individual lives and journeys over time and searches for changing self-concepts though an individual's own narrative account (Maruna, 2013). These two ways of conducting research have been positioned as being in opposition to each other.

Genders and Player (1995) faced a similar dilemma, and their answer was to employ an "eclectic" approach (p. 20). They needed to collect quantitative data to fulfil their research aim of describing their Grendon population as well as elucidating the key social processes involved in the interactions between inmates and between inmates and staff, which they did qualitatively. They were quite comfortable with having these as "overlapping" and "complementary" components that could be cross-checked to produce a more coherent picture of life at Grendon. In addition, the realities of conducting research in a living institution, in which key people may leave and changes occur in priorities, mean that research cannot be "neatly designed in advance and carried out according to some pre-ordained plan" (p. 17). In their case there had been a shift in Grendon from the TC being managed by a mental health professional to a prison governor. There was also a major upheaval during their field work due to a radical reorganisation and changes in pay and conditions of prison staff. Furthermore, there was a requirement for Grendon to make room for additional inmates, those on isolation Rule 43 incarceration, in a non-therapeutic wing. All of these changes combined to create an air of despondency and crisis. These conditions were clearly not conducive to an RCT, even if they had considered such an approach.

During our Dovegate research, we also experienced a change of director of therapy. We said earlier that Roland Woodward, in conceiving the Dovegate TC, did not want to replicate Grendon. In actuality, he thought Grendon had become "ossified and self indulgent" (Woodward in Cullen and MacKenzie, p. 129). He wanted to develop, as far as he could, the democratic ideals of a TC. He used Rapoport's (1960) guiding principles of democracy, permissiveness, communal and reality confronting in conceiving of the Dovegate approach. In addition, he was greatly influenced by Yalom's (1995) therapeutic factors, such as the instillation of hope and the idea of receiving through giving.

This departed from the more Adlerian, neo-Freudian approach of Grendon. Roland wanted to create "a living system" which was egalitarian and tried to fuse therapy and security as one way out of their inherent tension. In an interview with Ursula Smartt, Roland said:

> the community at Dovegate will be a synthesis of TC (shared power within a democratic framework) plus evidence-based cognitive behaviour co-lateral programmes... Our model will address criminogenic needs and future risk assessment. The inter-personal relationship and the developmental personal history will play a crucial role in our TC process.
>
> (Smartt, 2001, p. 205)

Smartt commented that this model of therapy was indeed different. Roland was characterised by Eric Cullen and Judith MacKenzie as a charismatic leader, although they speculated, rightly, that this was a label he was reluctant to accept. This is Roland's comment:

> my stance through the whole process was that charismatic leaders failed because they did not build sound organisational structures into the TCs. If a TC was to succeed, it had to do so because its organisational structures, internal skeleton, were strong enough to be independent of personalities. This is in part why I adopted the leadership style I did and insisted on clarity of structure and the involvement of the Community of Communities TC accreditation process in the organisation from an early stage of planning. I think that my awareness of my tendency to want to do "stand up" made me do all I could to take me out of the equation and place structures and mechanisms at the heart of the TC. How much I succeeded in this is for others to judge I guess.
>
> (personal communication, 2013)

He decided to leave Dovegate in May 2006 and was replaced by David Lynes. This was a difficult time for the TC, which struggled in the aftermath of Roland's departure and responding to a different style of leadership. These and other difficulties are discussed at greater length by Cullen and MacKenzie (2011). Our observation is that, for whatever reason, there was a period of instability at Dovegate, reflected in the Community of Communities assessments of the TC, which we discuss briefly in the next chapter.

David Lynes, was a psychotherapist with no prior prison experience. Compare his thoughts (elicited from an interview with JB shortly after he took over as director) on what Dovegate was all about with the view expressed by Roland, quoted above. For him, staff were custodians of the therapeutic process, which he likened to the mother [who] holds the wrath of the baby and gradually feeds this back in bits until the child develops the ability to process within its own right.

Ray Duckworth became the third director of the TC after David in 2008, and had a background as a prison officer with expertise in security and operations. He inherited some disarray in the TC, which faced criticisms from the Community of Communities and the Prison Service. He dismantled the original administrative structures and reinstated the distinctions between the therapeutic and security roles. He presented his view of the TC in an interview he gave to *The Custodial Review* (2012), in which he described the ethos of a therapeutic prison:

> therapy is devised to give individuals some control over their lives. We let them run everything that we can, they chose the décor, when to eat food, clean the community etc. However we do not forget that we are in a prison and we do not compromise on security, so our staff can veto decisions if they feel the residents have overstepped the mark. We must provide a safe and secure environment for therapy to work.

Thus, there were three very different characters running the TC in its first years, likened to the Three Wise Men by Eric Cullen and Judith MacKenzie in their book on Dovegate, each bringing different gifts at formative phases of Dovegate's evolution. Our research covered Roland's and David's time in the TC, and was completing by the time Ray took over.

As Grendon had before, Dovegate also experienced pressures on numbers. Stresses elsewhere in the prison estate meant that planned admissions and preparation procedures for entry into Dovegate TC had to be suspended, so that unsuitable people were accepted. This was compounded by operational difficulties preventing those no longer in therapy from moving on from the TC. By 2008, as our research was reaching its completion stage, a third of residents were actually out of therapy and had not been moved on (Cullen and MacKenzie, 2011).

Whilst it is true to say that we had decided not to use an RCT when we started our research, with hindsight these changes would have made it impossible to sustain the strict control requirements of an experimental design. Not only were there differences between the four TC communities, but the overall direction was different under the two directors covering the greater period of our research. We could not legitimately have held to the line that "all things were equal" in the content of the therapeutic programme during the period of our data collection. Our overall approach shares much with Genders and Player's in that we wanted to use qualitative and quantitative methods to cross-reference our results, described by some as methodological triangulation (Foss and Ellefsen, 2002), in order to find those that were sustainable, and so we opted for a multiple methods design.

Teddlie and Tashakkori (2003, p. 14) suggest that "mixed methods are useful as they provide better opportunities for answering our research questions", and are superior to single approach designs because they

- can answer research questions other methodologies cannot (i.e. they can address explanatory and confirmatory questions at the same time, thereby generating and verifying theory)
- provide stronger inferences (thereby complementing and overcoming weaknesses in single method approaches)
- provide greater diversity of divergent views (and, where findings converge, greater confidence can be expressed in the findings).

Furthermore, a mixed method approach places central importance on the experiences of the individual and alerts the researcher to the power differentials between themselves and those they research.

Conceptual signposts

Our research was not without some theoretical ideas, and we employed several conceptual notions that we thought would be particularly helpful.

Attachment

We were interested in attachment style when thinking about precursors to and desistance from offending behaviour. Adshead (2002) suggests that it would be unusual for offenders to have had early childhood experiences that would promote secure attachments. The research has focused largely on attachment styles in violent and sex offenders (see e.g. Ward et al., 1996; Baker and Beech, 2004). Essentially, childhood attachment is thought to affect future relationships throughout life. Originally established as a concept by Bowlby, an individual's attachment style is often described as secure or insecure. Secure attachment consists of feeling safe and results in positive emotional states, whereas insecure attachments revolve around fearful and avoidant responses to attachment figures (Ward et al., 1996). For Adshead (2002), attachment security profoundly influences the development of a capacity to imagine mental states in oneself or in others. This self-reflective function is critical in the development of an ability to empathise. Insecure attachments are likely to result in a lack of capacity to alleviate stress or to undertake care-giving on behalf of others and care-eliciting on one's own behalf. It follows that an examination of attachment styles was deemed especially useful in the context of a TC. Rex Haigh proposes that the first job of treatment is to establish a secure attachment, and then use that to bring about changes in deeply ingrained expectations of relationships, and patterns of behaviour. The culture in which this attachment needs to happen is one where community members can clearly feel a sense of belonging – where membership is valued and where members themselves are valued. This is harder than it sounds when people arrive with a life-long history of unsatisfactory relationships – expecting rejection, hostility, abandonment, trauma or abuse.

(Haigh, 2013, p. 8)

We used the four-category model of attachment conceived by Bartholomew and Horowitz (1991). They hypothesise two levels of self-image (positive vs. negative) and two levels of images of others (positive vs. negative), the intersection of which describes secure, dismissing, preoccupied and fearful attachment styles. We were also interested in the concept of "place" attachment, whereby people gain a sense of their identity through functional and emotional needs being met through their connection to places.

Therapeutic alliance

We supported the idea that the therapeutic alliance is a key issue relating to the effectiveness of therapeutic interventions. This can broadly be defined as the climate of the therapeutic relationship between a client, therapist and other members of a therapy group (Bachelor, 1995). A large body of research, across client populations and therapeutic modalities, has highlighted the importance of the therapeutic alliance in achieving positive therapeutic outcome (e.g. Horvath and Luborsky, 1993); it has been shown to account for as much of the outcome variance as particular treatments (Norcross, 2001). However, the majority of research has focused on individual or group therapy, with little effort to explore clients' experiences of the therapeutic alliance within a TC setting. One suggestion emanating from this body of research is the idea of ruptures in alliance (Clarkson, 1995) whereby crises, breakdown of trust and acting out can disrupt or, indeed, act as a catalyst in the therapeutic process. In a TC setting, group members may fail to recognise dysfunctional patterns in others, or, if levels of cohesion in the group are low, they may be unwilling to challenge or may possibly collude with other members. Genders and Player (1995) explain that, within the TC, each group member has a "central role to play in determining his own treatment" and that the aim is to empower individuals to "anticipate, and take responsibility for the consequences of their actions" (p. 14). We thought that the concept of the therapeutic alliance might offer a way in to exploring these layers, and also that the additional dimension that the community brings as a treatment instrument was a potential addition to the traditional notion of therapeutic alliance.

Culture shock

Given the contrasting environments that a TC and a prison present, we employed the idea of "culture shock", which occurs when:

> a sojourner [traveller] is unfamiliar with the social conventions of the new culture, or if familiar with them, unable or unwilling to perform according to these rules... Sojourners are not expected to adjust themselves to a new culture they learn selected aspects of it for instrumental reasons... These new practices need not become part of the permanent repertoire of the person but will be discarded when they are not functional.
>
> (Furhnam and Bochner, 1986, p. 250)

We thought this, and its mirror "reverse culture shock", the process of readjusting, reacculturating and reassimilating back into a familiar culture after having experienced a different one (Gaw, 2000), would provide useful explanatory tools to explain issues associated with entry into the TC and re-entry into mainstream prison.

Other issues

Researching in a prison

Finally, we wanted to draw attention to some practice issues which we discuss more fully in Chapter 12. These relate to the prison environment, therapeutic regimes and research. Similarly to Elaine Genders and Elaine Player before us, we were a team comprised mostly of women researchers collecting the data within Dovegate. They had fully appreciated their highly conspicuous presence in a largely all-male establishment, and observed that, as time passed, they became resources which could be utilised in the therapeutic process (p. 39). Complaints were made to them about staff misconduct, or admissions of offences for which there had been no prosecution, or disclosures of confidential confidences. Genders and Player tended to use each other as a sounding board in coming to a decision about how to respond to these. Some they ignored, others they reported anonymously. We took a rather more formal approach, perhaps having the advantage of some clinician-researchers, clinician consultants and advisors, and were careful not to be thought of as agents in therapy or conduits to make complaints to the management. Ethical conundrums were discussed in supervisory sessions, and a formal consent laying out the ground rules in the eventuality of disclosures was clearly communicated, understood and adhered to.

However, we did adopt a similar approach to Genders and Player in our efforts to fully inform residents and staff on what the research was about and how people could get involved. We, as they had, spent some time in explaining the research at the outset. We provided a six-monthly written report on progress, and formally presented our emergent findings orally to Dovegate staff and informally, by means of a newsletter, to residents. In this way, some adjustments could be made to the direction of the research as an organic and dynamic piece of work rather than a statically controlled RCT.

Working in a prison environment as our field setting had its problems. We were fortunate in having a room set aside within the TC to get access to computers. We had excellent liaison to help us try and iron out difficulties. But inevitably there were glitches, such as prison lock-downs in the event of an emergency, in which members of the research team were either inside and not able to get out or outside and not able to get in, the latter occurring more frequently. Tracking ex-residents to other establishments after their release from Dovegate was often frustrating. Records were sometimes incomplete and not in a form that was suitable for research purposes. Our efforts to secure a comparison group were particularly tough. We tried as far as possible to overcome or mitigate these difficulties, but they served to remind us as researchers of our reliance on the help and co-operation of others who had different priorities and whose timescales and agendas were different from ours. Sometimes we just had to compromise and do the best we could.

Reliability and validity

We had long and difficult discussions about our research methods, particularly the reliability and validity of our results. We felt, rather as had Genders and Player, that by using different methods we could cross-validate findings and demonstrate consistency of our evidence by its appearance in different types of data collection. We were aware of the pitfalls of qualitative data collection, such as demand characteristics, whereby those we interviewed might be telling us what we wanted to hear or might have other motives for the accounts they gave, such as presenting a positive picture of themselves as a precursor to a parole hearing. We accept that this may have happened some of the time, but we entered into the spirit of the TC's search for honesty. After all, this is what the residents were aspiring to achieve in their group sessions. Why, then, would they not try to do so when participating in the research? In some research techniques, such as the card-sorting task, it was not immediately obvious what we were trying to examine, so the likelihood of faking, good or bad, was reduced. Our research philosophy was one in which we started out with the belief that, if people voluntarily engaged with us to tell their stories, by and large they would try to do so authentically.

We realised that, in order to be as certain as possible that change was occurring as a consequence of the TC experience and not as some artefact of the passage of time during which a person might change because of some extraneous circumstances, we needed to construct a comparison group of prisoners not in a TC. We used this means to benchmark progress as measured by the battery of psychometric measures.

Prison-based TC

We also had to think about the tensions inherent in therapy taking place not just in a prison, but in one that was run privately. It seemed a definitional contradiction to establish a therapeutic unit which sought to alleviate pain and suffering in an institution that is primarily as punishment, exists to separate criminals from society and where most criminals want their stay to pass as quickly and easily as possible (Cullen, 1997). The basic ethos of a democratic TC comes into direct conflict with the underlying assumptions of security, good order and control that are inherent in the prison system (Cullen et al., 1997a).

Additionally, there is the physical constraint of being incarcerated. Locked doors and gates hinder the free and democratic culture granted to those in a TC. The prison TC is frequently expected to fit into the establishment's routines at the expense of its own timetable; for example, meals supplied to all wings by a central kitchen are delivered at a set time irrelevant to the timetable on each wing (including the TC's therapeutic regime). As mentioned above, Dovegate's first director paid considerable attention to the environment, as far as was practicable within the constraints of a prison. By encouraging staff to mimic processes designed for residents, the belief was that some of the barriers could be broken down. Certainly, the Grendon research (Shuker and Sullivan, 2010) had shown some positive results, and Fiona Warren's systematic review (Warren et al., 2003) demonstrated successes in prison-based TCs. It was our task to find out whether and what progress might be made in Dovegate, notwithstanding the obvious limitations.

Clearly, Roland Woodward had agonised about the issue of privatisation before taking the post as the first director of therapy (Woodward's chapter in Cullen and MacKenzie, 2011). There is the moral argument of the appropriateness of a private company making a profit from imprisonment and the possibility of commercial imperatives overriding the therapeutic interests of the residents. In accepting the grant, was this in the same moral terrain as the tobacco industry providing research funds? On balance, we decided that the overarching aim of the TC at Dovegate was to achieve a social good. Smoking, on the other hand, kills people. There had been a huge amount of creative work put into designing the programme and the training of staff. The TC staff worked hard, and the men entering the TC did so in good faith. We felt it important to assess the worth of these endeavours.

Prisoners' rights

Working with an incarcerated group of potential research participants, we were mindful of according the same entitlements to the TC residents as to anyone participating in research. Men joining the TC routinely agreed that anonymised psychometric assessment data would be used for research purposes. We then sought individuals' consent to volunteer for other parts of the research. We used the British Psychological Society's guiding principles for research participation, in that it was voluntary and consent was an informed process; participants could drop out of the research at any time with no detriment or implications for their TC residency; and, as mentioned previously, we made clear the limits to our confidentiality assurances. A number of students undertook masters' dissertations and three students successfully completed doctorates during the life of the study. These received ethical approval from the University of Surrey's ethics committee alongside other relevant permissions and approvals.

Did Dovegate TC "work"?

Finally, did Dovegate TC work? The answer is not straightforward. It depends on what criteria of success are used and the limitations of each of the methods we deployed. We hope the following pages will explain in some detail in what way and for whom Dovegate had some positive outcome, and we try to draw this together in Chapter 11. For now, let us conclude this Introduction with an insight offered by one of our residents:

> [Dovegate TC] has made me think a lot more, it has made me .... I had a lot of problems with me family and that and my mother and that and our relationships weren't too clever so now I can talk to them about it, think about me own feelings and talk to me family and things like that .... it has made me think about the consequences more .... that is really it, I have got a lot more patience, a lot more tolerance for people, me aims and goals are a lot different now ... I am more realistic about things, I don't really want to get involved in the same kind of stuff that I used to.

2
The "What Works" Debate and the Fit of Prison-Based Democratic TCs

Introduction

This chapter opens with a brief overview of the "nothing works/what works" debate. It sets out the history of research which initially concluded that interventions with prisoners were ineffectual until later evaluations adopted better designs and offered a more optimistic view of intervention outcomes. We also describe the originating therapeutic community (TC) in 1947, the Henderson Hospital. This has been identified as the first TC targeting an offender population within the UK. The ethos behind the democratic TC will be explained and the chapter will briefly review the history of how TCs have been adapted for prison settings. This will also involve touching on the debate over whether a TC can operate effectively within a prison setting and what limitations it faces in striving to do so, arguments we develop in the next chapter.

The success of the HMP Grendon TC has been established through the various studies conducted on outcomes, which have consistently reported a "dosage effect" of treatment (e.g. Cullen, 1992, 1994; Genders and Player, 1995 Taylor, 2000). By and large, graduates from Grendon TC released after 12–18 months of therapy have lower reconviction rates (particularly for violence) than those released earlier.

We also give a brief synopsis that describes current policies, standards and oversights of TCs, and Dovegate in particular.

History of treatment interventions – "nothing works" to "what works"

A considerable amount of practical work has been carried out in the past in an attempt to treat offenders and to reduce levels of criminality. However, when various evaluations were undertaken the results led to the conclusion that "nothing works". Martinson's (1974) seminal paper "What Works? Questions and Answers about Prison Reform" is seen as the benchmark, establishing the doctrine that "nothing works" in offender treatment. Martinson reviewed 231 controlled outcome studies conducted between 1945 and 1967 and found that only a very small number of prison-based treatment programmes produced positive results. He concluded that education and psychotherapy, at their best, cannot overcome, or "even appreciably reduce, the powerful tendency for offenders to continue in criminal behaviour" (p. 49). This pessimistic attitude found ready acceptance as a result of the political climate of the 1970s and 1980s, when crime and reoffending rates were escalating rapidly and there was widespread disillusionment with the concept of rehabilitation of offenders (Howells and Day, 1999).

The "nothing works" position also found acceptance in academic research, and the view became more widely supported. Robinson and Smith (1971), for example, stated that criminals could not be treated either by longer sentences, more intensive treatment or even closer supervision. With this level of academic and political scepticism, the policies and practices generated were extremely limited or abandoned, and few interventions or treatment programmes were developed or introduced during this time (Hollin, 1990).

However, with a lightening of the political climate and new academic interest, this position came to be modified. A number of studies (most notably Gendreau and Ross, 1979, 1987) proposed that effective treatment of offenders was possible and, moreover, this could be measured to show that group programmes were a success. In the light of new and more positive research, Martinson revised his position in 1979 and recanted his original assertion, noting the error of his previous reviews. The introduction of meta-analytic methods meant that it was possible for researchers to begin to strengthen the evidence base, and this precipitated a major reassessment of the "nothing works" doctrine. One of the largest of these meta-analyses was conducted by Lipsey (1992), who found that in the studies he reviewed 64.5% of interventions illustrated positive effects of treatment in terms of reducing recidivism. On average, the reduction of recidivism for treated offenders was found to be between 10% and 12%, but some high-effect studies led to reductions in excess of 20%. Martinson was led to conclude that the evidence in favour of successful interventions was, in fact, "too overwhelming to ignore" (Martinson, 1979, p. 252).

The original Martinson study was heavily criticised by Thornton (1987), who stated that a large proportion of the studies informing the "nothing works" doctrine had methodological flaws, such as selectively reported results, and that the treatments chosen for evaluation were often poorly applied. Thornton's conclusions were that the work reviewed by Martinson had either demonstrated that it was not possible to draw any conclusions from the studies analysed or had actually shown the effect of treatment on reoffending rates. These new studies spelt the end of the "nothing works" attitudes to the treatment of offenders and paved the way for a more positive approach to prison interventions, and the alternative "what works" movement began to develop.

What works

The foundation of the "what works" approach, according to McGuire (1995), is that intervention programmes designed to reduce criminality must be strongly skills and evidence-based, must have a coherent, legitimate and robust theoretical grounding, and should be administered in a reliable and audited way. The principle of "what works" is that reoffending can be reduced by using methods that address factors that have played a causal or contributory role in the offending. If risk factors for reoffending are addressed, then a successful intervention should be possible. A key resource in the "what works" debate is McGuire's book, *What Works: Reducing Reoffending. Guidelines from Research and Practice* (McGuire, 1995). This outlines some of the more successful interventions for reducing reoffending. Box 2.1 details the premises of the "what works" approach and expands on the foundations introduced above. McGuire believes that an intervention will be successful if it focuses on these elements. Moreover, McGuire's (2002) position is that offenders usually have multiple criminogenic needs, and, for this reason, interventions are required to tackle a range of problems in order to be successful.

Box 2.1 McGuire's requirements for successful interventions

- **Risk classification.** The level of risk should be matched to the degree of intervention an offender receives, i.e. those deemed higher risk receive more intervention.
- **Criminogenic needs.** These are factors that contribute to offending and differ from person to person. Criminogenic needs must be addressed as part of the goals of the intervention.
- **Responsivity.** Learning styles of staff and participants in the intervention must match. On the whole, offenders are more responsive to active, participatory methods. Furthermore, the individual offender's requirements and capabilities must be considered when allocating a form of treatment which aims to maximise impacts bearing on their criminogenic needs.
- **Community based.** Programmes based in the community tend to be more effective, mainly because it is easier to provide real-life learning situations in the community.

Box 2.1 (Continued)

- **Treatment modality.** The most effective programmes tend to be multi-modal, i.e. they address a variety of an offender's problems. They also use skills-orientated methods and techniques derived from cognitive-behavioural approaches (see also Hollin, 1999).
- **Programme integrity.** The aims of the programme are directly related to the methods being used. The staff are properly trained and supported to ensure accurate and consistent implementation of the programme. The intervention must be systematically monitored and evaluated.
- **Explicit model of the causes of crime.** Interventions that aim to reduce reconviction rates should target risk factors for offending behaviour (e.g. attitudes, behaviours, skills, psychological measures). It is important that these are based on empirically sound data.

The therapeutic community modality

The term 'therapeutic community' (TC) describes a complex psychosocial intervention which has been used to treat people with personality disorder, substance abuse and other addictions. Democratic TCs are cohesive groups whose members (staff and residents) participate together in daily decision-making regarding matters affecting group functions and in the development and delivery of therapeutic insight to self and others (Rutter and Crawford, 2005). The hierarchy between staff and residents is removed, and in this way some of the decision-making is entrusted to residents themselves within a "culture of enquiry" – openness to questioning so that understanding is owned by all, not merely the professionals (Main, 1983). In a secure setting, the hierarchy within the TC cannot be totally removed, but prison residents participate in decision-making and often in the provision of therapy. All members of the TC are seen as valuable, bringing individual strengths to the group, and the peer group is perceived as being fundamental in establishing a strong therapeutic alliance (Warren, Preedy-Fayers, McGauley, et al., 2003). However, staff in prison TCs in particular must provide strong leadership and have a responsibility to provide a safe therapeutic "frame" (Lees and Kennard, 1999).

There are also hierarchical TCs that are based on an environment in which there is a tier of roles, with staff being higher in rank than the residents. This is the model that is most popular in the USA for the treatment of substance abusers.

The modern TC movement traces its origins to residential programmes aiming to rehabilitate traumatised military casualties of the Second World War. Haigh (1999) identified five universal qualities of a modern TC:

- attachment (a sense of belonging)
- containment (safety)
- communication (openness)
- involvement (participation)
- agency (empowerment).

Furthermore, a TC has been defined as having four basic features: an informal atmosphere; regular meetings; participation in running the community; and residents as auxiliary therapists (Kennard, 1983).

The first established democratic TC in England was Henderson Hospital, which was founded in 1947 and took in those with and without criminal convictions. Democratic TCs have been run within the prison service since the 1960s and the first of these was HMP Grendon, which opened in 1962. The modern-day prison-based TC combines the supportive environment generally found in community TCs with the more formal programmes found in the Prison Service. Grendon is the only prison in England that is purely run as a TC. Other TCs comprise small units based inside larger mainstream prisons but separated from the normal prison regime wings. The TC at HMP Dovegate was the second to be established within the UK prison system, and the first to be privately managed. The Dovegate TC is a discrete unit, separate from the main prison, and consists of four TCs, an assessment unit and a high-intensity unit, with an overall capacity of 200 residents.

The TC at Grendon was designed to run in a similar way to the TC at Henderson Hospital, in that the population is composed of residents with personality disorder. The treatment model used in the TC at Dovegate is similar in some regards, although with a different focus. The population is not exclusively personality disordered, and, as Roland Woodward explained to Ursula Smartt (Smartt, 2001), there was to be a very strong emphasis on the development of skills that will be useful on release. It is also different from Grendon in that the TC at Dovegate has a stronger psychology rather than psychotherapy orientation.

The various strengths of the TC model include its ability to work within the everyday activities and discourse of the residents. The residents offer empathy and mutual support and can aid each other to avoid dysfunctional coping strategies, for example poor emotion regulation. New members of the TC should experience initial tolerance, support and sympathy; however, if they do not appear to work hard to change they will become the focus for peer challenge and, eventually, expelled from the regime. It is necessary for all TC residents to volunteer for admission as treatment is, by its nature, participatory (Rutter and Crawford, 2005).

It is a requirement of most TCs that referred patients or prisoners are of at least average intelligence and are without major psychiatric illness. This is to ensure sufficient responsivity to the intensive therapeutic regime. Residents sign up to a "contract" of rules, which usually include: no sex, no alcohol, no drugs (unless prescribed), no aggression or violence, and attendance at specified group therapy sessions. However, the TC regime is voluntary and there are often problems with high attrition rates. Residents at the TC in Dovegate can be de-selected for contravening the rules of the contract, or they can elect to leave by giving 48 hours' notice. If the resident changes his mind before 48 hours has passed he can withdraw his request to leave therapy, affording emotional cool down and the opportunity for self-reflection.

The TC is considered an effective treatment option for offenders with personality disorder because it utilises a multi-modal treatment approach that manages the variety of pathological manifestations of the personality disorder (Hollin, 1999). In addition, the TC can effective because it intentionally sets up an anti-criminal culture that challenges antisocial behaviour and experiences. This approach allows vigorous debate and disagreement without the possibility of resorting to criminal, particularly violent, behaviour. The TC is primarily a social treatment milieu, in which residents can come to understand and amend habitual psychological, cognitive and behavioural problematic responses.

An assumption underlying the TC philosophy is that the optimal functioning of residents in the milieu promotes better functioning in the external community (Chiesa, 2000). However, the TC, with its mixture of therapeutic culture and democratisation, is vastly different from the realities and demands of external society. Those who improve after a period of treatment in a TC may find it difficult to maintain this improvement once they leave and return to life outside it. This is a particularly pertinent issue for prison-based TCs, as the environment is enormously different from life in the community, and, whilst advances may be made in a secure setting, these may be difficult to sustain once the resident returns to the community or another non-therapeutic prison establishment.

HMP Grendon was originally evaluated by Marshall (1997) and the study was replicated by Taylor (2000). The findings from these studies show that prisoners selected for Grendon tended to be high-risk. Lower rates of reconviction were found for those admitted than for those remaining on the waiting list, and also for those who stayed for at least 18 months, most notably for life sentence prisoners. These studies found some reduction in reconviction rates for violent offences in the samples studied, and a reduction in sexual and violent offences in repeat sexual offenders. These results were clearly promising, illustrating the success of Grendon for various types of offenders.

Dosage and process

Jones (1997) found a pattern of deterioration during the initial stages of Grendon TC, with improvement occurring in the later stages. He found this change to occur alongside changes in self-perception, with residents viewing themselves as aggressive during the initial stages of therapy and less aggressive during the later stages. Jones proposed a model of therapeutic change brought about by confronting core criminogenic beliefs about the self and others, inducing a degree of cognitive dissonance accompanied by deterioration in self-esteem. Jones found that at this point in the therapeutic process a resident could *either* develop self-esteem enhancement strategies (and incorporate the value system that came with these strategies) *or* resort to old self-esteem maintenance strategies (including varieties of offending behaviour), thereby reinforcing the criminogenic value system. In the case of the latter outcome, the therapeutic process was "now construed as painful and ineffectual and perhaps even punitive" (1997, p. 125).

Genders and Player (1995) conducted semi-structured interviews with just over a hundred HMP Grendon TC residents in their study of "Therapeutic Achievements". Participants were divided into three groups according to time spent in therapy (less than 6 months; 6–12 months; and 12 months or longer). Residents who had been in therapy for fewer than six months nearly all reported that their perception of their problems had changed. All but one reported discovering new problems and coming to the realisation that their difficulties were considerably more complicated than they at first anticipated. They also found clear reduction in alienation at this time, and three-quarters of residents described lowering traditional prison barriers, such as pecking order and the "them–us" division with staff. Of those residents in the TC for at least 12 months, the majority were in favour of officers listening and contributing to group therapy. Genders and Player (1995) also found that men who had been in therapy for over a year were more likely to "stand out against the crowd . . . to assume personal responsibility" (p. 113), particularly in view of illicit activities occurring in the TC, such as drug supply and use. At this time, men were also more likely to claim that their problems emanated from difficulties in close relationships. Overall, residents in the 6–12-month group reported an increase in self-confidence, improved communication, socialisation skills and heightened tolerance of others. Interestingly, there was no reported increase in these areas in residents who stayed longer than a year.

Genders and Player (1995) concluded that the first six months in Grendon is defined by a settling-in period or an *"acclimatisation"* process (whereby traditional prison culture is pulled apart and replaced with the new traditions); the period between 6 and 12 months is a process of *"resocialisation"* (adjusting modes of social relations, reviewing social skills and consequently gaining more from relationships, especially with authority figures); and the period after 12 months is characterised by a *"consolidation"* phase (achievements are consolidated alongside an increase in confidence and trust in staff and movement towards greater social responsibility).

This innovative research shed light on processes that facilitate successful outcomes and highlight that the optimum period residents should spend in the therapeutic community is around 18 months. There are implications for premature withdrawal from therapy. If residents only complete six months of therapy and have not learnt to "resocialise" or had the opportunity to "consolidate", they may be inclined towards poor longer-term outcomes.

Oversight

Community of communities

In 2002 the Community of Communities was established as a means for achieving quality improvement within prison TCs. The Community of Communities is part of The Royal College of Psychiatrists' Centre for Quality Improvement and works in partnership with the Consortium for Therapeutic Communities and the Planned Environment Therapy Trust. The aim of the Community of Communities is to identify and share good TC practice, and it provides a mechanism for self- and peer-assessed review.

The joint review process is based on compliance with two sets of standards: the Service Standards for Therapeutic Communities, which contain items pertaining to the emotional health of a TC, and the Service Standards for Prison Service Democratic Therapeutic Communities, which have more to do with performance management. A team comprising a TC and non-TC specialist, a psychologist, a prison service representative and a lead reviewer spend two days in the TC. They undertake observations and interview staff and clients examining aspects of institutional support, treatment management and integrity, and quality of delivery. Standard compliance is scored: 2 if met, 1 if partially met and 0 if not met. Minimal levels of compliance should be 60% of PSO 7100 and at least 50% for each section (Paget and Turner, n.d.).

The review for 2007/2008 (Larkin and Paget, 2008) commented that there had been an overall improvement compared with the preceding three years "with the exception of HMP Dovegate which has experienced its poorest year so far" (p. 8). In particular, Dovegate was struggling to maintain support for residents in the continuity of care and resettlement. The report noted progressive improvement in the early years but a "worrying" downturn after 2005/2006. The review team for 2007/2008 noted a general lack of preparedness for the inspection, variability in treatment integrity between the TCs, and problems in supervision and training for staff. This does seem to correspond with a particularly difficult period for Dovegate TC, documented by Cullen and MacKenzie (2011) in the aftermath of Roland Woodward's departure and the ensuing de-stabilisation. The review for 2011/2012 (Thorne and Paget, 2012) commented on the improvement achieved by Dovegate, which corresponded with some restructuring and rebranding of the four Dovegate communities.

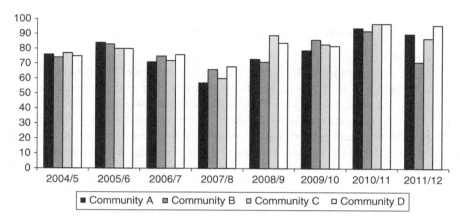

Figure 2.1 Community of communities overall evaluation of Dovegate TC's compliance rate

Figure 2.1 shows the scores achieved by the four Dovegate communities and a discernible drop in ratings from 2006 to 2008.

Her Majesty's Inspectorate of Prisons

Her Majesty's Inspectorate of Prisons for England and Wales (HMI Prisons) reports on conditions for and treatment of those in prison. Its role is to provide independent scrutiny and to promote the concept of "healthy prisons" whereby staff work effectively to support prisoners to reduce reoffending or achieve other agreed outcomes.

HM Chief Inspector of Prisons is appointed by the Justice Secretary from outside the Prison Service, for a term of five years. The Chief Inspector reports directly to the Justice Secretary and ministers on the treatment of prisoners, conditions in prisons in England and Wales, and other matters as directed by the Justice Secretary. The Inspectorate also reports to the Home Secretary on conditions and treatment in all places of immigration detention in the UK. There have been a number of inspections carried out on the TC. Early inspections reflected some of the teething problems, but noted the enthusiasm of staff and offered a conclusion that "some serious and often extremely difficult offenders are clearly helped to readjust to a level of appropriate and law abiding behaviour while they are in the TC, with every prospect of this learning assisting progress with the remainder of their sentences and, hopefully, on release" (HM Chief Inspector of Prisons, 2004, p. 5). In Box 2.2 we summarise some of the key positive and negative assessments of the Dovegate TC made by HM Prison Inspectorate after its first couple of years of operation.

Box 2.2   HM Prison Inspectorate comments on Dovegate TC in 2004

The pros

There were good induction arrangements, few instances of self-harm and little evidence of bullying. Relations between staff and prisoners were extremely good, with evidence of "genuine mutual support".

The TC had achieved a good balance between therapy and purposeful activity. Prisoners enjoyed a good amount of time out of their cell. Therapy was the major activity but there was also a range of education and vocational activities to meet the needs of the population. These activities were well managed and organised, and well integrated with therapy.

The cons

Some systems, such as the incentives and earned privileges (IEP) scheme, were unnecessary in the context of a TC but others, such as racist incident complaints, needed to be reinforced and there was a general need to tackle diversity issues.

Healthcare was delivered entirely from the main prison and needed to be more integrated with the work of the TC.

The TC was not performing sufficiently well on resettlement into the community and reintegration into the prison system and needed further development. There were many good basic resettlement systems but delivery was hampered by a lack of appropriately skilled staff. The drugs strategy did not match the needs of the TC.

There was concern that selection of residents was being "skewed by commercial imperatives."

Residents who had withdrawn from therapy "hung around listlessly."

By 2006 HM Inspectorate of Prisons (2006) reported that about 30% of prisoners on the TC were not in therapy and that this was still putting strains on all aspects of the TC. The tardiness in moving these prisoners was blamed by the prison on crowding elsewhere in the system. The report expressed a view that there was a "commercial imperative to keep numbers up on the unit" and concluded "whatever the cause, or combination of causes, the situation was unsatisfactory". However, the inspection noted improvements in education, training and resettlement planning. Staff–prisoner relationships for those in therapy were very good.

In 2008 there remained a large numbers of men still in the TC not participating in therapy, about 40%, and the inspection noted how damaging this was to staff morale and that it undermined progress by engaged residents.

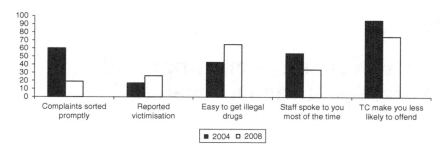

Figure 2.2 Selected variables comparing TC residents' self-reported assessment of Dovegate in 2004 and in 2008

As a consequence, the report gloomily observed that two of the TCs had failed to meet the required standards of the Independent Correctional Services Accreditation Panel. Notwithstanding the inspection praising the positive relationships between staff and residents, the results also revealed some deterioration that confirmed the difficulties noted by the Community of Communities review (HM Chief Inspector of Prisons, 2008). In Figure 2.2 we highlight some of the problems identified from the survey of residents' assessments carried out during the 2008 inspection.

Cullen and Mackenzie (2011, p. 70) noted a high attrition rate in therapy managers; nine had left by the end of 2008. They suggested that the combining of the security and therapeutic responsibilities, in their terms, was "not do-able". But by 2012 the Inspectorate reported a turnaround: the numbers of drop-outs or completers remaining within the TC had declined significantly, and the delivery of therapy had much improved, with appropriate levels of staff on each community and improved family support to help residents transition away from the TC. The therapeutic day had been reorganised, better structures had been put in place to manage sentence plans, and there were "impressive" levels of peer support and self-management among residents that distinguish successful TCs. Reception and induction were effective, as bullying was under control, levels of self-harm were low, and there was little evidence of drug misuse and little use of force and segregation.

Thus, between 2006 and 2008 there was a discernible decrement in the measured quality of the Dovegate TC's delivery, reflected in both the Community of Communities and HM Prison Inspectorate assessments as well as those of the residents. After the 2008 reorganisation instigated by Ray Duckworth, quality improved. It is hard to say with any precision what impact this may have had on the therapeutic gains of residents, but it is a background factor that needs to be taken into consideration when evaluating outcomes.

3
Controversies, Beginnings and Workings of the Dovegate TC

Introduction

On 21 November 1997 an invitation was issued to build a prison at Marchington, Staffordshire for an 800 Category B prison for adults with a facility for a 200-place therapeutic community (TC) (Genders, 2003). This was a legacy of the private finance initiative (PFI) of the early 1990s. The successful consortium, led by Premier Custodial Services, built and opened the prison containing the TC at HMP Dovegate in 2001 as the first purpose-built prison TC in the UK. Roland was Dovegate's first director of therapy and had previously worked in TCs at HMP Gartree and Grendon.

The TC has been defined as:

> a residential, social environment where the primary treatment agents are the group and the community. All activities are the focus of therapy and the TC approach retains primacy but provides a context for other forms of treatment.
>
> (Woodward et al., 2000)

The setting up of a TC within a prison is itself problematic (Genders and Player, 1995) and especially so in a privately run prison (Woodward chapter in Cullen and MacKenzie, 2011). A new enterprise of this kind is bound to have teething problems, which, indeed, Dovegate TC had (Cullen and Miller, 2010). This chapter describes the setting up of the Dovegate TC and discusses the paradox of a TC within the confines of a prison environment and the dilemmas presented by privatisation. We then go on to explain the Dovegate TC regime. In particular, we examine the underlying originating philosophy of the Dovegate TC deriving from the work of Rapoport (1960) and Yalom (1995) and developed by Roland Woodward with Eric Cullen. We touch on the training of the Dovegate TC staff and we also present some of the ideas that informed the design of the Dovegate physical environment.

Controversies

Therapeutic communities in prison: An oxymoron?

It appears a definitional contradiction to establish a therapeutic unit in an institution that is seen by some as for punishment, which exists to separate criminals from society and where most offenders want their stay to pass as quickly and easily as possible (Cullen, 1997). TCs are small cohesive communities where residents have a significant involvement in decision-making and the practicalities of the day-to-day running of the environment. TCs are deliberately structured so that residents are encouraged to take personal responsibility for their lives and to minimise dependence on professionals. The peer group is essential for forming a therapeutic alliance, although there is a need for strong leadership from staff in order to provide a safe "frame" in which therapeutic work can occur (Association of Therapeutic Communities, 1999).

The basic ethos of a TC may come into direct conflict with the underlying assumptions of security, good order and control that are inherent in the prison system (Cullen et al., 1997a). Often, TCs are set up in already established prisons and/or occupy the physical space of a previously established specialist unit, such as the vulnerable prisoner unit, or hospital wing. On the one hand, prisoners and staff may associate the residents in the new TC with the original purpose of the wing, labelling and potentially stigmatising the TC residents. On the other hand, it is beneficial for TC staff and residents to be separate from the discipline culture prevalent in the main prison (Rawlings, 1998). In the case of Dovegate, it enjoyed the precedent of being a purpose-built prison within which the TC could be designed to meet its therapeutic purposes.

The physical constraints imposed by security requirements carry with them all the paraphernalia of a lock-up culture necessary to contain prisoners and constrain their movement. TCs outside prison walls are largely run and maintained by residents along democratic lines, creating an essential part of their work skills training, whilst a TC within a prison often has to adapt to prison routines. Mandatory drug testing and cell searches are components of prison life that are forced onto the TC. Prisons tend to be hierarchical and socially divided, with prison officers having a monopoly of formal power, and can, if required, use legitimate coercion to obtain compliance with the rules of the institution (Genders, 2003). Thus, prisons impose non-negotiable rules, intended to bring about obedience in a setting that de-personalises and limits personal choices.

TCs seek to develop individuals' personal identity in flattened social structures where all members can exercise power democratically. Regulation of conduct is through discussion and negotiation. In a democratic TC, residents discuss issues and behaviour they are unhappy with, decisions being made on group agreement. The TC regime aims to reduce social divisions and enfranchise community members, "involving them in the exercise of power through choice and engagement in the process of rule-making" (Woodward, 1999, p. 163). TC members comply with the rules because they internalise them during the process of making them.

TCs are generally viewed with suspicion when introduced to an established mainstream prison. When/if regular practices are removed or modified to meet the TC regime, other inmates can feel aggrieved that this new regime is receiving special treatment, whilst staff may feel challenged by a seemingly uncontrollable new system. Effort is required to build bridges between the two models (Woodward, 1999, p. 163). As Genders (2003) explains, "the successful operation of a prison therapeutic community depends upon the extent to which the dual requirements of treatment and control can be met" (p. 142). A good relationship, which is required between the two to enable a healthy TC to develop, needs those within the prison system to be educated so that myths regarding TCs are removed (Rawlings, 1998). A balance needs to be struck within the prison so that the relationship with the TC does not have too great a distance (this problem contributed to the closure of Barlinnie's Special Unit in 1995), but is not too close (jeopardising security issues or disrupting the therapeutic regime). Rawlings (1998) suggests that the problem is not one of "how do we make the TC fit into the prison culture but rather how do we manage the lack of fit?" (p. 17).

Staff almost invariably enter the TC with experiences of working in mainstream prisons. They have to lose the dominant, rule-setting requirement of a prison officer and adhere to a therapeutic, democratically run establishment, involving a rethinking of work ethic and attitude. TC staff have multiple roles within a complex setting and there is a requirement to uphold personal and professional boundaries, difficult within an environment where these roles are somewhat interchangeable and an amount of self-disclosure (verbal and non-verbal) is inevitable (Rawlings, 1999). Their role moves between group facilitator and community member, the boundaries of which have to be carefully set for the TC to run efficiently. The closure of Barlinnie Special Unit is a clear example of how the collapse of these boundaries can lead to the community's demise (Cooke, 1997).

Whiteley (1997), in response to concerns regarding ethical problems posed by the close relationships between TC staff and residents, concluded that the very nature of the contact allows the generation of a system of functional and prosocial values and moral behaviour in residents. Newell (1996 cited by Cullen, 1997, p. 87) states:

> The TC concept is based on the assumption that prisoners and staff form the community of care and respect which is committed to the development

of personal functioning, to address offending and offensive behaviour in order to change so that those who go through the process create no more victims.

The commercial imperative

Elaine Genders (2007) reminds us that contracting out the building and management of prisons was a legacy of the Thatcher Conservative government, driven by the ideological principle that private was better and more effective than public. Penal policy, which favours containment and deterrence, was considered easier to manage within tight contractual specification than the more difficult rehabilitative functions. The proponents claim that this is a good deal for the tax-payer. Opponents raise principled concerns that the state should not delegate the consequences of punishment administered by the courts and the well-being of prisoners for the purposes of private profit. Genders (2007) is pessimistic about the public interest being always served by the involvement of the private sector, and cites the example of the Dovegate TC to expose the potentially perverse effects of contractual obligations and financial penalties. She says that, because prisoners volunteer themselves for admission to the TC in order to keep up the contracted numbers (and because the Prison Service was slow in transferring prisoners both in and out), prisoners from Dovegate main prison were being given preference over men on the waiting list. Genders noted the concern of the Chief Inspector of Prisons, Anne Owers, discussed briefly in the previous chapter, that the Dovegate "volunteers" were often clearly unsuitable and that selection criteria were being overridden by financial imperatives. Owers had concluded in her 2006 HM Prison Inspectorate report that this was neither fair nor appropriate, and potentially threatened the therapeutic integrity by destabilising the community.

Cullen and MacKenzie (2011, p. 56) were more sanguine, in that "the procedures for selection and completion of therapy at Dovegate are recorded in great detail and are, unlike Grendon, subject to contractual obligations". They conclude: "all this was anticipated at the drafting stage even before the contract was even awarded. The transparency of these operational quality control measures and the Freedom of Information Act should serve to reassure concerns about profit-driven circumventions." Notwithstanding these reassurances, there were problems in moving prisoners out of the TC, not necessarily because of the commercial imperative but rather due to "arbitrary decisions made by a bureaucrat in the Prison Service based on the rationale that as people in therapy are volunteers, the choice to leave therapy is regarded as a non-priority action" (Cullen and Miller, 2010, p. 38). When the prison estate was under pressure, for example the riot in Lincoln prison in October 2002, 200 displaced prisoners had to be located somewhere. A consequence for Dovegate TC was that the planned admission and screening of suitable applicants were suspended, and the lack of suitable assessments meant the admission of many unsuitable prisoners. Later Cullen did admit an element of commercial pressure: the tyranny of the number 194, which was the contracted figure of occupancy for the TC, and this "hung like a sword of Damocles" over the heads of directors of therapy (Cullen and MacKenzie, 2011, p. 195).

The considerations for and against privatisation of prisons presented below are a summary drawn from arguments presented by Cullen and MacKenzie (2011, pp. 49–53). They are of the view that the case in favour of privatisation "just tip the scales" (and report that they have seen few of the feared effects of profit imperatives influencing how staff treated residents (pp. 53–54)) (Table 3.1).

Roland Woodward also came to the view that the private bid to build Dovegate and the prospect of building a new kind of TC was a challenge he could not resist, given the flexibility and innovation that the consortium was offering in contrast to the "ossification" paralysing imaginative development in the public sector (Woodward chapter in Cullen and MacKenzie, 2011, p. 132).

Table 3.1   Pros and cons of private prisons (after Cullen and MacKenzie, 2011)

Considerations	For	Against
Cost	Financing, siting, building done more quickly and cheaply "True" costs visible	Addition of profit margin needs to satisfy shareholders and pay dividends
Quality	Competition encourages creativity and imaginative solutions freed from restrictive working practices and entrenched operating principles	Risk of paring down costs by hiring younger, less experienced staff
Accountability	Raising of standards through contractual requirements, HM Prison Service-appointed controllers	Invocation of commercial confidentiality to inhibit open scrutiny
Security	Reputational risks in the event of breaches of security and contractual penalties motivate strengthening security standards	Threatened by high turnover and inexperience of staff (because of poorer pay and conditions)
Ethics	So long as treatment matches or exceeds that provided by the public sector, no problem	Moral concerns about making profit from incarceration, legal liability

Philosophy and principles of Dovegate TC

The fundamental philosophy applied at Dovegate is that: "the process of change in democratic TCs comes from a gradual growth of self-knowledge and a 'culture of enquiry'" (Woodward et al., 2000).

The TC's main principles are drawn from the development of the analytic–democratic TC in the UK, and consist of:

- an emphasis on unlabelled normal living, i.e. minimal use of professional jargon;
- an emphasis on personal growth through enhanced interpersonal relationships;
- a non-hierarchical decision-making structure;
- a belief in self-help and that residents can help each other, sometimes more so than professionals can through advice;
- an emphasis on "moral treatment", i.e. treated as normal within a consciously sustained social atmosphere;
- shared responsibility for every possible aspect of the life of the community;
- an emphasis on open, honest communication between all community members, staff and residents;
- an activation of "living-learning" situations;
- safeguarding the culture of enquiry;
- allowing space to play;
- support and activation of the belief that the more people are empowered, the greater your empowerment.

Dovegate TC is guided by Yalom and Rapoport's work. Rapoport (1960) suggests that there are four principles which characterise democratic–analytic TCs:

1. Democracy – democratic decision-making and power sharing;
2. Permissive – individual and collective tolerance of personal and interpersonal behaviour;
3. Communal – shared amenities, closer relationships and informality between staff and residents alike;
4. Reality confronting – encouraging everyone to express how each other's behaviour affects them in order to address interpersonal distortions, denial and avoidance.

In order to avoid "cloning" the Grendon approach, there was a departure from the Adlerian psychoanalytic bases. Roland was inspired by the writings of Yalom and drew on these to form a template from which to develop the Dovegate approach (see Box 3.1 for details).

Box 3.1   Yalom's 11 therapeutic factors (1980)

- Instillation of hope, which is significantly correlated with positive therapy outcome.
- Universality – realising others have been as lost as you??
- Altruism – for the genuine good of others: receiving through giving.
- Group cohesiveness – gaining public esteem and acceptance.
- Imparting information (guidance) – teaching by staff and fellow group members either directly or indirectly.
- Corrective recapitulation of the primary family group, i.e. returning group members to their own first group, the family, and exploring what went wrong, what experiences are with them and are influencing how they are today.
- Development of socialising techniques, e.g. ability to give and receive accurate feedback and to act on it.
- Imitative behaviour, i.e. practising new behaviours via modelling-operant learning.
- Catharsis, i.e. the purgative process of addressing the most painful and guilt-laden things and not being rejected.
- Existential factors refers to five things: life at times is unfair and unjust; there is no escape from some of life's pain or from death; no matter how close to anyone, life must be faced alone; facing issues of life and death, thus living life more honestly and being less caught up in trivialities; learning ultimate responsibility for the way your life is being lived.
- Interpersonal learning – the task of the group is to help the individual learn how to develop distortion-free, gratifying interpersonal relationships within a crime-free lifestyle. Gradually, an adaptive spiral is set in motion, with distortions diminishing and the ability to form rewarding relationships.

Building the environment

Elaine Genders (2003, p. 146) noted that the PFI competition for Dovegate gave an opportunity to design a therapeutic community *ab initio*. She goes on to say that the physical environment can enhance or dampen the success of the regime, and opined that Grendon's accommodation had little that assisted its therapeutic purposes. Her ideal specification included functionally adequate facilities for the scheduled activities, and a sufficient number of rooms with sizes compatible with small group meetings and larger community meetings.

Roland took personal charge and a great deal of care with the physical layout of Dovegate TC. He said: "the task for us was to create a physical environment that supported a cultural lifestyle that we would define. In order to do this we had to know how people would live in this space and what they needed the space to do for them" (Woodward chapter in Cullen and MacKenzie, 2011, p. 130). Peter Thomson, a Surrey University master's student, interviewed Roland about the environmental considerations in 2004. Roland's responses are given in Box 3.2.

Box 3.2 Roland Woodward on the physical environment of Dovegate

There were two things – we needed to design in all the spaces required for a therapeutic community for it to function properly so there had to be discreet group rooms, a room big enough for an entire community to meet in and then there had to be a serviceable space for each community to own as well. And in terms of the prison and the way it was designed, it was important that the office with staff in was actually in the community because the company builds prisons where the office isn't in that situation a lot of the time. The front doors of the community were actually manual and key operated whereas in a lot of the spaces that the company builds, they have sliders. So it was a different design for the company. So there was that – the discreet needs of it being a TC and then there was the overall design in terms of trying to build a low level complex of buildings which reflected a community. So there was a central focal point which is the water feature and then the chevrons, which contained the communities and amenities, all pointing onto that area. So there's a real sense of being drawn into the centre of it.

The other thing was most prisons or every prison of this size has internal zone fences so that areas of the prison are zoned off for security reasons. In our design, there are no zoned fences. So when you walk across or round the community, the only fence you see is the exterior wall. So it's a very, very open design and although it's a category B prison, we wanted the design to give the message that this was a place where people are trusted who came here voluntarily and our part of that was to demonstrate very quickly that you were in an open trusting kind of place. It's built to make you feel part of the community. Whereas most establishments would have exercise yards that are fenced off with high fences with wire round the top, here everyone exercises together in the market square so it is very much a community feel.

Box 3.2   (Continued)

And different colours that the cells were painted depending on whether they were on a cold side or warm side of the building and we coordinated bedding colours as well so a huge amount of thought went into that to start off with. We also made quite a bit of money available to the staff teams to personalise the spaces. So one of the things they did was buy an awful lot of plants so there's a lot of living stuff around the environment as well. We encouraged that and we encouraged the guys to personalise the living spaces as well by decorating them themselves and coming up with different designs. When I first looked at the designs and then saw it actually being built was that other big communities in prisons don't have all the cell doors looking out on a common area and it feels like a community where everybody can see everybody else's front door. And so if somebody comes out of a group and they're upset or whatever, everybody sees it and everybody knows. And that has had an impact so that's worked for us. We deliberately didn't put in fixed furniture. We just put in tables and chairs and said the residents can use that space how they will. So they determine what they put in that space and they have done and they've used those spaces not only to regulate how they live but they do drama in those spaces as well.

Mention has already been made of Roland's insistence on using a round table for staff group discussions. Roland wanted to give TC residents a role in the decoration too. He told Peter Thompson:

I think we're probably through our second set of murals in the joint vestibule; a common vestibule before they split off into the two communities. Every so often somebody will decide to do a mural. And you know it comes through like that. Then the next community comes in and decides nah we're not too keen on that so they'll paint over it and they do. So there's that constant change. But they also want to...I mean we had an arts festival in the summer. It's something that we try to do each year and there's... The first thing they wanted to do was have sculptures outside the represented groups so there's now a sculpture outside our window which is made of old chairs which have been welded together into a set of figures which have been set.

There is a considerable body of work from the environmental psychology literature that argues for the idea of attachment to place(s) (see, e.g., Raymond et al.,

2010 for a brief overview of conceptual and measurement issues). The case is made for a construct that comprises place identity, whereby aspects of the self, such as emotions and symbolic connections, embedded in places, help towards defining who we are; place dependence is more functional, in that it reflects the ability of physical aspects of a place to support the intended use. We can discern from Roland Woodward's reflections that both the symbolic dimension of supporting a sense of self and positive emotions engendered by the physical environment and care about the instrumental needs of TC residents were factored into the design.

The idea of place attachment and dependence is much richer than these two dimensions. Theorists argue that the developing self has highly meaningful associations to places as the person grows up, which figures in the construction of an individual's identity (Gustafson, 2001). Notions of community attachment, such as belongingness, being rooted and having a sense of connection to residents of a community, are mediated by physical proximity and the development of social bonds. Twigger-Ross and Uzzell (1996) propose that places offer people a point of reference for past actions and experiences, which, in turn, plays an important role in maintaining individual and group identities. This has a number of implications: first, can we tap into place attachment memories to provide an indication of positive or negative experiences; second, can we get a sense of the strength and influence of these attachments; and, third, can we create a positive place attachment and dependence in supporting the therapeutic goals, whereby the environment can assist in the reinstatement of healthy emotional and social bonding?

We use the idea of place as a means of accessing attachment in our study, and this is explained more fully in Chapter 8. Residents' identification of Dovegate as a place in which they can construct new relationships and enjoy a sense of community proved an important aspect of their therapeutic journey.

Training the staff

Roland Woodward, with Eric Cullen and colleagues, developed and delivered a training programme for TC therapists, managers and counsellors (Woodward et al., 2000). Training was cascaded to teams on the four TCs. For Roland, the crucial thing about the training was that it should be an articulation of the philosophy and treatment model of the TC. In essence, the training "was the translation from theory to the practical and operational day-to-day living in the TC" (Woodward's chapter in Cullen and MacKenzie, 2011, p. 145). He wanted the training to be accessible and provide an understanding of why things were done in a particular way. He invented the SMART – Social Milieu And Reintegration Therapist – role whereby staff could understand the reasoning and contribute to the development and evolution of the TC. As Cullen and

MacKenzie (2011, p. 192) put it, "Roland's vision of the growth and development of the [Dovegate] TCs depended on the therapy managers and their teams learning through mistakes and taking ownership of the process. He did not want other cultures from other places imposed upon his developing children."

The training programme ran over a period of four weeks, summary details of which are provided in Box 3.3.

Box 3.3   The Dovegate TC four-week training programme

Week one
History of TC, introduction to Rapport's four principles, definition of primary roles: prison officer, social milieu, group facilitator role, process/team support and recorder/data roles, explanation of SMART, i.e. understanding inter-group processes, continuity and group dynamics, coping with personal emotions, modelling reasonable rational behaviour.

Week two
Attachment theory, Stack Sullivan's self-dynamism and corrective emotional experience, group work and cognitive-behavioural therapy, practicing SMART skills.

Week three
Socialising, family re-enactment, social skills, social drive theory and experiential learning groups. Boundary issues, e.g. limits of sexual behavior, the making of inappropriate exceptions.

Week four
Group facilitator skills, role plays, issues of staff dissent, threats to the community, functional analysis of offending behaviours.

Structure and regime

Applicants for Dovegate can be made from any prison, and people may be recommended to apply or may self-refer. They are sent a referral pack to assess their suitability for assessment within the TC. Prisoners who report recent substance misuse, are taking psychotropic drugs or have recently engaged in self-harming behaviour are deemed not suitable for the assessment process. Prisoners are also required to have 18 months left of their custodial sentences to progress to the assessment stage and to have expressed motivation to take part in the TC.

On arrival at Dovegate TC, individuals reside in the Assessment and Resettlement Unit (ARU), where they are assessed for TC suitability by staff over four-week periods. The assessment includes how they respond to small group sessions to see whether they are able and willing to engage. They are then assigned to one of the four TCs, originally called A, B, C and D.

The High Intensity Programme (HIP) was designed to take difficult life-sentence prisoners who needed more detailed and sensitive assessment before being located on one of the TCs, and also to act as time out for those at risk because they had not adjusted to the regime or when it was appropriate to give them a break from therapy (Cullen and MacKenzie, 2011, p. 38).

During the period of the research, every weekday was split broadly into three parts. Mornings began with a business meeting, followed by a community meeting or a small therapy group. Afternoons were devoted to ordinary prison activities, such as offence-focused programmes, work or education. Residents also had the opportunity to take part in psychodrama. The evenings were free for the usual leisure activities available in the prison.

The five core parts in the TC were:

(i) Small Groups

The small groups and the community meetings are the core focus of the community. These serve to "create and develop the atmosphere of trust, respect and honesty which is so important in allowing the therapeutic process to take effect" (Woodward and Hodkin, 1996, p. 48).

A small group of up to ten residents with one or more members of staff meets three times a week for one hour. These groups are open-ended and non-hierarchical. Each member is gradually encouraged to share his life story with the group, starting with his earliest memories and including life moments to date which he feels have most influenced the way he is today. The member's criminal history, particularly his current offences, is explored. He will be expected to discuss his behaviour in the community as well. Such exploration will endeavour to identify in greater depth his previous patterns of problematic and antisocial behaviour, and to challenge the maintenance of such patterns. The group will also provide the opportunity to help make links between "here and now" feelings, thoughts and behaviours and their past ways, including offending and problematic patterns of behaving. Thus, it is in the small group that the core therapy work of the TC is done.

(ii) Feedback

Immediately after small groups, the community convenes to share a brief feedback session. Feedback involves a description of what took place, such as who said what, the group mood and dynamics. Feedback is not open to correction or discussion at this time (but may be returned to by groups and community in following meetings). Staff then meet to have their own feedback and analysis session.

(iii) Community Meetings

These meetings are held twice a week for one hour. The purpose and functions include:

- a forum where all community members and staff meet;
- an opportunity for residents to hold and practise positions of responsibility and power;
- a forum for presenting information to everyone, e.g. prison rules changes and work details;
- the venue for the community to nominate, discuss, consider and elect representatives to any, and every, aspect of the community's work and responsibilities;
- the appropriate setting for inter-group and intra/inter-community issues, e.g. issues concerning relationships between one community and another within the TC.

(iv) Staff Support, Feedback and Sensitivity Meetings

These meetings share a similar purpose to those of the community, e.g. giving feedback and making sense of therapy issues and function to help staff:

- monitor individual and group progress;
- deal with some of the issues associated with new arrivals in the community;
- reflect upon and manage their own feelings and thoughts.

(v) Informal Socialising

This includes both the natural mixing and activities within the community and the extra-communal experiences, i.e. inter-unit, TC-wide.

Aside from "Educom", an eliding of education and commerce described earlier, Roland's other innovation was "rezart", an abbreviation of residents' art. This was to be an annual festival of fun things to do with no explicit therapeutic goal. Activities included dance, poetry, film-making, sculpture, embroidery, electronic gaming and drama, with the hope that "if people in the TC found new activities that they enjoyed that they would incorporate into their lives and therefore have an additional way to occupy their time – and of course a way to express themselves" (Woodard, chapter in Cullen and MacKenzie, 2011, p. 153).

Administration

Staffing levels and roles

Dovegate TC staff initially comprised the director, four TC managers, managers for Educom, the ARU and HIP, a visiting psychiatrist and some administrative support. Roland's original conception was to break down the barriers between the therapy and security demands, which Genders and Player (1995) discussed as bringing about tension. Roland attempted to fuse the security and therapy roles by (a) asking all staff to wear uniform, (b) sharing training and exposing all staff to the requirements of the prison officer role, (c) making the therapy manager responsible for all aspects of therapy and operational function, and (d) giving a degree of autonomy to the therapy mangers to solve problems.

As mentioned earlier, HM Prison Inspectorate had expressed some concern about staffing levels and the numbers of men remaining in the TC who were not participating in therapy. In 2008, when Ray Duckworth became director of the TC, he instituted a clearer separation of therapy and security roles. Moreover, the TC was rebranded as a therapeutic prison and residents chose new names: Avalon, Camelot, Endeavour and Genesis. The Senate was disbanded and there was a definite shift back towards a more hierarchical administrative structure and a change of emphasis reflected by the shift from TC to a therapeutic prison.

The Senate

This comprised the operational and therapy managers, the psychiatrist, the Educom manager and, latterly, one of Roland's administrative support staff members. This forum was where people brought problems and issues and attempted to broker resolutions. As mentioned in the Introduction, there was also the fluffy, which was a more informal gathering. Although the Senate was disbanded in 2008, although the fluffy continued to meet informally for a little while longer.

Outcomes

This is a contentious area, which Genders noted with particular reference to Dovegate TC (Genders, 2002). She asks two key questions: can the processes of change be demonstrated, and are behavioural improvements, such as compliance with prison rules or desistence from offending, meaningful? Genders points out that in therapy all human resources (and some environmental ones) are mobilised to achieve therapeutic goals. She questions whether the relative contributions of all these ingredients can be isolated with any precision. We tried to address these by disaggregating and unpacking the constituent elements implicated in offending by looking at levels of self-esteem, propensity to aggression and other attitudinal changes that are the precursors to more constructive relationship-forming, increasing "other" awareness and self-management. By assessing change using psychometric measurement (and employing the reliable change index) and by asking residents to comment on their own experiences, we hoped we could demonstrate meaningful change. By meaningful change, we would argue that the Reliable Change Index (RCI) demonstrates discernible clinical movement in respect to psychological constructs, and residents' own commentaries allow us to map the interpretation that the men themselves gave to changes that were taking place.

Genders also asks how those incidents or moments, out of the totality of a prisoner's sentence, that might have contributed to change can be separated out. We tried to address this in two ways: by repeat data collection, i.e. the psychometric measurements, focus groups and our multiple card sorting task, to isolate changes to at least some degree to key points in time, and also by assessing residents' progress against any changes in a comparison group (non-TC offenders). Whilst acknowledging that comparison is not without its difficulties, we do not accept Genders' view that a direct comparison between prisons is "almost impossible" (p. 298). Whilst the comparison group barely changed, we did detect improvement in those receiving the TC treatment. Genders also questions whether the dosage framework is a legitimate approach, since there are individual differences in responsivity. As mentioned above, we argue that our use of the reliable change index goes some way towards mitigating this concern.

When he was describing appropriate outcomes of the TC, Roland's view was that

> any possible change in behaviour . . . if somebody has spent their life stepping into your personal space and they learn not to do that, it's a good outcome. Outcomes don't have to be big or spectacular it's about observable change.

This is rather a long way from the reconviction rate measurement required by the Home Office as an operationalisation of the success or otherwise of a prison treatment programme. David Lynes was more pragmatic about other forms of measurable success from the point of view of the prison and the political imperatives:

> From the point of view of our masters, I think that success needs to show a result in various measurable terms, when that person goes back out into society or then they go onwards into another establishment you can measure success in terms of number of adjudications, reduction in self harm, better engagement with programmes. Eventually the Holy Grail is that a person goes out and a) doesn't commit any more offences and b) lives a life which is worthwhile.

David elaborated his views about outcomes as follows:

> You can't put your residents through a psychological X-ray machine that tells you exactly what's wrong with them, and then measures them to see what is right with them when they get out. You may have a person who you work hard with, and they take away an experience, but nobody knows about it, and it grows later, and you think "that's a success", in terms of moral or humanistic terms. So that's the core of the success.... if a resident has an experience that endures, a positive experience that endures after the intervention, that's a success... that's a success in moral or humanistic terms.

Ray Duckworth says in his Custodial Review interview that the therapy groups allow prisoners to open up about their past feelings, motivators and key influences, and it is through challenge and patience that residents come round. With the support of the members of the therapy group and TC staff and help from psychotherapists, drama therapists and other specialists, the TC helps to break through the residents' mental barriers. Ray said: "in this way we alter the way the individual behaves and thinks about his interaction with people; he becomes more pro-social through this process" (Custodial Review, 2012).

Finally, a comment from a TC resident summarised what success in the TC looked like for him:

> If you can put the theory into practice, that would be a success, if you stayed off for more than two years that would be classed as a success. Getting a job, that would be a success. There are a hell of a lot of successes, not just one.

4
The Data

Introduction

A key aspect of our approach to the research was to examine the process of change and the meaning that was attached to that change. Our research brief had been set by Roland Woodward, as Dovegate's first director of therapy. As well as identifying the TC residents' degree of change on various psychological characteristics, such as self-esteem, anger and sense of alienation, each of which has been associated with maintaining criminal lifestyles, Roland wanted us to explore the process of treatment. This meant looking at the idiosyncratic needs and following the journeys of TC residents whilst in the Dovegate TC, as well as explicating what ex-residents took with them back into mainstream prison and also when returning to the world outside. In keeping with the ethos of the TC, we tried to encourage the TC residents and ex-residents as much as possible to comment on their own lived experiences, as we were anxious to recognise their expertise and value their insights about Dovegate. Being in the TC meant engaging with and doing the work of therapy. We wanted, as far as we could, to extend a sense of active engagement in terms of their research participation.

As the search for meaning was the impetus for our research investigation, it logically followed that "talk" was essential to our enquiries and that amassing words were critical to our data collection. This, in turn, dictated the use of qualitative methods, the most obvious being interviewing, to garner TC residents' own stories to derive a narrative account of the Dovegate experience. Using a qualitative methodology and analytical approach was also compatible with the conceptual shifts in offender treatment evaluation by taking the service-user perspective. Whilst such an approach allowed individuals to be heard, the challenge to the researcher is how to make sense of and present a coherent account amidst the cacophony of competing voices. Whose voice is privileged, can we capture individual differences and can we typify stories that draw out the strands of common experiences?

Many evaluations of treatment are undertaken by means of quantitative methods (Wakeling & Travers, 2010). Evaluators of interventions assess individuals before the intervention and then afterwards, making the assumption that any differences between the two measurements are attributable to the specific intervention. But there are several threats to such assumptions:

- lack of normative data against which to assess scores;
- ceiling or floor effects (in other words, the starting score of an individual and their subsequent change score may give an erroneous impression of change achieved);
- use of group aggregate scores can mask individual change by not fully appreciating the spread of scores;
- recognition that a person may regress before being able to progress in achieving the goals of the intervention;
- extraneous factors that might influence outcomes.

Even the "gold standard" RCT, which attempts to design out interference in the evaluation by strictly controlling potential sources of variation, has been criticised for its failure to maintain the same controls when applied in prison settings (Hollin et al., 2004). These criticisms notwithstanding, we did not dismiss quantitative methods, as they have their place in providing descriptive accounts and allowed us to use psychometric measurement to track changes in psychological characteristics over time. We also recognise the value of having a comparison group as a yardstick against which to compare the Dovegate residents' progression. Thus, we opted for a mixed method design of quantitative (QUANT) and qualitative (quals) techniques to provide as rounded a picture of the Dovegate experience as possible. In this chapter we explain our reasoning, provide details of the research techniques we used and give a description of the Dovegate residents who participated in the different component parts of the study. We also discuss how we dealt with issues of reliability and validity.

Methodological considerations

Randomised controlled trials and why we did not use this method

A common approach to assessing change within clinical settings is to measure a patient's traits, attitudes, beliefs and/or behaviour before receiving treatment and then to measure the same characteristics after treatment. Any change is assumed to be a function of the clinical or therapeutic intervention. One way to undertake such measurement is by using a randomised control trial (RCT) in which participants are randomly allocated to receive one of several clinical interventions (Jadad, 1998). The main aim of an RCT is to find out which intervention or treatment works. The interventions can consist of preventive strategies, diagnostic tests, screening programmes or treatments.

RCTs have three main components:

- Control, which refers to holding variables constant or at least varying them systematically so that their effect can be examined (Bower & King, 2000).
- Comparison, without which clinical trials cannot be considered RCTs. As for the interventions, one of them is usually regarded as a standard of comparison or control, and the group of participants who receive it is called the control group. Generally, the control can be conventional practice ("treatment as usual"), a placebo, or no intervention at all.
- Random allocation of participants to the study groups, which means that allocation is not determined by the investigators, the clinicians or participants. Randomization can be achieved through a variety of procedures, and, if the participants are randomly allocated to the study groups, the groups are described as being "balanced at baseline". There are different types of randomization. For example, *restricted randomization* ensures that the same number of participants are allocated to the study groups, while *stratified randomization* enables the characteristics of the participants (e.g. age) to be as similar as possible across the study groups (Jadad, 1998).

RCTs are most suitable for assessing small to moderate effects of health care interventions and are not appropriate for answering all clinical questions, especially questions relating to aspects of health care (Jadad, 1998). While RCTs undoubtedly have certain strengths, they have a number of shortcomings, which are summarised in Box 4.1.

Box 4.1   Limitations of RCTs

- Arbitrariness of the choice of a suitable comparator and its potential unavailability (Porter et al., 2003).
- Illusion of homogeneity that randomization creates (Grossman & Mackenzie, 2005).
- Patients' preference for treatment can be so strong that some refuse randomization or adversely affect the randomization process (Torgerson & Sibbald, 1998).
- Resentful demoralization may follow in those cases where it is not possible to blind patients to their treatment allocation. Conversely, patients assigned to their preferred treatment may bias the results and thus the efficacy and effectiveness of a trial (Torgerson & Sibbald, 1998).

- Intention-to-treat analyses (which compare the control group and the group that was originally intended to receive treatment instead of the group that actually received the treatment, e.g. the waiting list control) often ignore the reasons for drop-out rates (Grossman & Mackenzie, 2005).
- Do not answer "real life" questions in "real life" clinical situations, particularly in psychiatry (Mulder et al., 2003).
- Ignore other factors beyond treatment that contribute to psychological well-being, e.g. employment status, family relationships, social environment, social stigma against mental illness or offending, etc. (Warren et al., 2006).
- May be unethical and unjustified when a consensus already exists regarding the usefulness of an existing treatment (Mulder et al., 2003) and when effective treatments are already clinically available (Miller, 2000).

The adoption of the RCT paradigm has also been criticised in specific relation to psychotherapy and in psychosocial treatments for making a set of assumptions, which are:

neither well validated nor broadly applicable to most disorders and treatments: that psychopathology is highly malleable, that most patients can be treated for a single problem or disorder, that psychiatric disorders can be treated independently of personality factors unlikely to change in brief treatments, and that experimental methods provide a gold standard for identifying useful psychotherapeutic packages.

(Westen et al., 2004, pp. 632–633)

Given that RCTs cannot control the wider social structures within which repeat offenders are located, their applicability in the psychological and psychiatric fields may remain limited. For instance, repeat offending may not stem from a personality problem alone, but as a result of the interaction between problematic personality traits and social factors such as poverty, discrimination or lack of opportunities (Farrington, 2002). Extraneous factors such as religious beliefs or family history may also influence patients' psychological progress and therefore the success of the intervention.

Essentially, it is difficult to achieve full control over the variables involved in a study if participants are not being strictly supervised by investigators, but attempting to elicit such control would blight the ecological validity of the findings. While undergoing a therapeutic intervention, participants may be exposed to other factors, e.g. disliking the therapist, that may influence their psychological state, the quality of the therapeutic alliance and hence the outcome of the study. As we explained in the Introduction, Dovegate experienced several disruptions due to changes in therapy director, turnover of staff, admission problems, and difficulties in relocating ex-residents into other prison establishments. In Chapter 2, we showed a dip in quality of the TC's compliance to quality standards during the period of our data collection. Maintaining tight controls, i.e. assuming a standard model of treatment delivery, under these circumstances was impossible. Moreover, it has been pointed out that, when interventions are administered to people in groups, the group processes *per se* should be taken into account. These, such as their relationships with others in the group and the influence of group leaders, might bias an individual participant's responses to the intervention (Rapkin and Trickett, 2005). It was obvious from the Community of Communities evaluations and ours that there were differences between the four TCs in Dovegate, ostensibly all being exposed to the same treatment regime.

As for randomization, this works with the proviso of "all other things being equal", i.e. that participants' characteristics that might bias the study are equally distributed across the study conditions. However, study participants from the intervention and the control groups are not always fully equivalent, and other aspects of their disorder, such as degree of severity, may influence the study outcome (Bower & King, 2000). Particularly relevant for forensic populations is the complex task of gauging the degree of intervention readiness (McMurran & Ward, 2010). Readiness is likely to involve an array of factors such as level and nature of motivation to change, emotions, thoughts, skills/competencies ("person" factors), as well as "contextual" factors such as the properties of the treatment, resources (availability, quality, timing) and interpersonal supports available. It is conceivable that a participant's preference for treatment may influence the outcome (Brewin & Bradley, 1989). Therefore, in the context of psychological interventions, patients' preferences should be taken into account rather than them being allocated randomly to the treatment groups.

We thus concluded that an RCT design was not appropriate for methodological and practical, and, indeed, ethical reasons, and so we instead adopted a mixed-methods approach.

A mixed-methods approach

There is now a large body of research using mixed methods in applied psychology, driven by a need for greater understanding of results derived from traditional quantitative methodologies (Waszak and Sines, 2003). On the one hand, as Hammond and O'Rourke (2007, p. 85) point out it is useful to tap into the unique experience and construal system of individuals undergoing an intervention, and we agree with Bower and King (2000, p. 95) that "the subtle psychological changes that occur are not amenable to the relatively crude quantitative measurement methods available". On the other hand, monitoring the psychological movement, even if crudely, over time by using standardised (and validated) psychometric tests is a useful way to demonstrate progression (or otherwise) as a consequence of engagement in a therapeutic intervention (Hammond, 2000). We are sympathetic to the position taken by Shadd Maruna (Maruna, 2013), who suggests a remarkable commonality between what he dubs in shorthand the experimental "what works" and the qualitative "desistence" approaches (i.e. they are both empirical, they emerge from theory, and both aim to support decreases in recidivism and increases in community safety through the reintegration of former prisoners). A mixed-methods approach involves both quantitative and qualitative techniques of data collection and analysis, either sequentially or in parallel, and offers a rapprochement between the two perspectives.

There have been major shifts in the way in which offender rehabilitation programmes are conceptualised and have consequently been evaluated. The first concerns an advancement within the "what works" paradigm to "how does it work?" Day et al. (2006) recommend that there needs to be an examination of the *process* of change, as understanding the mechanisms of change can help to explain why rehabilitation programmes are successful for some and not for others and go some way towards creating more responsive and, therefore, more successful treatment programmes.

Another important shift concerns the traditional method of measuring treatment effectiveness using recidivism rates. The limitations associated with recidivism rates as an outcome measure have been described in detail elsewhere (e.g. Rawlings, 1999) and we have already touched on this subject. But perhaps the most important point to reiterate is that a decrease in reoffending is only *one* of the expected objectives of a prison TC. A prison TC is also expected "to create an atmosphere in which an individual can explore and acknowledge his pattern of behaviour, understand the motives underlying it, and modify his behaviour..." (Home Office, 1987). Therefore "in-therapy" indicators of positive psychological change have an important role to play in evaluating the effectiveness of a prison TC.

The final shift in the way that treatment programmes are being evaluated emanates from mental health providers' recognition that "service-user" involvement has ethical and practical benefits. In a recent literature review commissioned by the National Institute for Mental Health in England (NIMHE), Glasby et al. (2003) concluded that service users "are experts in their experience" and offer "an important resource that can help to improve individual packages of care as well as services more generally" (p. 5). Glasby et al. (2003) also identified that service users often have very different perspectives about service provision, and suggested that "involving users can provide extremely rich data which prompts practitioners to re-evaluate their work, challenges traditional assumptions and highlights key priorities which users would like to see addressed" (p. 5). Finally, as Glasby and colleagues rightly point out, it can be therapeutic in itself for service users to know that they are being listened to and that their contributions are valued by researchers. Clients' perceptions and theories of change are not a new concept. As early as 1955, Hoch referred to the benefit of patients' own ideas and expectations about psychotherapy, and within more recent psychotherapy literature there is a suggestion that making use of the client's theory of change (i.e. the client's ideas held about aetiology and resolution) brings about favourable relationships and increases client involvement, therefore enhancing positive outcome (Hubble et al., 1999).

The data collection methods

Secondary documents

The documents within the therapy case files that were examined included:

- Referral pack containing a brief exploratory questionnaire about motivations to attend the TC.
- Social History Questionnaire
- Police National Computer records
- Psychiatric reports
- Psychometric results (PDQ-4 and Ravens)
- Individual Treatment Plans
- End of TC contact sheets
- Termination confirmation letters

In the absence of many of the above, the following documents were examined (if present):

- Lifer parole board documents
- Correspondence regarding transfers, etc.
- Pre- or post-sentence probation reports
- Sentence plans and/or risk assessments.

In addition, ethnicity and religion data were collected from Educom administrative records. From this we conducted a census of all residents who had attended the assessment unit at Dovegate TC, regardless of the length of their residence, until the data collection "cut-off" date, 31 May 2004 (for the census). Of the maximum possible sample of 452, data were obtainable for 375 (83% of cases), with varying degrees of success. Further details are provided in the Appendix.[1]

Psychometric measures

Dovegate residents

The psychometric measures were administered and the results recorded throughout each resident's time at Dovegate at intervals of six months for a sample of 250 men. After they left Dovegate, follow-up psychometrics were administered every six months from the date of discharge. Therefore, the time intervals were not necessarily six months throughout the research period, because the time from their last psychometric in Dovegate may have been up to a year before their six months' follow-up post-Dovegate. A full list of the psychometric measures is included at the end of this chapter.

Comparison group

We also collected a set of psychometric data from our comparator group of mainstream prisoners ($n = 57$). These participants had at least 18 months remaining of their sentence, were not receiving peer group therapy and had no history of residence in a TC, or suffering any mental illness. We recruited volunteers from HMP Blundeston and HMP Woodhill. Demographically, our comparators were not statistically significantly different from the TC residents, except with respect to age. The comparators were slightly older, with an average age of 38 years as opposed to 33 years for the TC residents. Also, the TC residents tended to start their offending at a younger age and there were more sex offenders within the comparison group. The four repeated psychometric measures we used were:

- Revised Gudjonsson Blame Attribution Inventory (GBAI-R)
- Culture-Free Self Esteem Inventory 2 (CFSEI-2)
- Hostility and Direction of Hostility Questionnaire (HDHQ)
- Inventory of Altered Self Capacities (IASC)

Leavers' questionnaire

A sample of 60 TC residents left the TC because they were de-selected or they requested to leave early (through the 48-hour procedure). This questionnaire was designed to explore ex-residents' experiences of leaving the TC. The questionnaire covered participants' reasons for leaving the TC, their experiences of being in the TC and their transitions to a mainstream prison.[2]

Interviews with ex-residents

We undertook follow-up interviews with ex-residents who had been transferred to mainstream prisons. Visits were made over a period of two years, from July 2005 to July 2007. In the process of data collection approximately 50 different prisons, ranging from low to high security, were visited across England and

Wales. Ex-residents were traced to their mainstream establishments with the help of the Prisoner Location Index.

All participants had been residents at Dovegate TC and had been transferred back into the mainstream prison system to complete their sentences. Participants had left the TC under one of the following conditions: voluntarily via a 48-hour notice; had been de-selected by the TC community and told to leave; or left because they had completed therapy. Lengths of time spent in the TC varied from under six months to over two years. We reinterviewed ex-residents either once, twice or three times in mainstream prisons, resulting in a total number of 124 interviews with 73 participants.[3]

Focus groups

A total of 16 focus groups, involving 40 residents overall, were conducted with men from each of four TCs over a two-year period to explore the process and extent of therapeutic change from residents' perspectives. Participants had to have spent a specified time in therapy, so that the focus groups represented these time points: ≤6 months in therapy; 6–12 months; 12–18 months; 18–24 months. This was done so that potential psychological change over time could be monitored.

Multiple Card Sorting Task Procedure

The Multiple Card Sorting Task Procedure (MCSTP) is a data elicitation technique that gives insight into how individuals categorise a set of concepts or things. Sixty TC residents were asked to take part in card sorts, at baseline and every 12 months thereafter. One card sort focused on "people" in the resident's life and the second on environmental "places".

Post-release case studies

The Dovegate research team had on file the locations of ex-residents of the TC. A number of these ex-residents who were now situated in the community, 12 under the supervision of the probation service, were chosen randomly, and six agreed to participate. They were contacted via their probation officer and meetings were then arranged to be conducted in the probation office.

A schedule was produced to guide the semi-structured interviews, and themes covered included: their opinions of Dovegate and the TC regime and whether it "worked"; after Dovegate, the reintegration process and any change they felt; and life before Dovegate, what led them to a life of crime and evaluating life now.[4]

Adjudications

Details of TC residents' adjudications ($n = 250$) one year prior to and one year after being in the TC were collected. These were infractions of prison rules, arbitrated by the governor and formally noted on a prisoner's record. The same information was collated for our comparison group ($n = 54$).

Reconviction rates

The effectiveness of the TC was measured in relation to reconviction rates. The rate and nature of reconvictions were obtained using the Inmate Information System (IIS). Any reconvictions (offences resulting in a guilty court conviction) were recorded for $n = 250$ residents. As well as the rate, result and nature of reoffending, the following factors considered likely to affect reconviction were accounted for: mode of release, passage of time post-release, length of TC residency (treatment dosage), age and criminal history.

Analytic procedures

Reliable Change Index

One way to overcome the threats, listed above, of a purely quantitative group analysis approach is to use idiographic analyses. Researchers have noticed that using inferential statistics and comparing means ignores variability in treatment; for example, some people may actually be deteriorating after having completed the treatment (Ogles et al., 2001). This belies the question of whether change occurring for the group overall is reflected at the individual level. Such a shift in focus would provide an arguably more clinically pertinent perspective on the efficacy of therapy. Jacobson and Truax (1991) proposed a useful method for statistically examining therapeutic change at this individualised level, their technique becoming known as the Reliable Change Index (RCI).

The changes of score observed between times of administration were analysed for significance using the RCI by dividing the difference in test scores between two time points by the standard error of difference (S diff) for the psychometric measure being used. The value of S diff is based on variance and reliability indices for the measure, which are obtained from normative samples. The use of S diff as a denominator provides an adjustment for natural instabilities in the measure, and the resultant RCI value thus provides an estimation of whether the test score change is greater than would be expected by chance alone (O'Neill, 2010). The exact formula is as follows:

$$\text{RCI} = \frac{x2 - x1}{\text{S diff}} \quad \text{where S diff} = \sqrt{2(\text{SE})^2}$$

The RCI values are equivalent to standardised z-scores and thus can be interpreted for statistical significance through comparison with that probability distribution. Scores greater or less than 1.96 can consequently be deemed significant at $p < .05$, i.e. there is less than a 1 in 20 chance that no statistically meaningful change occurred. RCI scores were examined for all psychometric data where appropriate normative statistics required for the calculation of S diff were available.

The kappa coefficient

The kappa coefficient (Cohen, 1960) is used as a descriptive statistic indicating the degree of beyond chance agreement between two ratings per subject, based on a dichotomous response. If the two ratings are in complete agreement, kappa $= 1$; if they are in total disagreement, the rating <0. The level of agreement was further clarified in criteria laid down by Landis and Koch (1977), which have now been widely accepted. Although it should be noted that these criteria are described by the authors themselves as "clearly arbitrary", they do provide "useful benchmarks" (p. 165).

Kappa statistic	Strength of agreement
<0.00	Poor
0.00–0.20	Slight
0.21–0.40	Fair
0.41–0.60	Moderate
0.61–0.80	Substantial
0.81–1.00	Almost perfect

(Landis & Koch, 1977, p. 165)

Bonferroni correction

Given the number of scales on some of the psychometric measures administered to participants, it was important to adjust for any possibility of increased Type I errors by applying a correction for multiple testing. This was achieved using a Sequential Bonferroni Adjustment, which is a modification of the probability cutoff, ordered according to degree of significance, such that the most significant result must have a lower probability of a correct null hypothesis than the most stringent corrected probability cutoff (.05/ "Number of tests within a family of analyses"). If the test statistic remains significant with this criterion applied, then the next most significant test statistic is measured against a slightly less strict cutoff (.05/"Number of tests" – 1), and so on. This procedure is described more fully in Holm (1979).

Ex-resident interview analyses

Taped interviews were transcribed verbatim and in an anonymised form so that no individuals could be identified from the transcripts. Transcripts were then entered into a qualitative software package, MAXQDA, for coding, analysis and data management.

Multiple card sorts

The multiple card sorts were recorded in the form of matrices and the relationships between the variables were ascertained using multi-dimensional scaling (MDS). The card sorts were analysed using Multiple Scalogram Analysis (MSA; Lingoes, 1979), allowing idiographic psychological progression to be considered. Therefore, this piece of analysis was very much concerned with the process of change as experienced at the individual level. The MSA procedure tests the relationship each variable (in this case, card) has to every other variable by producing an association matrix. A visual summary of the relationships is produced, in which the distances between the variables reflect their actual ranked correlations. The shorter the distance between two variables (i.e. cards), the higher their inter-correlation, whereas the further apart two variables are, the smaller the inter-correlation. As distances reflect co-occurrence between variables,[5] regions can be identified and partitioned by the researcher using the principles of sensitivity and selectivity.[6] In keeping with the co-researcher approach, residents received MCSTP feedback sessions during which they were presented with a diagram showing their card sorts, which they commented upon.

Common space analysis (COSPA) is a procedure that enables researchers to examine similarities across individuals in their responses on a fixed (i.e. all cards are the same for all participants) sorting task. It permits three-way multidimensional scaling (MDS) analysis without distorting the relationships in the data. The variables used in the card sorting tasks for each participant were coded and subjected to MSA, as explained above. From these, triangular Euclidean (standard) distance matrices are then calculated for the purpose of the COSPA. On inputting the distance matrices into the COSPA, configurations in the chosen number of dimensions are calculated, denoting plot similarity between individuals in the MDS output. Configurations are provided separately for both the test variables and the participants.

Smallest Space Analysis (SSA) tends to look at the relationships between variables, amalgamating responses from individuals. The programme has a number of correlation coefficient options depending on the type of data, e.g. rating scales or dichotomous scoring, and thereby generates a lower triangular correlation matrix in which every variable (item) is correlated with every other variable or item. These are converted into linear distances so that the higher the correlation, the shorter the equivalent distance. The goodness of fit between the correlation coefficients and the relative distance is assessed by a measure called the coefficient of alienation (CoA), varying between 0 and 1, with the former designated a perfect fit. A rule of thumb suggests that a coefficient of alienation of 0.15 is usually considered to be a good fit, although interpretable SSA can be undertaken with CoA that are higher (Donald, 1995). The output of an SSA is in the form of a map with the variables projected as points in an *n*-dimensional space. Co-ordinates anchor the points in terms of the number of dimensions. Thus, a two-dimensional solution is anchored by co-ordinates that may be thought of as longitude and latitude or length and breadth. A third dimension, such as time or depth, could provide other co-ordinates, thereby creating a three-dimensional space.

Focus groups

Interpretative Phenomenological Analysis (IPA; Smith, 1996a, b; Smith et al., 1999) was used to analyse the focus group transcripts in order to gain an "insider's perspective" (Conrad, 1987). The analysis is "phenomenological" as it involves detailed examination of the individuals' world and it is "interpretative" because it recognises the dynamic and engaged role of the researcher as interpreter.

The transcripts were analysed separately for each TC. This seemed logical because each TC is viewed within the Dovegate prison estate as an independent unit, existing and functioning as its own community. The transcripts were also analysed in chronological fashion, starting with the first focus group undertaken (six months or less in therapy) and finishing with the last focus group (18–24 months in therapy).

Using the IPA directions put forward by Smith and colleagues (1999), the first stage of analysis involved a detailed, line-by-line examination of each focus group transcript, leading to a comprehensive set of themes represented by key words or "abstract theme titles" (Smith et al., 1999, p. 221). Preliminary exploration of relationships or connections between the theme titles was then undertaken, allowing a clustering of themes. These theme clusters are kept "grounded" by returning to the transcripts, re-examining participants' words and making use of direct quotations from the transcripts. Once these stages were completed for each transcript across the different time phases for each TC, the theme clusters were amalgamated using diagrams to capture relationships and connections. This led to an emergent "master list of themes" (Smith et al., 1999, p. 226) describing the change process for a particular TC. In line with recent guidelines for qualitative research, credibility checks of the evolving analysis were undertaken (see Elliott, Fischer & Rennie, 1999) by a second researcher independently examining the detailed coding and clustering of themes.

Research design

Objective one: Assessment of the extent and process of psychological and behavioural change within Dovegate TC

Objective one was addressed by measuring psychological and behavioural change in a group of residents whilst they were in the Dovegate TC. As well as measuring change across groups of residents using standardised psychological tests, a variety of idiographic measures of change were employed. The combination of traditional procedures, i.e. psychometrics, alongside novel qualitative techniques, i.e. multiple card sorts and focus groups, enabled comparison with previous findings as well as the opportunity to answer the following questions:

- What is the optimal treatment dosage?
- Who benefited most from the TC?
- What does the process of change involve? (Figure 4.1)

Objective two: Assessment of TC residents' behaviour and experiences after transfer to another prison

Objective two considered the sustainability of the TC treatment effect using a repeated battery of psychometrics. Qualitative interviews with ex-residents also explored this issue and considered the process of reintegration into mainstream prison. A quantitative survey followed up premature TC leavers. In addition, a comparison was undertaken looking at psychological outcomes for premature leavers, those who stayed in the TC for at least 18 months and a non-TC mainstream prison sample, in order to look for change in prisoners experiencing a TC and those who did not.

The secondary research questions included the following:

- What does the process of change continue to look like?
- What is the process of reintegration into mainstream prison, post-TC?
- Thinking about change: what personal changes did men attribute to their TC involvement?
- Sustaining positive change in a mainstream prison: is it possible and how?
- Does a TC experience result in greater change compared with prisoners not experiencing a TC? (Figure 4.2)

Objective three: Assessment of TC residents' behaviour and experiences after release into the community

The purpose of objective three was to consider the longer-term effect of TC therapy. Treatment outcome was measured using adjudication and reconviction data. Treatment sustainability was also considered using semi-structured view case studies including the individual's psychometric test scores. Here the more detailed research questions comprised:

- How effective is the TC in reducing recidivism severity and frequency?
- How effective is the TC in reducing adjudication severity and frequency? (Figure 4.3)

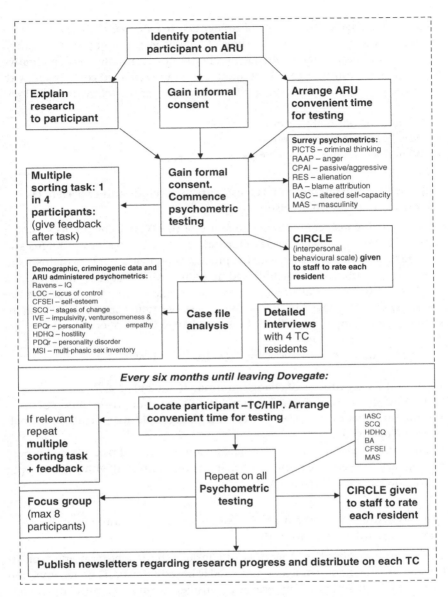

Figure 4.1 Research design to address objective one

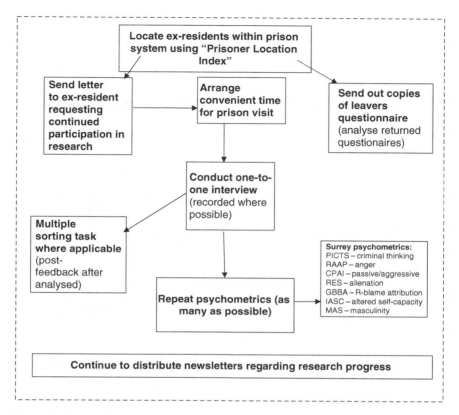

Figure 4.2   Research plan to assess change on return to mainstream prison

To help guide readers through the analyses associated with the research objectives, a summary table indicating the methods used is provided in Table 4.1.

Some further technicalities

Note on premature leavers and drop-out

Generally, therapy drop-out is seen as problematic not only for research designs, but for the prison service in terms of time and cost, and also for the individual. There is an assumption that dropouts are "treatment failures" because of the association between programme attrition and increased risk of reoffending. Whilst "treatment failures" are of concern to the service provider and the service user, drop-out from groups in TCs is especially important, as high drop-out rates are likely to impact the therapeutic milieu and can be unsettling for the

62

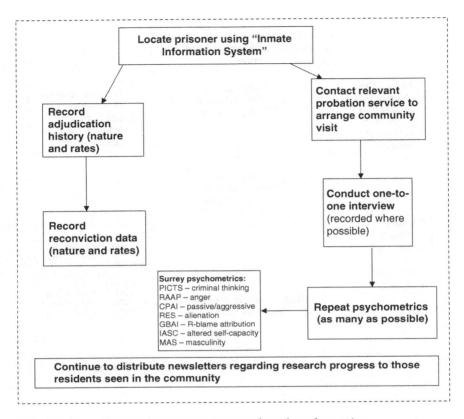

Figure 4.3 Research plan to monitor outcomes after release from prison

Table 4.1 Summary of methods used to address research objectives

Extent and process of psychological and behavioural change within Dovegate TC	TC residents' behaviour and experiences after transfer to another prison	TC residents' behaviour and experiences after release into the community
Psychometric measurement (QUANT)	Psychometric measurement (QUANT)	Psychometric measurement (QUANT)
Focus groups (Quals)	Leavers survey (QUANT)	Adjudications (QUANT)
Multiple sorting task (QUANT + Quals)	Interviews (Quals)	Reconvictions (QUANT)
Interviews (Quals)	Comparison study (QUANT)	Interviews (Quals)
Comparison study (QUANT)		

dynamics within a TC (Campling, 1992). So, investigating and understanding therapy drop-out is important in order to avoid loss of resources and maintain a safe therapeutic milieu for residents.

Generally, therapy drop-out is associated with resistance, particularly early on in treatment (Miller & Rollnick, 2002). Resistance, or "those aspects of clients' functioning that seek to maintain the status quo in their psychological lives" (Newman, 2002, p. 166), has often been regarded as an obstacle to treatment and therapeutic change. Newman (2002) lists several examples of resistance, such as strong reactions to the therapist, failure to adhere to the treatment programme and other avoidance behaviours. However, contemporary thinking conceptualises resistance as part of the therapeutic process. Resistance to change is not construed as the client's problem, but is understood in a relational context, in which the client's resistant behaviour is a "signal of dissonance in the relationship" (Miller & Rollnick, 2002, p. 45). Resistance in a group or community setting appears to be even more complex, and this is further complicated by the prison context. This context is one with a "self-same culture" (Doctor, 2001, p. 57), which can promote an attitude of pride about the crimes committed. This, in turn, may lead to an unwillingness and inability to express feelings or insight so as to maintain the necessary respect to survive in the prison culture. Thus, it is not surprising that TC residents may be ambivalent about or show resistance towards change.

Within this research study the terms "drop-out" and "therapy leaver" are used interchangeably. "Therapy leaver" refers to individuals who were members of the TC and who left before completing the programme, who were

(1) either de-selected from the TC by other members for breaking rules or failing to make an effort, or
(2) themselves asked to leave early (within the 48-hour procedure) for personal reasons.

In both instances leavers are transferred back to mainstream prisons.

Completers

It is problematic to declare when a TC resident is deemed to have successfully completed therapy. One of the directors of therapy put this problem thus:

> Well, I generally speaking don't use the word "complete" in terms of therapy. I ask people in their assessments to look at whether the therapeutic community remains the most appropriate environment for an individual to live in given various different factors: the length of their sentence that's remaining is one factor we take into consideration in that judgement; whether they have exhibited sufficient progress in their ability to cope with their

emotions. To, you know, be able to go somewhere else and carry on the work on their own is another, but I don't think that in psychotherapy there is something that is ever complete. I would hope, if you learn the ability to reflect, that's then something that is a useful tool, useful as walking is even though you're not a perfect walker, it depends on what you wanna to do with it, really, I suppose. So, you know, there's a lot of talk in therapeutic communities about, "I've been signed off, I have finished", well, it's not like that, really, although when you think of the processes being one of slowed-down examination of every aspect of your life... I think I want it to be finished!

The TC residents themselves are not sure about when the therapy has come to an end, e.g.

for some reason they keep mentioning this two year thing, so maybe sub-consciously when you get to your two years, you think that you're fucking done. For me, I don't know if that is the case.

In this report we are not seeking to define completers precisely in terms of their period of time spent in Dovegate, but where appropriate we do refer to periods of time the resident spent within the TC.

Chapter annex

(1) Details of psychometric tests used

Revised Gudjonsson Blame Attribution Inventory (GBAI-R)

The GBAI-R (Gudjonsson & Singh, 1989) evaluates offenders' attribution of blame and feelings of remorse in relation to their offending behaviour. In our study, the various scales of the GBAI-R demonstrated adequate internal consistency, ranging from .71 for the *External Attribution* subscale to .76 for the *Guilt* subscale (see Appendix 3 for a full listing of reliabilities).

- External Attribution assesses levels of blaming the crime on social circumstances, victims or society (higher scores indicate more external attribution).
- Mental Element Attribution assesses the blaming of responsibility for the crime on mental illness or poor self-control (higher scores indicate more mental element attribution).
- Guilt Feeling Attribution assesses feelings of regret and remorse concerning the offence.

Higher scores denote greater levels of guilt.

Culture-Free Self Esteem Inventory 2 (CFSEI-2)

The CFSEI-2 (Battle, 1992) assesses perception of self-worth overall and in relation to three lower-order components: *General, Social* and *Personal Self-Esteem*. It also assesses defensiveness in responding through a *Lie* subscale. The questionnaire had moderate to excellent reliability in our sample, ranging from an alpha coefficient of .58 for its Lie subscale to .91 for the *CFSEI Total* scale.

- General Self-Esteem assesses the aspect of self-esteem that refers to individuals' overall perceptions of their worth.
- Social Self-Esteem assesses the aspect of self-esteem that refers to individuals' perceptions of the quality of their relationship with peers.
- Personal Self-Esteem assesses the aspect of self-esteem that refers to individuals' most intimate perceptions of self-worth.
- Lie subtest assesses defensiveness.

For all scales, higher scores indicate higher levels of the respective aspects of self-esteem or defensiveness.

Chart of Interpersonal Reactions in Closed Living Environments (CIRCLE)

The CIRCLE (Blackburn & Renwick, 1996) is an observer-rated measure developed to assess patients in forensic psychiatric hospitals in relation to an octagonal conceptualization of interpersonal functioning, emphasising concepts of power and affiliation. Its inclusion in this study enables an exploration of its utility as a psychometric tool within TC settings. Within our sample, reliabilities obtained for the CIRCLE ranged from a low alpha of .55 for the *Submissive* scale to .87 for the *Coercive* scale.

High scores on each represent high levels of the respective construct.

Hostility and Direction of Hostility Questionnaire (HDHQ)

The HDHQ (Caine et al., 1967) assesses negative, aggressive or punitive cognitions and feelings towards self and others. It comprises a series of scales, ranging from evaluation of specific attributes such as self-criticism to higher-level components assessing broader categories of inwardly and outwardly directed hostility, as well as an overall hostility scale. The internal consistencies obtained for the HDHQ amongst our participants varied from .61 for the *Paranoid Hostility* scale to .89 for the overall HDHQ *Total Hostility* scale.

High scores indicate higher levels of the respective constructs.

Inventory of Altered Self Capacities (IASC)

The IASC (Briere, 2000) evaluates disturbed functioning in identity, affect regulation and relationships with others. It is comprised of 11 scales, assessing a variety of such attributes. The reliabilities for this scale varied in our study from an alpha coefficient of .77 for the *Tension Reduction Activities* scale to .92 for the *Affect Dysregulation* scale.

- Interpersonal Conflicts assesses problems in relationships with others and a tendency to be involved in chaotic, emotionally upsetting relationships.
- Idealization-Disillusionment assesses a predisposition to dramatically change one's opinions about significant others, generally from a very positive view to an equally negative one.
- Abandonment Concerns assesses a general sensitivity to perceived or actual abandonment by significant others and the tendency to expect and fear the termination of important relationships.
- Identity Impairment assesses difficulties in maintaining a coherent sense of identity and self-awareness across contexts. It comprises two subscales: Self-Awareness and Identity Diffusion, which respectively assess respondents' sense of self and their tendency to confuse their cognitions with those around them.
- Susceptibility to Influence assesses a proclivity to follow the directions of others without sufficient self-consideration and to accept uncritically others' statements or assertions.
- Affect Dysregulation assesses problems in affect regulation and control, including mood swings, problems in inhibiting the expression of anger, and inability to easily regulate dysphoric states without externalization. It includes two subscales: Affect Instability and Affect Skills Deficits, which respectively assess mood fluctuations and poor emotion control.
- Tension Reduction Activities assesses the tendency to react to painful internal states with externalizing behaviours that – although potentially dysfunctional – distract, soothe or otherwise reduce internal distress.

Lower scores on all scores reflect more appropriate modes of functioning.

University of Rhode Island Change Assessment Scale (URICA)

The URICA (McConnaughy et al., 1983) is a quantitative assessment of therapeutic progress, assessing four stages from preparation for change to the maintenance of progress achieved. In our sample, the reliabilities for the URICA ranged from .77 for the *Precontemplation* scale to .82 for the *Contemplation* scale.

- Precontemplation: which reflects a lack of awareness about the need to change. The person is entering into a therapy situation but does not think s/he has a problem or knows s/he not want to change; may feel pressured by others to be there; may admit to having a problem but has no desire to change. S/he is either not aware of or is ignoring the problem.

- Contemplation: The person is beginning to be aware that a problem exists or that s/he is bothered by something about him/herself. S/he is struggling to understand the problem (i.e. cause, solution); is seeking more information; but has not made a commitment to change.
- Action: The person has actively started to change the behaviour or the environment; is struggling to change; has not been very successful on his/her own and needs help. S/he has not attained the desired change.
- Maintenance: The person has already changed and made significant gains but is either slipping or coming in to prevent a relapse. S/he might have found it difficult to maintain the changes (i.e. new behaviours, new attitudes) on his/her own, and is therefore seeking help. S/he has already attained the desired change and is better off than s/he was initially.

Cork Estrangement Scale (CES)

The CES (Hammond, 1988) is an assessment of estrangement in various forms, along with an overall estrangement scale. The internal constancy of the scales varied from $\alpha = 0.48$ for the *Rule-Group* scale to $\alpha = 0.82$ for the *Total Estrangement* scale.

- Existential Estrangement: Higher scores indicate more existential estrangement.
- Social Estrangement: Higher scores indicate more social estrangement.
- Rule-Group: Higher scores denote a more negative view of societal rules/regulations.

Cork Passive Aggression Inventory (CPAI)

The CPAI (Hammond, 2010) comprises three scales assessing overall passive aggression, as well as its subcomponents. The scales ranged in reliability from $\alpha = 0.88$ for the *Aggressive Impulse* subscale to $\alpha = 0.93$ for the higher-order *Passive Aggression* scale.

- Passive Aggression scale is the sum of the Aggressive Impulse and Resistance to Demands subscales.
- Aggressive Impulse scale items assess the subtle expression of anger, spite and stubbornness.
- Resistance to Demands scale items assess decisiveness, distractibility, concentration and steadfastness.

Locus of Control of Behaviour (LCB)

The LCB (Craig et al., 1984) is an assessment of respondents' understanding of controlling factors in their personal behaviour. The scale demonstrated a reliability of $\alpha = 0.65$. This single-scale assessment measures the extent to which subjects perceive responsibility for their personal problem behaviour. Higher scores indicate a more internalised locus.

Psychological Inventory of Criminal Thinking Styles, version 4 (PICTS-4)

The PICTS (Walters, 2002) is an assessment of crime-supporting attitudes, beliefs and other cognitions supportive of criminal behaviour. It comprises two general content scales (split between current and historical variables), four factor scales, eight thinking style scales and one additional *Fear of Change* scale. It also includes a series of validity scales. The reliability of the scales in the present sample varied from $\alpha = 0.66$ for the *Sentimentality* thinking style scale to 0.93 for the *Fear of Change* scale.

- Mollification: reflects a tendency to blame one's criminal involvements on others, whether the focus is family members, the government or victims of past crimes.
- Impulsivity: measures impetuousness and the tendency to rely on phrases such as "fuck it" to eliminate common deterrents to crime. Drugs and alcohol are another popular form of cutoff.
- Entitlement: reflects a sense of ownership, privilege and uniqueness that the individual uses to give him or herself permission to violate the laws of society or the rights of others. Misidentification of wants as needs is also common in entitlement.
- Power Orientation: is elevated in respondents who crave power and control over others. These individuals are commonly referred to as "control freaks".
- Sentimentality: pinpoints the belief that performing good deeds erases the harm done as a result of one's involvement in a criminal lifestyle. Such individuals often fail to see the harm they inflict on themselves, their families and their victims (both known and unknown) because of the blinders that sentimentality places over their vision and insight.
- Superoptimism: captures the belief that one will be able to postpone or avoid the negative consequences of lifestyle involvement that others engaged in a similar level of criminal involvement suffer daily.
- Cognitive Indolence: typically is elevated by individuals who take short-cuts and the easy way around problems. Such individuals are continually in trouble because their shortcuts invariably catch up with them sooner or later. Persons scoring high on this scale are frequently characterized as lazy, unmotivated and irresponsible.
- Discontinuity: reflects a tendency to lose sight of one's goals and be easily side-tracked by environmental events. Respondents who score high on this scale are often characterized as fragmented, flighty and unpredictable.

RAMAS Anger Assessment Profile (RAAP)

The RAAP (O'Rourke & Hammond, 2000) provides a profile of respondents' anger problems on ten scales, ranging from assessments of sensitivity to possible provocations to awareness of consequences of the expression of anger. In the current sample, the internal consistency of the scales ranged from $\alpha = 0.76$ for the *Attitude* scale to 0.94 for the *Assaultative* scale.

- Expression Scale (EXP): Individuals vary in the way they deal with and express anger and angry feelings. The Expression Scale attempts to measure the degree to which the respondent expresses anger inwardly (Anger-in) or outwardly (Anger-out).
- Provocation Scale (PRO): A wide range of threats, frustrations and annoyances can activate anger. The Provocation Scale is designed to gauge how easily provoked to anger the respondent is.
- Somatic Tension Scale (SOM): The presence of physical tension is predisposing for anger, aggression and assault. The Somatic Tension Scale measures the degree of awareness of physiological arousal when anger is experienced.
- Duration Scale (DUR): Once feelings of anger have been activated, it can be prolonged, intensified or revived by continued arousal. The Duration Scale seeks to identify individual differences in relation to the timescales of anger once aroused.
- Irritability/Sensitivity (SEN): The tendency to be irritable and very sensitive is a dimension of emotion that is related to anger, aggressive behaviour and assault. Irritability and oversensitivity may lead to increased arousal in the face of small frustrations or annoyances.
- Victimisation Scale (VIC): An individual's experience of other people's anger or aggressive behaviours, i.e. victimisation affects the way they themselves respond to anger arousal. It affects aggression tolerance and also their personal schemas and cognitions in relation to anger. The Victimisation Scale is made up of questions relating to a wide range of abuse and assault experiences in which the respondent is the victim.
- Abuse and Assault Scale (ASS): The Abuse and Assault Scale uses self-reported acts of abuse and assault to gauge an individual's assaultative history.
- Attitude Scale (ATT): The scale assesses the degree to which the justification of assaultative behaviour is related to the attitudes that we have towards anger. The Attitude Scale assesses the degree to which the respondent sees the expression of anger as positive or negative. Those manifesting a high positive attitude are conceived as those who are not likely to excuse angry excesses.
- Consequences Scale (CON): The behavioural/interpersonal outcomes of anger are an important element in the definition of anger as problematic or non-problematic. This scale assesses the degree to which the respondent links negative consequences to their own anger.

- Anger Control (CNT): When anger is activated, behavioural and cognitive responses and response inclinations play an important role in the outcome. In stressful situations, anger control or anger management depends on cognitive and behaviour problem-solving strategies or skills. The anger control scale contains questions relating to adaptive and maladaptive reactions to anger. A high score indicated a rational style of anger control.

Structured Clinical Interview for DSM-IV personality disorders (First et al., 1997)

The SCID II closely follows the language of the DSM-IV Axis II personality disorders criteria, increasing the face validity of the measure. In the SCID II, questions are grouped together according to sets of DSM-IV criteria, and all questions pertaining to a single personality disorder are listed together. There are 12 groups of questions corresponding to the 12 personality disorders. Most criteria are assessed using a single question; however, interviewers are encouraged to ask any additional questions to clarify ambiguous responses. The clinical judgement of the interviewer determines whether a particular criterion has been met. Using the SCID II, the interviewer is able to judge whether the interviewee is meeting the criteria for each personality disorder. Scoring is simple: either the trait is absent, sub-threshold or present or there is "inadequate information to code".

The reliability of the SCID II has been examined in a number of studies. Moran and colleagues (Moran et al., 2003) state that "the instrument demonstrates acceptable test–retest ($k = 0.68$) and inter-rater reliability ($k = 0.71$)" (p. 229). Another example, by Maffei and colleagues (Maffei et al., 1997), examined the inter-rater reliability and calculated kappa scores for each of the personality disorders using the SCID II in a study with over 200 participants. Kappa scores for the ten main DSM personality disorders ranged from 0.83 (obsessive-compulsive) to 0.98 (narcissistic). A wide variety of demographic information was collected about the research participants and the following tables provide an overview of the data obtained.

(2) Sample details of Dovegate research participants

Demographics

Table 4a.1   Ethnic background of the participating residents

Ethnicity	Frequency	Percentage
White – British	192	76.8
White – Irish	1	0.4
White – Other background	10	4
Black – Caribbean	17	6.8
Black – African	3	1.2

Black – Other background	11	4.4
Asian – Pakistani	3	1.2
Asian – Other background	3	1.2
Mixed – White and black Caribbean	2	0.8
Mixed – Other background	3	1.2
Unknown	5	2.0

Table 4a.2   Marital status of the participating residents

Status	Frequency	Percentage
Single	148	59.2
Married	25	10
Relationship/cohabiting	33	13.2
Divorced/separated	30	12
Widowed	6	2.4
Unknown	8	3.2

The mean age of the sample was 32.98 (SD = 8.18), ranging from 21 to 63. The largest ethnic group was White British, which represented over 75% of the sample. About 23% of the sample were in a relationship of some sort, although the majority (59.2%) of participants were single. Just over half (55.6%) had children, while 23.2% did not.

The mean age at which participants had left school was 14.84 (SD = 1.56); 18% of the sample had no history of employment, while 13.2% had held a long-term job in the past. A further 37.6% had worked in less stable jobs, while the work history of the remaining 31.6% had not been recorded.

Records for 105 participants, or 42% of the sample, showed they had been abused during their childhoods, either physically, sexually or emotionally. An examination of their mental health history showed that 63% of participants had at some point attempted or been considered at risk of committing suicide.

Criminal history

The mean age at first conviction for the sample was 15.91 (SD = 4.16). The average number of preconvictions was 18.25 (SD = 17.82), with approximately 5.4 sentences (SD = 7.03) served prior to the current.

The estimated mean age at which residents received their current conviction was 29.78 years old (SD = 7.66). The average current sentence length was 112.6 months (SD = 85.97).[7] The sample comprised 83 lifers, 79 Cat B inmates and 86 who were designated Cat C. The residents' index offences were coded according to the Home Office's Offenders Index coding scheme.

Table 4a.3   Index offence types[8]

Type	Number of participants	Percentage of sample
Violent	103	41.2
Sexual	19	7.6
Burglary	28	11.2
Robbery	69	27.6
Theft	1	0.4
Fraud	0	0
Criminal damage	6	2.4
Drug	13	5.2
Motoring	0	0
Other	11	4.4

Table 4a.4   Nature of preconvictions[9]

Type	Number of participants	Percentage of sample
Violent	152	60.8
Sexual	31	12.4
Burglary	101	40.4
Robbery	77	30.8
Theft	125	50
Fraud	35	14
Criminal damage	79	31.6
Drug	64	25.6
Motoring	54	21.6
Other	83	33.2

Table 4a.5   Residency figures of research participants

Length of residency	Frequency	Percentage
0–5 months	52	20.8
6–11 months	47	18.8
12–17 months	29	11.6
18–23 months	32	12.8
24 months+	90	36

Table 4a.6   Reason for leaving TC

Reason	Frequency	Percentage
n/a, still in therapy	39	15.6
De-selected	48	19.2
48 hr	72	28.8
End of therapy	19	7.6
Released	23	9.2
Progressive move	11	4.4
Medical hold	1	0.4
Failed assessment	29	11.6
Unknown	8	3.2

(3) Sample details of follow-up psychometric assessment

Data collection continued once residents left the TC and moved elsewhere in the prison system. In total, 60 former residents underwent follow-up assessments. The following is a breakdown of the sample sizes for these follow-up assessment points.

The follow-up sample had an average age of 32.4 (SD = 7.3) at their baseline assessment, almost exactly the same as the mean for the total set of participants. The ethnicity of the follow-up sample is presented in Table 4a.8, which, again, is

Table 4a.7   Post-TC assessment sample sizes

Length of within-TC participation	6-month follow-up	12-month follow-up	18-month follow-up
0–5 months	12	15	7
6–11 months	17	9	5
12–17 months	7	2	0
18–23 months	9	1	1
24 months+	2	1	0
Total	47	28	13

Table 4a.8   Ethnic background of the follow-up participants

Ethnicity	Frequency	Percentage
White – British	48	76.8
Black – Caribbean	5	6.8
Black – Other background	3	4.4
Asian – Other background	1	1.2
Unknown	3	2.0

Table 4a.9   Index offence types[10]

Type	Number of participants	Percentage of sample
Violent	20	33.3
Sexual	6	10
Burglary	7	11.7
Robbery	17	28.3
Theft	1	1.7
Fraud	0	0
Criminal damage	0	0
Drug	6	10
Motoring	0	0
Other	3	5

quite representative of the overall sample, albeit with some of the less frequent ethnicities no longer included.

In comparison to the overall sample, this post-TC subgroup included slightly fewer participants with a violent index offence and more with drug offences (see Table 4a.9). All other offences were represented in approximately the same proportions as in the overall sample.

In terms of the follow-up sample's history of criminal offending, they had served on average 5.1 (SD = 4.4) prior sentences and held 20.2 (SD = 16.1) previous convictions. The proportional representation of the types of preconvictions was again very similar to that seen in the overall study sample.

5
Personality Disorder

Introduction

This chapter describes the links between personality disorder and criminality; it will explore the treatability debate and provide an outline of the treatments available for personality disordered offenders. In addition, the chapter will provide an examination of the methods of assessment of personality disorder, comparing a self-report method and a semi-structured clinical interview.

The inclusion of the focus on personality disorder within this book was due to the important relationship between personality disorder and criminal behaviour. So many of the men housed in our prisons struggle with the symptoms of personality disorder that it is essential to understand how this can affect their progress through the prison system. An understanding of prisoners with personality disorder can also help us to answer a number of the research questions at the centre of our work, particularly:

- Which kinds of individuals benefited most from the TC?
- Which resident characteristics best predicted/impeded treatment participation and completion?

If we are to evaluate whether prisons can be therapeutic, we have to understand their effect on residents with personality disorder. In order to do this reliably we must also ensure that we are diagnosing personality disorder accurately, which is the rationale for exploring methods of assessment, namely clinical interview vs. self-report.

There are currently two manuals available for the classification and diagnosis of personality disorders. The first is the Diagnostic and Statistical Manual of Mental Disorders, presently in its fifth revision (DSM-IV-TR, APA, 2000). The second is the International Statistical Classification of Diseases and Related Health Problems, 10th Revision (ICD-10; WHO, 1992). The ICD-10 definition of personality disorder is as follows: "a severe disturbance in the characterological condition and behavioural tendencies of the individual, usually involving several areas of the personality, and nearly always associated with considerable personal and social disruption".

The Diagnostic and Statistical Manual of Mental Disorders, Version IV – Text Revision (DSM-IV-TR; APA, 2000) describes personality disorder as *"an enduring pattern of inner experience and behaviour that deviates markedly from the expectations of the individual's culture"* (p. 686). The continuing pattern is inflexible and persistent across a broad range of personal and social situations, and is not a result of another mental disorder. Neither is the disorder the consequence of the direct physiological effects of a substance (e.g. a drug of abuse; a medication; exposure to a toxin) or a general medical condition (head trauma, for example). Onset is usually in late adolescence or early adulthood and the pattern is stable and of long duration.

Personality disorder can affect cognition and volition, without significantly impairing them, and this can increase the propensity for violence and criminality. However, the relationship between personality disorder and antisocial behaviour is complex, and often indirect, which can be problematic for the criminal justice system. Personality disorder does not *cause* violent behaviour or criminality *per se*, but may contribute to antisocial activity. A diagnosis of personality disorder is rarely sufficient to explain a serious offence. There is a stronger relationship between specific forms of personality disorder and criminality, although the functional link is complicated and not always clear.

Personality disorders and criminal behaviour

Antisocial personality disorder (APD)

Prison populations contain large numbers of people with personality disorder. The Office of National Statistics survey found that 78% of male remand prisoners, 64% of male sentenced prisoners and 50% of female prisoners were diagnosed as having personality disorders (Singleton et al., 1998). The most prevalent personality disorder for male prisoners is antisocial personality disorder (APD). APD is characterised by use of deception, disregard for the rights of others and lack of remorse for their behaviour. The association between APD and criminal behaviour in large part reflects the fact that criminal behaviour is one of the diagnostic criteria for APD (Moran, 2002).

In order to be diagnosed with antisocial personality disorder an individual must be at least 18 years of age, and a history of conduct disorder must have been present prior to 15 years of age. For formal diagnosis a person must demonstrate a persistent disregard for and violation of the rights of others, as indicated by at least three of the criteria listed in Box 5.1.

Box 5.1   Diagnostic criteria for personality disorder

- Failure to conform to social norms with respect to lawful behaviours, as indicated by repeatedly performing acts that are grounds for arrest;
- Deceitfulness, as indicated by repeated lying, use of aliases, or conning (swindle by persuasion) others for personal profit or pleasure;
- Impulsivity or failure to plan ahead;
- Irritability and aggressiveness, as indicated by repeated physical fights or assaults;
- Reckless disregard for safety of self or others;
- Consistent irresponsibility, as indicated by repeated failure to sustain consistent work behaviour or honour financial obligations;
- Lack of remorse, as indicated by being indifferent to or rationalising having hurt, mistreated, or stolen from another.

The definition of APD in the DSM-IV (APA, 1994) was updated to ensure more of a combination of personality and behaviour than in the earlier DSM-III-R (APA, 1987[1]). Typically, each symptom describes a personality attribute with a behavioural operational definition, for example: "irritability and aggressiveness, as indicated by repeated physical fights or assaults". The pervasive pattern of behaviours outlined above tends to result in a number of negative outcomes, often including an individual's imprisonment or legal problems; for example, many people with APD develop substance dependence and many incur injuries and violent deaths (Moffitt, 2003).

Other personality disorders of interest

Whilst APD has the most obvious link to criminality, a number of the other personality disorders can lead to violent or criminal behaviour due to various deficits resulting from the disorder. For example, paranoid personality disorder is characterised by a pattern of pervasive distrust and suspiciousness of others. Someone with this disorder will often interpret others' motives as threatening, making it relatively easy to understand how such a disorder could lead to violence.

Borderline personality disorder has been found to be highly co-morbid with APD (Becker et al., 2000), and possibly involves common psychological mechanisms, such as affective instability and impulsiveness (Paris, 1997). People with BPD often have marked instability in mood and problems with interpersonal control. They characteristically display inappropriate and intense anger and have very little control over this. This recurrent, intense anger is often associated with a history of physical violence and threats against others, with research showing that the prominent characteristics of BPD tend to be exaggerated in people with histories of extreme violence (Raine, 1993).

In a community survey of more than 600 people, carried out recently by Coid and colleagues (Coid et al., 2006), it was found that those with cluster B personality disorders (antisocial, borderline, narcissistic and histrionic) were more likely to have had a criminal conviction, to have spent time in prison and to have been in local authority or institutional care.

The particular case of psychopathy

Much attention has been given to psychopathy as a personality construct associated with violence, and the word "psychopath" describes someone who is: "grandiose, arrogant, callous, superficial and manipulative; affectively, they are short tempered, unable to form strong emotional bonds with others, and lacking in guilt and anxiety; and behaviourally, they are irresponsible, impulsive and prone to delinquency and criminality" (Hare, Cooke and Hart, 1999). The link between psychopathy and crime has been established for some time. Hare (1998) tells us that psychopathy is "the single most important clinical construct in the criminal justice system" (p. 189). Psychopathy is most closely related to APD within the DSM framework.

The method of diagnosing an individual with psychopathy is the Psychopathy Checklist – Revised (PCL-R; Hare, 1991). The PCL-R consists of two stable and distinctive factors. Factor 1 measures and identifies core personality characteristics of psychopathy, such as grandiosity and callousness, whilst Factor 2 assesses those aspects of psychopathy related to impulsive, antisocial behaviour and unstable social background. It is Factor 2 that is more often associated with antisocial and borderline personality disorders, criminal behaviour, socio-economic background, and self-report measures of socialisation and antisocial behaviour (Hare, 1991).

Perhaps the most salient aspect of psychopathy is the violation of society's rules (Hare, 1999). Interestingly, criminal versatility is also a feature of psychopathy as measured by the PCL-R, and we acknowledge the concerns raised by Skeem and Cooke (2010) about the danger of conflating measures with constructs. They question whether criminal behaviour "is a central component, or mere downstream correlate, of psychopathy" (p. 1). Nonetheless, in 1995, Hare estimated that 15–20% of all prisoners were psychopaths, as he saw them, and these individuals accounted for a considerable proportion of serious crimes which involved violence. Psychopaths commit violent and aggressive offences at a particularly high rate. For example, in a sample population of 244 inmates it was found that PCL-defined psychopaths were significantly more likely than other criminals to engage in physical violence and other forms of aggressive behaviour, including verbal abuse, threats and intimidation, both in and out of prison (Hare and McPherson, 1984).

Research carried out by Herpertz and colleagues (Herpertz et al., 2001) supports the theory that psychopaths are characterised by a pronounced lack of fear in response to aversive events. In addition, their findings suggest a general deficit in processing affective information, regardless of whether stimuli are negative or positive. These deficits may help to explain why psychopaths are more violent and more prone to criminal behaviour than non-psychopaths. Psychopaths may lack fear, and this is what usually inhibits people from behaving in dangerous or violent ways. The hypothesis of low levels of fear in those with APD was expressed by Lykken (1995): "The fear of punishment and the coercive [restraining] voice of conscience both are, for some reason, weak and ineffectual" (p. 134).

Dangerous and severe personality disorder

In 1996, a mother and her two children were attacked when returning home from school. The attack led to two fatalities and left the surviving child with a permanent disability. The assailant, Michael Stone, was known to psychiatric services, and many questioned why this violent assault had not been prevented. The incident triggered the introduction of a programme that aimed to provide treatment to those assessed as having "dangerous and severe personality disorder" (DSPD). Units were set up in two special hospitals (Broadmoor and Rampton) and two prisons (HMPs Frankland and Whitemoor). The programme allowed the detention of those suspected of having DSPD if they satisfied all three of the following criteria (Home Office and Department of Health): (i) they were more likely than not to commit an offence within five years that might be expected to lead to serious physical or psychological harm from which the victim would find it difficult or impossible to recover; (ii) they had a significant disorder of personality; (iii) the risk presented appeared to be functionally linked to the significant personality disorder. Those whose offending is linked to severe forms of personality disorder present complex and difficult challenges to the criminal justice system in terms of public protection and meeting the mental health needs of the offender. The DSPD programme aimed to address these needs.

The DSPD programme was introduced as a bold attempt to address the difficult problem of dangerousness linked to personality disorder. To its credit, the programme has helped focus attention on a group of individuals who previously received little in the way of mental health care. However, the associated costs of the service were extremely high and research showed that the level of gain was unjustified in terms of cost (Barrett et al., 2009; Tyrer et al., 2010).

Assessment of personality disorder

In order to examine the effectiveness of a treatment for personality disorder, in whatever setting, it is important to first decide how best to assess the presence of a personality disorder. The Personality Disorder Questionnaire-4 (PDQ-4; Hyler, 1994) is routinely used by the prison service. This is a self-report measure, completed by prisoners by themselves using a computer programme. However, the semi-structured interview has been seen for some years as the "gold standard" of personality disorder assessment because it uses clinical skill (Tyrer, 2001). Although there is frequent debate surrounding the best method of assessing personality disorder, at the present time the semi-structured interview remains the most widely used method in research (Zimmerman et al., 2005).

The PDQ-4 is currently the only method of assessment used by the prison staff when evaluating prisoners for suitability for admittance into the therapeutic community (TC) at HMP Dovegate. The Royal College of Psychiatrists (1999) has expressly stated that self-report techniques should not be recommended in the routine clinical assessment of prisoners, and that self-administered tests cannot substitute for clinical interviews due to the extent of false positive results obtained using this method. A false positive result is when a person tests positively for an illness, but they are, in fact, healthy. Typically, self-report measures have been found to under- and over-diagnose personality disorders when compared with structured interviews (Hyler et al., 1990; Bodlund et al., 1998). Hyler's own research (Hyler et al., 1990) concluded that his revised version of the PDQ (PDQ-R) was not a substitute for a structured clinical interview.

Structured clinical interviews for Axis II disorders were developed in order to improve the reliability of assessments of personality disorder (Hyler et al., 1990). They are used in our research as the true positive result against which the PDQ-4 results are measured. A true positive result is obtained when a person tests positive when they actually have the disease.

Although the Personality Diagnostic Questionnaire is now available in its fourth version (PDQ-4; Hyler, 1994), and this most recent adaptation is used in the current research rather than the PDQ-R, it is proposed that the self-report method of diagnosing personality disorders has limited reliability when employed as the sole method of assessment. Sensitivity and specificity analyses were performed in order to prove that results using a self-report measure are not accurate enough to be solely relied upon, and, therefore, use of a semi-structured interview, such as the SCID II, is warranted when assessing an offender population.

The reliability of the SCID II has been examined in a number of studies. Moran and colleagues (Moran et al., 2003) state that "the instrument demonstrates acceptable test–retest ($k = 0.68$) and inter-rater reliability ($k = 0.71$)" (p. 229). Another example, by Maffei and colleagues (Maffei et al.,

1997), measured the inter-rater reliability of the SCID II and found that kappa scores for the ten main DSM personality disorders ranged from 0.83 (obsessive-compulsive) to 0.98 (narcissistic). Furthermore, internal consistency coefficients were found to be satisfactory (0.71–0.94). Whilst these results for test–retest reliability and inter-rater reliability are certainly "acceptable", they tend to be centred at the mid-range level of kappa scores, with only a few results at the higher levels of reliability.

The treatability of personality disorders

Treatability is a complex concept and essentially refers to two main issues: amenability and suitability. Amenability refers to a person's readiness and willingness to engage in an intervention. Personality disorders are ego-syntonic (i.e. consistent with a sense of self) and, therefore, people often do not recognise a need to change. They may not be self-reflective, so establishing a therapeutic alliance is an essential part of the programme (Chiesa et al., 2000). Suitability refers to the intervention that is available to the person with personality disorder. Often, if a patient is not having success with a particular programme it may be that the programme is not specifically tailored to their needs.

Treatability is an important concept in mental health. In its legal sense it limited the involuntary admission of patients with particular mental health issues – patients could not be admitted if they did not meet the treatability criteria, which stated that treatment for a patient must be "likely to alleviate or prevent a deterioration of his treatment". However, this has changed since the revision of the Mental Health Act in 2007, which states that patients can be admitted involuntarily as long as "appropriate medical treatment is available" – the "appropriate treatment test". This means that those deemed dangerous due to severe personality disorder can be detained without their consent, as long as a particular intervention is available, even if it may not be effective for that person. Some professionals working with personality disordered patients remain convinced that it is untreatable, whilst others hold firm that it is. Consequently, it is one of the most controversial categories of mental disorder within psychiatry and other associated disciplines (MacLean Committee, 2000).

At present, personality disorders are separated from other mental illnesses in the classificatory systems of the DSM-IV and the ICD-10 due to their enduring and potentially lifelong nature. It is this aspect of the definition that inhibits mental health professionals from seeing personality disorders as treatable.

An interesting piece of work by Duggan (2004) states that there are three questions fundamental to any inquiry into the treatment of personality disorder: (i) does personality disorder change? (ii) if it does, what changes? and (iii) how can one demonstrate that a change in personality has actually occurred? A number of studies have shown a change in personality disorder symptoms over time. Several thorough long-term follow-up studies of borderline patients (e.g. Paris et al., 1987) show that numbers of participants meeting the threshold for BPD decrease over time. The stability of personality disorder diagnoses was further questioned in the Longitudinal Study of Personality Disorder (Lenzenweger, 2006).

If, then, we accept that PD is amenable to treatment, the next question is how to design interventions. The Fallon Inquiry (Fallon et al., 1999) directly addressed this issue. It found that treatment varies depending on whether people are in a general NHS setting, an inpatient unit, a special hospital or a forensic setting. Fallon's specific recommendation regarding personality disorder services is that they should be delivered within small specialised units in both high-security hospitals and prisons, with easy transfer between the two and the development of nationally agreed assessment and treatment protocols. These recommendations reflect the poor state of research knowledge about treatability (Dolan and Coid, 1993) and the therapeutic ambivalence and consequent uncertainty about whether the disorder is managed most effectively by therapy (i.e. in hospital) or by custody (i.e. in prison). The results of the Fallon Inquiry made the treatment pathway for those with personality disorder no clearer for practitioners.

To summarise, although there are few well-controlled studies, research findings seem to suggest it is possible to treat personality disordered individuals successfully. There is, as yet, no clear evidence of the superiority of one type of treatment approach over another or for a particular method of service delivery (inpatient, outpatient, day programme). However, treatment benefits appear most evident when treatment is intensive, long-term, theoretically coherent, well-structured and well integrated with other services, and where follow-up to residential care is provided (Alwin et al., 2006).

Treatments for personality disorder

The evidence-based literature on treatments for people with personality disorder has tended to concentrate on psychological or mental health need, with little mention of offending behaviour (Craissati et al., 2002). Traditionally in mental health services there has been little faith that treatment is able to impact offending behaviour. In contrast, the "what works" literature (as explained earlier) almost exclusively addresses offending behaviour and the reduction of risk to others. The Policy Guidance for Services for People with a Personality Disorder (Department of Health, 2003) outlines a model for personality disordered offenders which should tackle three areas of functioning: mental health need; offending behaviour (and risk); and social functioning.

Approaches to treatment

There are essentially four main approaches that have been used in the treatment of personality disorders. Broadly, these include: pharmacological; psychodynamic; cognitive and behavioural psychotherapy; and the TC model. Before detailing the TC approach, a brief description of the three other approaches is given in Box 5.2.

Box 5.2   Personality disorder treatment approaches

Pharmacological – There are no drug treatments that have been specifically developed for the treatment of personality disorders. Medication is simply helpful for alleviating some of the symptoms. Short-term treatments usually involve either anxiolytic or neuroleptic drugs, often prescribed at times of severe stress. Longer-term treatments might involve the prescription of neuroleptics for increased periods, and this is particularly successful in the treatment of paranoid and schizotypal personality disorders. Treatment may improve symptoms but is unlikely to impact personality pathology, particularly in borderline patients (O'Rourke and Hammond, 2001). Whilst this will have a positive effect on inhibiting the expression of personality disorder symptoms, pharmacological intervention is not addressing the psychopathology itself, and so the long-term benefits for personality disordered patients remain unknown (Silk, 2000).

   Psychodynamic – This emphasises personality organization and development and helping patients who commit anti-social acts to access and process their subjective mental states to try to limit impulsive and aggressive behaviours (Cordess, 2001). Some partial success to date, but outcome research suggests those with anti-social personality disorder have a worse outcome than others. Limited evidence of the benefits in outpatient settings for people with personality disorder and low levels of functioning, modest improvement for people with Cluster B personality disorders, i.e. anti-social, borderline, narcissistic and histrionic PD (Bateman and Fonagy, 2000). Forensic history better suited to inpatient treatment. Furthermore, the beneficial effect of psychodynamic intervention may diminish over time and the continuation of support or contact after treatment is recommended (Dolan and Coid, 1993).

   Cognitive and behavioural psychotherapy – E.g. Cognitive Therapy (Beck and Freeman, 1990); Dialectical Behaviour Therapy (DBT; Linehan, 1993); Interpersonal Psychotherapy (Benjamin, 1998) and Cognitive Analytical Therapy (CAT; Ryle, 1997). Most cognitive-behavioural approaches

Box 5.2   (Continued)

endeavour to address specific thoughts, feelings and behaviours and do not claim to treat the personality disorder as a whole. As Dolan and Coid (1993) noted, it is rare to find a cognitive-behavioural therapy treatment that has been specifically developed for people with very "severe" personality disorder.

The fact that these treatments aim to treat the associated aspects of the disorder may be the reason why they have the greatest value for the short-term management of personality disorders. The longer-term promise of these approaches is beginning to show some progress (McGuire, 1995), but more research is required. When these treatments are well designed, there is evidence that reoffending can be drastically reduced. Blackburn estimates an average reduction of 20%, with some interventions showing a reduction of up to 50% (Blackburn, 1998).

Therapeutic community

Whilst a number of interventions have been employed for the alleviation of personality disorder symptoms, the TC is the only offender model which specifically targets personality disorder. However, often the focus is on reconviction rates, even in those studies that used TC methods with personality disordered offenders, which does not do justice to the actual targets of the treatment (Harris et al., 1994). It has been suggested that the success of a prison-based therapeutic community, such as Grendon, should be determined by the residents' progression in their "therapy career" rather than subsequent criminal behaviour (Norton and Dolan, 1995). A therapy career can be seen as a patient's progress in therapy – from initial engagement in the assessment process through to engaging in meaningful therapeutic work, whether that be group work or individual sessions with a psychologist or prison counsellor. A prisoner further on in his "therapy career" may be more open to being challenged by others during community meetings, or able to share his wisdom with those just starting to engage in the therapeutic process.

Many mental health professionals agree that the TC is "the treatment of choice for personality disorder" (Roberts in Cullen et al., 1997b, p. 7). This may be because it fits with many of the principles set out by McGuire (1995) in his contribution to the "what works" literature. For example, the TC targets risk factors for offending by correcting maladaptive social functioning, and attitudes and behaviours associated with offending. Furthermore, according to McGuire (1995), offenders respond better to more active and participatory methods.

Multi-modal interventions are said to have a more positive effect on offending behaviour, and the TC provides the structure within which other programmes can be applied. However, it has been postulated that prison TCs may enhance psychopathic traits by providing the opportunity to exercise and develop the capacity to manipulate and deceive. If this is the case, those entering the TC with a low psychopathy score may actually leave with a higher one (Rice, Harris and Cormier, 1992). It is important to view this finding objectively, as the institution in the study conducted by Rice and colleagues (1992) does not fit the generally accepted criteria for a TC. The programme was strongly hierarchical and incorporated some unusual therapies.

Additional research has shown that treatment in a TC can be effective against a range of psychological and behavioural aspects of personality disorder in the medium term. Warren and colleagues (Warren et al., 2006) investigated the outcome of specialist TC treatment for personality disorder at Henderson Hospital; a one-year post-treatment effect was evident. Those who received the TC treatment were significantly more improved than the group who did not on borderline personality disorder symptoms, irritability, depression, anxiety, impulsive feelings and impulsive actions.

Dovegate analyses

Due to extensive criticism of self-report methods of assessing personality disorder (most notably by the Royal College of Psychiatrists, 1999), we felt that it was essential to compare the accuracy of this type of assessment with an additional method in order to assess accuracy. To this end, the Structured Clinical Interview for DSM-IV personality disorders (First et al., 1997) was also administered to participating residents of Dovegate TC and the results were compared.

The advantage of self-report questionnaires for the assessment of personality disorders is that they are quicker to complete and do not involve time-consuming and expensive clinical expertise in order to make a diagnosis. Therefore, the research presented here aimed to investigate whether an assessment of personality disorder obtained using a self-report measure (i.e. the PDQ-4) is adequate, or whether the greater time and effort involved in conducting a semi-structured interview are warranted in terms of the accuracy of the diagnosis.

The residents recruited for the Dovegate sample all had more than 18 months remaining of their current sentence (in order to allow time for follow-up). All participants considered here were recruited from the Assessment and Resettlement Unit (ARU) at the TC at HMP Dovegate, where they were being assessed for suitability for admittance and had not yet entered into the therapy. The average population on this wing is 20 residents at any one time. Every participant had submitted voluntarily to the therapeutic regime at HMP Dovegate, and the baseline SCID II was carried out over the period between June 2005 and July 2006. During this time 58 initial interviews were completed with residents. Corresponding PDQ-4 results were only available for 53 of these participants, and it is these residents, for whom both measures have been completed, who are included in the following analyses.

The residents mostly started their criminal histories early, with a third committing their first offence before the age of 16. A further third started offending between 16 and 21 years of age. The largest number were serving sentences for murder (20.8%) or robbery and burglary (both 15.1%). Nearly a third were serving life sentences (28.3%), just over a quarter sentences of between 10 and 14 years. For full details of this group, see the annex at the end of this chapter.

The measures we used for this study were the Personality Diagnostic Questionnaire – 4 (PDQ-4; Hyler, 1994) and the Structured Clinical Interview for DSM-IV Axis II personality disorders (SCID II; First et al., 1997). The PDQ-4 was included because it is the measure currently used on the ARU unit of the therapeutic community at Dovegate. It assesses the 12 personality disorders listed in the DSM-IV and includes scales for "Too Good" and "Suspect" responses. Participants were asked to complete each of the 99 true/false questions using computer software at the prison. Completion of this questionnaire usually took less than 20 minutes.

As with the PDQ-4, the SCID II also contains questions relating to each of the 12 personality disorders listed on the DSM-IV. However, in both cases only the ten main personality disorders were considered, as those listed in the appendices of the DSM-IV, including depressive and passive-aggressive personality disorders, are not yet recognised as separate and distinct personality disorders. In the SCID II it is the clinical judgement of the interviewer that determines whether a particular criterion for each personality disorder has been met. Scoring is as follows: either the trait is absent, sub-threshold or present, or there is "inadequate information to code".

Participants were approached whilst on the ARU of the TC at Dovegate. Residents are required to complete the PDQ-4 as part of their assessment for suitability for therapy. This is administered by prison staff, in small groups, and self-completed using the prison computer system. Participants were supervised by the prison staff whilst filling in the questionnaire. The results of the PDQ-4 were accessed if possible, along with other case file data, prior to the resident's interview with the research (SN). Before the semi-structured interview was conducted, the aims of the research was outlined for residents, and they were asked whether they would like to participate, and, if so, to sign a consent form. Participants were then invited into a private room where the SCID II interview was conducted by SN. This was not done on the same day as the PDQ-4. The assessment was explained as a "personality assessment", as it was felt the term "personality disorder" might have been disturbing or confusing for the residents.

Interviews took, on average, one hour, and it was made clear to participants that they were free to leave at any time, could refuse to answer any questions if they wished, and were required to be honest in all of their responses.

The SCID II covers all of the DSM-IV personality disorders, and it was elected not to use the two disorders listed in the appendix (depressive and passive-aggressive personality disorder) as they have not yet been proven to be separate and distinct from the other disorders. Therefore, questions concerning these two personality disorders were omitted from the interview process. At the conclusion of the interview, the summary score sheet was completed, providing an assessment of presence or absence of each personality disorder.

The findings

The average number of personality disorders per resident is three, and is not significantly different between methods ($t = 0.108$, df = 52, $p = .915$). However, the standard deviation around the mean is higher for the PDQ-4 than the SCID II. This implies that there is greater variation in diagnoses obtained using the PDQ-4 as opposed to the SCID II.

Sensitivity and specificity are the most widely used statistics to describe a diagnostic test. The sensitivity analysis is a statistical measure of how well a test correctly identifies a condition, or the probability that a symptom is present (or a screening test is positive) given that the person has the disease or disorder. It is often referred to as the "true positive" rate. The results of a screening test are compared with an absolute, or "gold standard", and the sensitivity is the proportion of true positive results of all diseased or disordered cases within a population. A sensitivity value of 100% means that the test recognises all personality disordered people as such, in this case. Sensitivity is not the same as the "positive predictive power" of a test, which is the ratio of true positives to all true and false positives combined.

Specificity is a statistical measure of how well a test correctly identifies the negative cases in a study, or those who do not meet the condition being investigated. The specificity analysis calculates the probability that a symptom is not present (or a screening test is negative) given that the person does not have the disease or disorder; that is, the proportion of true negatives of all negative cases within a population. Specificity is, therefore, also known as the "true negative" rate. The "negative predictive power" of a measure is the proportion of patients with negative test results who are correctly diagnosed.

Table 5.1 shows that sensitivities for the PDQ-4 compared with the SCID II ranged between 0.00 and 0.78, and were >0.50 for five of the ten personality disorders. According to the sensitivity analysis, the PDQ-4 was most effective at diagnosing paranoid and schizotypal personality disorders, with 78% and 60% true positive diagnoses, respectively. The self-report method

Table 5.1   Sensitivity analyses

Personality disorder	Positive diagnoses		Sensitivity (True positive)	Positive predictive power
	PDQ-4 n (%)	SCID II n (%)		
Paranoid	36 (67.9)	32 (64.4)	0.78	0.69
Schizotypal	14 (26.4)	5 (9.4)	0.60	0.21
Schizoid	9 (17.0)	7 (13.2)	0.14	0.11
Histrionic	6 (11.3)	1 (1.9)	0.00	0.00
Narcissistic	11 (20.8)	17 (32.1)	0.10	0.33
Borderline	19 (35.8)	23 (43.4)	0.34	0.63
Antisocial	27 (50.9)	44 (83.0)	0.52	0.85
Avoidant	23 (43.4)	14 (26.4)	0.57	0.35
Dependent	3 (6.0)	2 (3.8)	0.00	0.00
Obsessive-compulsive	20 (37.7)	25 (47.2)	0.52	0.65

performed particularly poorly when diagnosing histrionic, narcissistic, schizoid and dependent personality disorders, with between 0% and 14% true positive results. For antisocial, avoidant and obsessive-compulsive personality disorders, only approximately half of the positive assessments using the PDQ-4 are true positives.

The positive predictive power of the PDQ-4 ranged between 0.00 and 0.85, and was good for APD only. In this case the probability of a resident having this disorder when a positive diagnosis is made is 85% (positive predictive power = 0.85). Again, the PDQ performs particularly poorly for dependent and histrionic personality disorders, where the probability of a positive diagnosis being accurate is 0%.

Specificity analyses

The specificity analyses show that the true negative assessments made by the PDQ-4 range between 0.46 and 0.94. The PDQ-4 performs particularly well for dependent, histrionic and schizoid personality disorders, with between 83% and 94% of negative assessments being true negatives. However, the measure performs relatively poorly for paranoid and anti-social personality disorders, with roughly half of the diagnoses made by the PDQ-4 being false negatives.

Table 5.2 displays the proportion of residents diagnosed above threshold for each of the personality disorders, according to the PDQ-4 and the SCID II. These figures show that the self-report method diagnoses more people with six of the ten personality disorders than the interview method, but under-diagnoses antisocial personality disordered residents most noticeably.

Table 5.2 Specificity analyses for PDQ-4 and SCID II

Personality disorder	Negative diagnoses		Specificity (True negative)	Negative predictive power
	PDQ-4 *n* (%)	SCID II *n* (%)		
Paranoid	17 (32.1)	21 (39.6)	0.46	0.59
Schizotypal	39 (73.6)	48 (90.6)	0.77	0.95
Schizoid	44 (83.1)	46 (86.8)	0.83	0.86
Histrionic	46 (86.8)	52 (98.1)	0.89	0.98
Narcissistic	42 (79.3)	36 (67.9)	0.64	0.33
Borderline	34 (64.2)	30 (56.6)	0.61	0.32
Antisocial	26 (49.1)	9 (17.0)	0.56	0.19
Avoidant	30 (56.6)	39 (73.6)	0.62	0.80
Dependent	50 (94.3)	51 (96.2)	0.94	0.96
Obsessive-compulsive	33 (62.3)	28 (52.8)	0.75	0.36

Table 5.3 Kappa scores

Personality disorder	PDQ-4 *n* (%)	SCID II *n* (%)	Kappa	Chi-square
Paranoid	36 (67.9)	32 (64.4)	0.27*	3.86*
Schizotypal	14 (26.4)	5 (9.4)	0.21	3.20
Schizoid	9 (17.0)	7 (13.2)	−0.03	0.04
Histrionic	6 (11.3)	1 (1.9)	−0.03	0.13
Narcissistic	11 (20.8)	17 (32.1)	−0.05	0.15
Borderline	19 (35.8)	23 (43.4)	0.30*	4.71*
Antisocial	27 (50.9)	44 (83.0)	0.05	0.18
Avoidant	23 (43.4)	14 (26.4)	0.16	1.46
Dependent	3 (6.0)	2 (3.8)	−0.05	0.13
Obsessive-compulsive	20 (37.7)	25 (47.2)	0.27*	4.10*

Note: $^*p \le .05$.

The negative predictive power of the PDQ-4 is reasonably good overall (range between 0.29 and 0.98). The probability of a resident not having schizotypal, dependent or histrionic personality disorders when a negative diagnosis is made is over 95%, which is extremely accurate. The PDQ-4 performs most poorly when diagnosing APD. The probability of a participant not having this disorder when a negative diagnosis is made is only 19%.

Table 5.3 shows the Kappa scores indicating the overlap of the two approaches in measurement of particular PDs. According to the structure developed by Landis and Koch (1977), the rates of agreement between assessments using the PDQ-4 and the SCID II vary between poor (schizoid, histrionic, narcissistic and dependent personality disorders); slight (antisocial and avoidant personality disorders); and fair (paranoid, schizotypal, borderline and obsessive-compulsive personality disorders).

Conclusion

The descriptive statistics show that the PDQ-4 is over-inclusive when assessing personality disorder. Although the average number of personality disorders diagnosed per resident is not statistically different for each method used, the standard deviation is greater for the PDQ-4. The values are more widely spread for the PDQ-4 than the SCID II, suggesting that a broad net is being cast.

Sensitivity and specificity analyses were performed to investigate the accuracy of the PDQ-4 compared with the SCID II in detecting personality disorders when they were present (true positive) and not diagnosing them when they were absent (true negative). The results of the sensitivity analysis show that the PDQ-4 is not particularly successful at positively diagnosing offenders when a personality disorder is present. The PDQ-4 does not correctly identify any participants with histrionic or dependent personality disorders, and all diagnoses using the self-report measure for these personality disorders are false positives. The PDQ-4 notably over-diagnoses histrionic, dependent, narcissistic, schizoid and borderline personality disorders, compared with the SCID II.

The PDQ-4 correctly identifies only half of the residents who actually have APD, according to the sensitivity analysis. This is a worrying result, as it is extremely important to diagnose accurately those TC residents who have APD. APD is akin to psychopathy, and these residents can be amongst the most difficult and disruptive offenders, violating the social rules of the therapeutic regime and disrupting therapy for other residents. Therefore, it is particularly important to correctly identify these individuals. The sensitivity analyses indicate the level of inaccuracy of assessments made using a self-report measure compared with a structured clinical interview, and support criticisms found in the literature of the tendency for self-report measures to over-diagnose (Bodlund et al., 1998).

The relatively low values for positive predictive power show that when the PDQ-4 makes a positive diagnosis it is most likely to be a false positive diagnosis. The only exception is for APD, which has a high positive predictive power, but unfortunately the sensitivity result shows that the PDQ-4 is under-diagnosing this disorder in the first place. On the whole it would appear that the PDQ-4 cannot be relied upon to correctly assess the majority of personality disorders when they are present and has a tendency to over-diagnose.

The results of the specificity analysis demonstrate that the PDQ-4 is more accurate when making true negative diagnoses for the sample of residents from the TC, and accuracy is particularly high for five of the ten personality disorders. However, low specificity values for paranoid disorders and APDs indicate that the PDQ-4 under-diagnoses these.

The high values for negative predictive power indicate that when the PDQ-4 fails to make a diagnosis the disorder is most likely absent. Negative diagnoses for schizotypal, histrionic and dependent personality disorders are more than 95% accurate. The low accuracy score for APD is the notable exception to the otherwise reasonably good negative predictive power of the PDQ-4. A large proportion of TC residents with this disorder are missed due to the self-report assessment providing a false negative result, and this is detrimental to the assessment process for suitability for admittance to the therapeutic community.

In Hyler and colleagues' (1990) research they found that the PDQ most over-diagnosed schizoid and histrionic personality disorders, with a large number of false positive diagnoses. This result is replicated in the current research, with the addition of over-diagnosis of dependent personality disorder, evidenced by the 100% rate of false positive assessments. The PDQ-R over-diagnosed personality disorders rather than under-diagnosing, and this appears to be the case here. The PDQ-4 makes a large number of false positive assessments but performs rather better in not diagnosing a personality disorder when none is present. With the exception of antisocial and paranoid personality disorders, the PDQ-4 makes relatively few false negative assessments and, according to the current research, appears to be more prone to making false positive diagnoses.

They also reported excellent sensitivities, but stated that specificities ranged from "poor" for histrionic to "excellent" for APD. The opposite is found in the current research, with poor sensitivities (perhaps with the exception of paranoid personality disorder assessments) and rather better specificities.

The kappa results demonstrate that there is very little agreement between the self-report and semi-structured interview methods of diagnosing personality disorders in offenders. A notable proportion of results show that the agreement between diagnoses obtained using the two measures is "poor". For four of the disorders (schizoid, histrionic, narcissistic and dependent) the agreement between ratings is less than zero, and this illustrates that there is no agreement whatsoever between the two measures when diagnosing these disorders. The two measures are, therefore, diagnosing different people with these disorders, with no corresponding assessments.

Assessments obtained using both measures achieved a level of agreement interpreted as "fair" for paranoid, schizotypal, borderline and obsessive-compulsive personality disorders. This suggests that similar diagnoses are obtained when using either self-report or interview techniques. For three of these personality disorders (excluding schizoid), the relationship between assessments using the PDQ-4 and SCID II is statistically significant. The two methods are, therefore, diagnosing the same individuals for these personality disorders.

PDQ-4 and the SCID II do not diagnose the same residents with personality disorders, and assessments obtained using these two measures do not correspond to each other, as the assessment of personality disorder using self-report and interview methods produces differing results. The agreement between diagnoses using the PDQ-4 vs. the SCID II is fair at best, and this is the case for fewer than half of the personality disorders examined.

In his early study, Hyler and colleagues (1990) found only "modest" agreement between the PDQ and two interview measures, and suggested that the self-report method of assessment of personality disorders was best used as a screening measure only. This study also found that agreement between the self-report and interview measures was modest. In addition, the sensitivity of the PDQ-4 was poor, leading to over-diagnosis of many personality disorders. Its specificity was somewhat better, but indicated that APD was being under-diagnosed – an important personality disorder in prison populations, for which an accurate diagnosis is essential. Hyler concluded that his results showed that the PDQ-R was not a substitute for a structured interview, and the same conclusion must be drawn here for the more recent version of the PDQ. The inaccuracies reported here further support the recommendation made by the Royal College of Psychiatrists (1999), that self-report measures should not be relied on for the sole assessment of personality disorders in offenders.

Due to these inaccuracies, it must be concluded that the PDQ-4 is not valid for use as the sole measure for diagnosing personality disorders within a prison setting. It may be useful as a screening measure to give some indication of the presence of personality disorders, but for a definitive assessment a structured clinical interview is recommended.

Chapter annex

Table 5a.1 Demographics of the Dovegate TC residents taking part in the PD assessment

	n	%
Ethnicity		
White	43	81.1
Black	6	11.3
Asian	1	1.9
Mixed	1	1.9
Missing data	*2*	*3.8*

Marital status

Married	6	11.3
Single	29	54.7
Cohabiting/in a non-marital relationship	7	13.2
Divorced/separated	6	11.3
Missing data	*5*	*9.4*

Note: The sample population was male, with the majority being white (81.1%, $n=43$). Slightly more than 11% of participants were black ($n=6$). Most of the participants were single (54.7%, $n=29$).
The age range of participants was 22–63 years with a mean age of 32.45 years (SD $=9.38$).

Table 5a.2   Criminal history of the Dovegate TC residents taking part in the PD assessment

	n	%
Age at first offence		
<16 years	19	35.9
16–21 years	17	32.1
>21 years	2	3.8
Missing data	*15*	*28.2*
Index offence		
Murder	11	20.8
Robbery	8	15.1
Burglary	8	15.1
Armed robbery	3	5.7
GBH	3	5.7
Drug offences – supply or possession	3	5.7
Rape – adult or child	3	5.7
Manslaughter	2	3.8
Arson	2	3.8
Conspiracy to rob	1	1.9
Attempted murder	1	1.9
Missing data	*8*	*15.1*
Length of current sentence		
Up to 4 years	5	9.4
5–9 years	9	17.0
10–14 years	14	26.4
15–22 years	2	3.8
Life	15	28.3
Missing data	*8*	*15.1*

6
Changes over Time: The Psychometric Data

Introduction

Psychometric assessment tools have a long history of application in the evaluation of psychological interventions, their utility being their ability to produce quantitative and generalisable measures of therapeutic change. However, the majority of research that has been conducted into the efficacy of the democratic form of the TC model has been marked by a reliance on descriptive methodologies (Rawlings, 1998; Haigh, 2002). Furthermore, the results of such work have been critiqued for their inconsistency (Manning & Morant, 2004). This has left the treatment open to claims that the success of particular TCs comes down to issues of charisma and idiosyncratic leadership styles (Manning, 1991). Recent years have, however, seen a growth in the implementation of more structured, quantitative research designs, and this has subsequently offered a more systematic insight into the workings and impact of the TC approach (Lees, Manning & Rawlings, 2004).

This chapter will present the findings that emerged from the psychometric evaluations of the residents' psychological and behavioural functioning during their time in the TC. A sample of 250 TC residents was assessed at six-monthly intervals from the beginning of their participation in the programme. The results demonstrate that the TC residents had impaired functioning at the commencement of their time in therapy when compared with prisoners in mainstream establishments, i.e. with our control comparison group. While relatively little change occurred during the initial six months of therapy, there was a demonstrable increase in prisoners' self-reported contemplation of change by their first year. This was further reflected by measurable decreases in observed behaviour, i.e. dominance, gregariousness and nurturance, and by increases in self-reported hostility. This is consistent with the acclimatisation phase and somewhat regressive responses to the early stages of therapy reported in the literature (Jones, 1997). After this initial period, residents appear to benefit from a more distinctly positive impact of the therapy, with improvements occurring in self-esteem and hostility levels by 18 months. Some improvements in affect regulation also occurred, although these lacked long-term stability. After 18 months, there was some further improvement in self-esteem and hostility, but rates of improvement decelerated, suggesting that 18 months is the optimum length of participation in Dovegate TC.

Studies conducted at Grendon have reported reductions in hostility amongst TC residents (Newton, 1973; Miller, 1982), as well as decreases in psychoticism and neuroticism (Newton, 1998). Conversely, prisoners who have undergone TC treatment have been found to show greater extroversion (Newton, 1998) and improved interactive skills (Gunn et al., 1978). Shuker and Newton (2008) employed idiographic assessment techniques to examine individual-level change on tests of self-esteem, hostility and overall personality and so account for variability in participants' length of residency in the TC. They demonstrated that longer length of stay (one year or more) generally corresponded to larger proportions of the residents showing improvements on both mental health and risk variables. Shorter-stay residents conversely only showed limited changes and no demonstrable reduction in risk. Recidivism studies have also shown the importance of the length of residency on therapeutic outcome, but have suggested that the completion of 18 months in therapy is the most important threshold for ensuring positive treatment outcome (Cullen, 1993, 1997; Genders & Player, 1995).

Maxwell Jones (1968), who is credited with the being the original proponent of the TC model, believed an important aspect of the TC is an attention to process, rather than a focus on the outcome alone, yet, as Neville et al. (2007) note, the mechanisms effecting change during TC residency remain underexplored. This chapter will describe an effort to address this gap.

Methodological considerations

As part of the longitudinal evaluation of the TC programme at Dovegate, a diverse psychometric test battery was established and administered to TC residents at regular intervals during their time in the intervention. This work aimed to examine the extent and nature of any psychological and behavioural changes achieved by these therapy participants, and the process by which these developed across participants' residency in the programme.

In fulfilling these aims, the test battery was administered to therapy participants at six-monthly intervals during their time in the TC. Initial testing occurred during the prisoners' induction period within the Assessment and Resettlement Unit (ARU), and was repeated regularly throughout participants' period of engagement in the TC proper. In total, 250 participants were recruited, and the length of their participation in the data collection varied according to their length of residency in the TC, with the longest lengths surpassing 24 months. Thus, this work will offer a comprehensive insight into the workings of the intervention, and the pattern and extent of any quantifiable change that it elicited.

A profile of the residents

Prior to examining the psychometric results, it is important to examine the characteristics of the participating residents. Case file analyses at the point of recruitment into the study were conducted to gauge the demographic details and offending histories of this group. These details provide a useful initial insight into the recruited residents and enable comparison with the overall population of the TC as well as the wider prison population.

The average age of the participating residents was 32.98 (SD: 8.18), ranging from 21 to 63 years old. The residents were predominantly of a white British ethnicity, with the next most common ethnicity being black Caribbean (6.8% of sample; see Table 6a.1 in the chapter annex for full details). Almost 60% of the sample were single, while 23.2% reported themselves to be in an ongoing relationship (see Table 6a.2 in the chapter annex). Just over half (55.6%) had children, while 23.2% did not. It could not be established for the remaining prisoners whether they had children, as case file data were incomplete.

These residents tended to leave school early, the average age being about 15 years old ($M = 14.84$, $SD = 1.56$). Almost a fifth (18%) had no history of employment, while 13.2% had held a long-term job in the past. A further 37.6% had worked in less stable jobs, while the work history of the remaining 31.6% had not been recorded. Records for 105 participants, or 42% of the sample, showed they had been abused during their childhoods, either physically, sexually or emotionally. An examination of their mental health history showed that 63% of participants had at some point attempted or were considered at risk of committing suicide.

Interestingly, the age of first conviction corresponded with the age at which these TC residents left school ($M = 15.91$, $SD = 4.16$). However, by the time the residents received their current conviction, they were on average nearly 30 years of age ($M = 29.78$ years old, $SD = 7.66$). They comprised 83 lifers, 79 Cat B inmates and 86 who were designated Cat C. The average current sentence length was 112.6 months ($SD = 85.97$).[1] The residents' index offences were coded according to the Offenders' Index coding scheme as originally proposed by the Home Office. The summary of index offence types (Table 6a.3 in the chapter annex) demonstrates that violent offences (41.2% of the sample), followed by robbery (27.6%), were the most common index categories.

A similar pattern is also reflected in the preconviction history of the participants (Table 6a.4 in the chapter annex): a majority (60.8%) of the sample had prior convictions for violent offences, while 50% of the sample also had a history of robbery offences. Most offenders had more than one preconviction, however. In fact, the average number of preconvictions was 18.25 (SD = 17.82), while the research participants had served approximately 5.4 sentences (SD = 7.03) prior to the current incarceration.

TC engagement indices

The participating residents varied in terms of the length of their engagement in the TC programme. One-fifth dropped out within the initial six months, prior to the first follow-up stage of the psychometric assessments. A similar number left with the subsequent assessment interval (6–11 months). Fewer residents left during the next two assessment periods, and the largest proportion of residents were in the category that survived up to two years within the community. Full details on the proportions are provided in the chapter appendix (Table 6a.5).

It was also possible to evaluate the participants' eventual reason for departure. The most common reasons were due to a request by the prisoner to be moved out of the TC (termed a "48 hr request"), followed by occurrences of "de-selection", where the prisoner was required to leave the programme due to disruptive behaviours. A full breakdown of the differing reasons for participants' departure from the TC is provided in Table 6a.6 in the chapter annex.

Psychometric tests used

A range of psychometric measures comprised the test battery administered to prisoners during their participation in the data collection. These are listed in Box 6.1. For full details please refer to the annex in Chapter 4.

The findings

The six psychometric measures, administered in the test battery at six-monthly intervals, were subjected to a series of repeated-measures analyses. To account for dosage effects of the therapy, the residents were split according to the length of their participation in the data collection process. Residents were excluded from assessments once they had dropped out of therapy, and thus the grouping method adopted for these analyses approximated the prisoners' length of participation in the TC therapy proper. Furthermore, this grouping factor maximises sample sizes and thus the power of the analyses. Table 6.1 outlines the breakdown of sample sizes for each group defined by this partitioning.

Box 6.1   Psychometric measurements

Revised Gudjonsson Blame Attribution Inventory (GBAI-R)

Higher scores on each scale are indicative of higher levels of blame attribution for that particular construct.

Culture-Free Self Esteem Inventory 2 (CFSEI-2)

For all scales, higher scores indicate higher levels of the respective aspects of self-esteem that they operationalise.

Chart of Interpersonal Reactions in Closed Living Environments (CIRCLE)

The eight indices of interpersonal functioning assessed by this observational tool are as follows: *Dominant, Gregarious, Nurturant, Compliant, Submissive, Withdrawn, Hostile* and *Coercive*. High scores on each scale represent high levels of the respective construct.

Hostility and Direction of Hostility Questionnaire (HDHQ)

High scores indicate higher levels of each form of hostility assessed by the HDHQ.

Inventory of Altered Self Capacities (IASC)

Lower scores on all scales reflect more appropriate modes of functioning, i.e. lower levels of the dysfunctional characteristic being operationalised.

University of Rhode Island Change Assessment Scale (URICA)

This is a quantitative assessment of therapeutic progress, assessing four stages from preparation for change to the maintenance of progress achieved. The four stages operationalised by the measure are defined as follows: *Precontemplation, Contemplation, Action,* and *Maintenance*.

Although research participation offers an important grouping factor for exploring dosage effects of TC residency, we acknowledge some issues with this method. The staggered mode of recruitment across time needed for a longitudinal study means that some residents continued in therapy once the data collection end-point was reached, or were what is technically termed "right-censored". Additionally, 24 participants dropped out of the research prior to its completion.[2] Almost all, however, dropped out of the research at approximately the same point as they dropped out of therapy, ensuring comparability

Table 6.1 Sample sizes for participation groupings

Length of participation	n	%
0–5 months	73	29.2
6–11 months	72	28.8
12–17 months	46	18.4
18–23 months	30	12
24 months+	29	11.6

between research and therapy participation lengths. It must be acknowledged, nonetheless, that a small number of residents remained in the TC facility awaiting transfer despite having dropped out of therapy, and it is possible that these may have benefited indirectly from simply residing in the TC, but it was not possible to quantitatively evaluate such benefits in the current instance.

After data collection, preliminary data cleaning was performed to prepare the data for statistical testing. Exploratory analyses indicated variance from the normal distribution in some scales, and consequently non-parametric tests were employed for subsequent inferential analyses. Friedman's tests were performed on the data, and any significant results were subjected to appropriate post-hoc follow-ups. This offered a standard group-level perspective on the participants' therapeutic progress during their time in the TC, but, given the clinical basis of this treatment modality, an additional perspective was sought through the use of idiographic change tools to ensure that the focus on therapy impact at an individual level was also obtained. The Reliable Change Index (RCI) methodology (O'Neill, 2010), fully described in Chapter 4, enables such idiographic testing, by adjusting for each psychometric measure's reliability. This adjustment means that the changes in participating residents' test scores over time can be examined for statistical meaningfulness after inherent fluctuations in the assessment tools are accounted for. In conjunction with knowledge about the direction of such test score changes, the RCI approach consequently represents a valuable measure for detecting whether change occurring over time for each participant is relevant in both a statistical and a clinical sense.

Measuring therapeutic progress at group level

6–11 months group (n = 72)

The progress demonstrated by TC residents who participated for between 6 and 11 months (and thus were assessed on two occasions) is outlined in Figure 6.1. Little change was evidenced during this group's time in the intervention, but Box 6.2 provides a summary of where any change did occur.

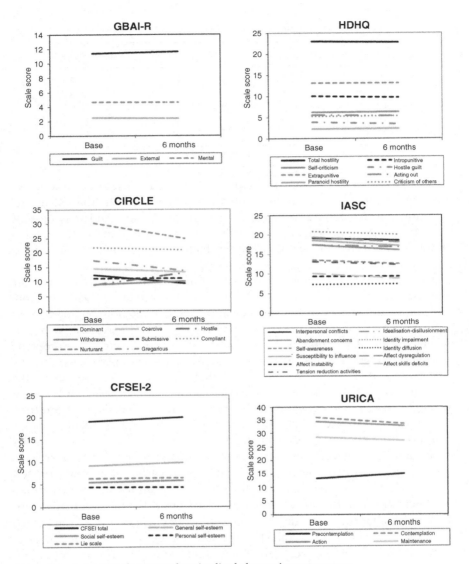

Figure 6.1   6–11 months group: longitudinal change in mean scores

12–17 months group (n = 46)

TC residents who participated for between 12 and 17 months were assessed at three time points. The charts presented in Figure 6.2 provide an overview of the change demonstrated by this group on the six primary psychometric measures. These residents showed some changes, but most lacked statistical meaningfulness, as shown in the summary of the inferential results achieved (Box 6.3).

Box 6.2 Patterns observable in residents staying between 6 and 11 months

Barely noteworthy shifts occurred in how residents perceived their own self-esteem levels (CFSEI-2) and in their self-reported dysfunctional relating and affect regulation (IASC). Test score shift was even less evident in hostility (HDHQ) and blame attribution (GBAI-R). Inferential analyses conducted using Friedman's tests underlined the absence of statistical significance for any changes on these measures.

Interpersonal functioning, however, as identified through staff ratings of residents (CIRCLE) and self-reported preparedness for change (URICA), did show more notable change. On the CIRCLE, statistically significant decreases were evident on the *Dominant* ($\chi^2(1) = 8.07$, $p = .005$), *Gregarious* ($\chi^2(1) = 6.9$, $p = .009$) and *Nurturant* ($\chi^2(1) = 11.66$, $p = .001$) scales, suggesting that these residents became less outgoing in this time. This change was mirrored by a non-significant increase in hostility amongst these patients: *Hostility* ($\chi^2(1) = 15.52$, $p = .06$).

In terms of self-reported change, these residents were more likely to show increased *Precontemplation* ($\chi^2(1) = 9.68$, $p = .002$), which may denote a more entrenched resistance to change. This corresponded with an overall decrease in *Contemplation* about change ($\chi^2(1) = 12$, $p = .001$) during this time, and similarly a decrease in actual efforts towards achieving any such change (*Action*: $\chi^2(1) = 8.33$, $p = .004$).

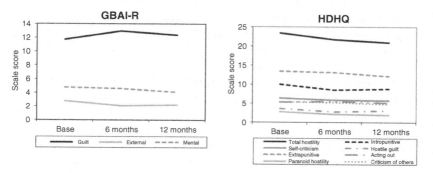

Figure 6.2   12–17 months group: longitudinal change in mean scores

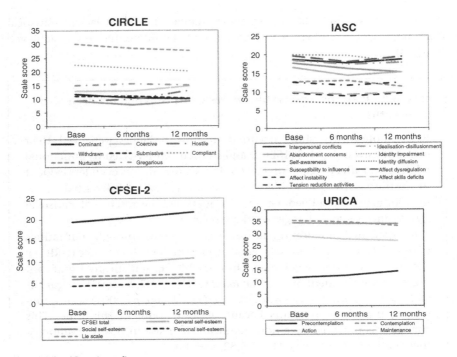

Figure 6.2   (Continued)

Box 6.3   Patterns observable in residents staying between 12 and 17 months

The residents showed increases in self-esteem (CFSEI-2), most markedly in General Self-Esteem and the measure's total score, but these were not of a sufficient magnitude to be statistically significant.

There were observable decreases in overall hostility (HDHQ), but again this pattern was not statistically significant. Moreover, some improvements in inwardly directed hostility that were achieved by 6 months began to revert to earlier levels by 12 months.

This reversal of improvements achieved was likewise seen to occur in measures of poor affect regulation and some dysfunctional interpersonal behaviours (as assessed by the IASC and CIRCLE, respectively). This pattern could point to factors relevant to therapeutic resistance or ruptures or possibly to increased likelihood of drop-out subsequent to this final assessment point. However, none of these trends remained statistically significant once adjustment to the statistical inference cutoffs was implemented to account for the number of tests performed.

Conversely, feelings of *Guilt* about offending, as assessed by the GBAI-R, showed a similar pattern, but were statistically significant ($\chi^2(2) = 10.54$, $p = .005$). Follow-up analyses showed that the significant increase that occurred on this scale by 6 months was reversed by the 12-month point.

Two scales on the URICA additionally showed significant change, but with the changes occurring between baseline and 12 months. These were *Precontemplation* ($\chi^2(2) = 8.1$, $p = .017$) and *Maintenance* of change ($\chi^2(2) = 9.05$, $p = .011$), with an increase in the former being matched by a drop in the latter.

18–23 months group (n = 30)

Thirty residents completed 18 months of therapy, but subsequently dropped out before the next assessment point at 24 months. Summary charts illustrating the therapeutic progress of this group are presented in Figure 6.3.

Residents in this group showed an increase in self-esteem and a drop in self-reported feelings of hostility. However, unlike the earlier study leavers, the

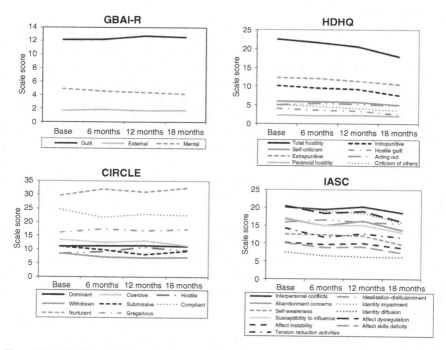

Figure 6.3   18–23 months group: longitudinal change

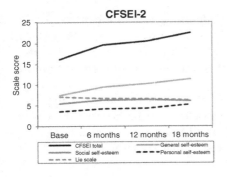
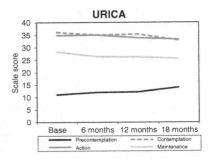

Figure 6.3   (Continued)

changes demonstrated by the 18–23-month survivors on these characteristics were more frequently statistically significant. Moreover, they were accompanied by noteworthy changes on a number of other scales. Box 6.4 is a summary of these results.

Box 6.4   Patterns observable in residents staying between 18 and 23 months

Increases in *General Self-esteem* ($\chi^2(3) = 18.21$, $p < .001$) were reflected in a corresponding increase in the overall self-esteem factor (*CFSEI Total*; $\chi^2(3) = 14.31$, $p = .003$). Post-hoc tests showed that significant stages of change for these scales occurred both between baseline and 12 months, and between baseline and 18 months. A simultaneous drop occurred in *Hostile Guilt* ($\chi^2(3) = 13.01$, $p = .005$), as assessed by the HDHQ; however, in this case, significant change only occurred between baseline and 18 months. A decrease on the outwardly directed *Criticism of Others* scale also approached significance.

The group showed further improvements in the psychoanalytically relevant area of *Identity Impairment* ($\chi^2(3) = 17.54$, $p = .001$), specifically in terms of *Self-Awareness* ($\chi^2(3) = 18.38$, $p < .001$). The importance of 18 months' residency was underlined here by post-hoc tests, with scores from this assessment showing significant improvement on each preceding stage for the *Self-Awareness* scale. Affect regulation also significantly improved, with *Susceptibility to Influence* ($\chi^2(3) = 14.18$, $p = .003$) and *Affect Skills Deficits* ($\chi^2(3) = 13.21$, $p = .004$) scales both showing increases. Post-hoc tests established that the period between baseline and 18 months was again the source of this significance. Interestingly, a number of scales on IASC showed trends by 12 months where participants were either regressing to earlier levels of dysfunction or, at best, maintaining progress achieved by the six-month assessment. The subsequent six months leading up to the 18-month assessment point, however, showed further improvements on all scales of the measure.

As with the earlier study leavers, *Precontemplation* of change ($\chi^2(3) =$ 11.53, $p = .009$) increased over time, particularly between 12 and 18 months. A significant difference in the *Maintenance* of change ($\chi^2(3) =$ 11.19, $p = .011$) was also evident, albeit in the opposite direction. An overall decrease was similarly evident for the *Contemplation* scale ($\chi^2(3) =$ 16.52, $p = .001$), with the significant change occurring between baseline and 18-month assessments.

There was marked variation in the patterns of change across the CIR-CLE scales, which is perhaps understandable given that the measure assesses interpersonal behaviour in terms of two orthogonal, or unre-lated, bipolar axes. Of these changes, however, only the *Submissive* scale approached significance, which, as illustrated in Figure 6.3, was on account of a reduction in behaviours classified as such between baseline and the end of residents' first year in therapy.

24 months+ group (n = 29)

The final sample grouping examined was residents who completed assessments up to the two-year point. The graphs presented in Figure 6.4 offer a concise overview of these results, while details about the statistical meaningfulness of these results are summarised in Box 6.5.

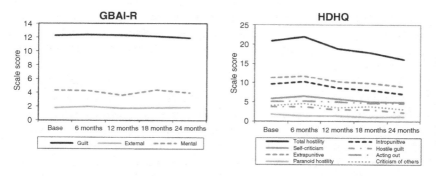

Figure 6.4 24 months plus group: longitudinal change

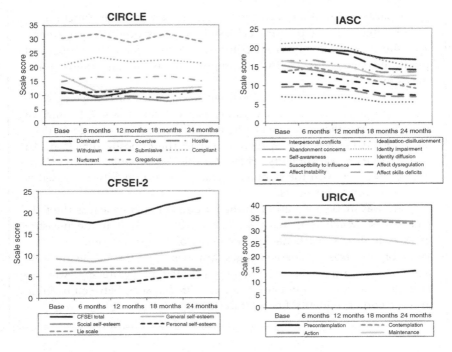

Figure 6.4   (Continued)

Box 6.5   Patterns observable in residents staying over 24 months

Interpersonal behaviour as assessed by the CIRCLE showed perhaps even more pronounced variation than was seen with the 18–23 month group. Initial reductions in *Coercive* and *Dominant* behaviours are apparent, as are peaks at 6 and 18 months in the more pro-social scales of the measure: *Nurturant, Compliant* and *Gregarious*. No overall significance was identified however.

Self-esteem was again a notable area of improvement, with increases occurring in *General Self-esteem* ($\chi^2(4) = 21.34$, $p < .001$) and *Personal Self-esteem* ($\chi^2(4) = 22.48$, $p < .001$), as with the higher-order *CFSEI Total* scale ($\chi^2(4) = 23.49$, $p < .001$). Almost all these findings were down to differences of the 24-month scores from earlier assessments.

Likewise, significant changes were demonstrated in self-reported hostility. *Total Hostility* ($\chi^2(4) = 13.84$, $p = .008$) also showed a significant improvement, with a consistent decrease across assessments. Post-hoc tests, however, point specifically to the change that occurs between

6 months and 24 months. This decrease in hostility appears to be particularly related to that which is inwardly directed, with *Intropunitiveness* ($\chi^2(4) = 17.1$, $p = .002$) and *Hostile Guilt* ($\chi^2(4) = 15.57$, $p = .004$) scale scores also showing significant drops. Interestingly, a plateau effect is apparent on the *Self-Criticism* and *Acting-Out* scales of this HDHQ measure between 18 and 24 months.

A similar plateau pattern is also evident on a number of significant scales from the IASC questionnaire. Affect regulation scales on this measure point to increasingly large improvements up to 18 months for these participants, with a subsequent deceleration prior to the 24-month mark. This is the case for *Affect Dysregulation* ($\chi^2(4) = 30.03$, $p < .001$), *Affect Instability* ($\chi^2(4) = 31.89$, $p < .001$) and *Affect Skills Deficits* ($\chi^2(4) = 17.28$, $p < .002$), as well as scales assessing dysfunctional behaviours and modes of relating, namely *Susceptibility to Influence* ($\chi^2(4) = 16.32$, $p = .003$), *Tension Reduction Activities* ($\chi^2(4) = 33.74$, $p < .001$), *Identity Diffusion* ($\chi^2(4) = 19.72$, $p = .001$) and *Idealisation-Disillusionment* ($\chi^2(4) = 18.51$, $p = .001$).

This plateau effect was not universal across these measures, however. Some of the post-hoc tests of *IASC* data suggest that continuation to the 24-month stage can carry some benefits. For example, participants showed consistent decreases across 18- and 24-month in *Identity Impairment* ($\chi^2(4) = 32.3$, $p < .001$) and in impaired *Self-Awareness* ($\chi^2(4) = 29.83$, $p < .001$).

Looking at the URICA data, *Contemplation* ($\chi^2(4) = 21.9$, $p < .001$) of change also shows a steady drop over time, which was mirrored by a non-significant increase in *Action* over change.

Idiographic change: An alternative perspective

In addition to the group-level analyses, Reliable Change Indices were calculated for each measure and the results are presented in Tables 6.2 through 6.6. The tables show the number and percentage of individuals in each dosage group who increased or decreased on each of the specific psychometric scales during their time participating in the intervention. The RCI technique also enables an evaluation of sample frequencies where no change occurs. These proportions can be inferred from the tables, but are also directly reported in the complete tabulations in the appendices. (It should be noted that the RCI includes an adjustment for each psychometric measure's reliability, so that individuals who show no change may be making some movement, but this does not reach statistical significance.) Where scores were statistically significant at $p < .05$, the direction of the change was noted and recorded as either an

Table 6.2   Within-TC CIRCLE idiographic change

Scale	Change	6–11 Months	12–17 Months	18+ Months
Dominant	Increase	20% (13)	20% (8)	26% (14)
	Decrease	54% (35)	42% (17)	30% (16)
Coercive	Increase	25% (16)	33% (13)	22% (12)
	Decrease	36% (23)	23% (9)	46% (25)
Hostile	Increase	40% (26)	46% (19)	26% (14)
	Decrease	20% (8)	27% (11)	24% (13)
Withdrawn	Increase	34% (22)	34% (14)	24% (13)
	Decrease	26% (17)	34% (14)	39% (21)
Submissive	Increase	26% (17)	29% (12)	22% (12)
	Decrease	28% (18)	34% (14)	33% (18)
Compliant	Increase	29% (19)	27% (11)	24% (13)
	Decrease	37% (24)	51% (21)	35% (19)
Nurturant	Increase	14% (9)	20% (8)	37% (20)
	Decrease	39% (25)	38% (15)	26% (14)
Gregarious	Increase	17% (11)	32% (13)	43% (23)
	Decrease	52% (34)	29% (12)	24% (13)

Table 6.3   Self-esteem (CFSEI-2) RCI results: % (*n*)

Scale	Change	6–11 Months	12–17 Months	18+ Months
CFSEI total	Increase	20% (11)	32% (9)	47% (25)
	Decrease	13% (7)	11% (3)	9% (5)
General	Increase	29% (16)	46% (13)	47% (25)
	Decrease	13% (7)	14% (4)	11% (6)
Social	Increase	28% (15)	21% (6)	28% (15)
	Decrease	9% (5)	7% (2)	8% (4)
Personal	Increase	6% (3)	25% (7)	26% (14)
	Decrease	13% (7)	11% (3)	4% (2)

Table 6.4   Blame attribution (GBAI-R) RCI results: % (*n*)

Scale	Change	6–11 Months	12–17 Months	18+ Months
Guilt	Increase	6% (3)	6% (2)	2% (1)
	Decrease	0% (0)	3% (1)	2% (1)
External	Increase	0% (0)	3% (1)	0% (0)
	Decrease	4% (2)	3% (1)	4% (2)
Mental	Increase	10% (5)	9% (3)	4% (2)
	Decrease	14% (7)	19% (6)	12% (6)

Table 6.5 Self-reported hostility (HDHQ) RCI results: % (*n*)

Scale	Change	6–11 Months	12–17 Months	18+ Months
Total hostility	Increase	12% (6)	13% (4)	10% (5)
	Decrease	18% (9)	32% (10)	38% (19)
Self-critical	Increase	10% (5)	3% (1)	8% (4)
	Decrease	12% (6)	29% (9)	26% (13)
Hostile guilt	Increase	2% (1)	0% (0)	6% (3)
	Decrease	12% (6)	13% (4)	22% (11)
Acting out	Increase	8% (4)	10% (3)	14% (7)
	Decrease	6% (3)	3% (1)	24% (12)
Paranoid hostility	Increase	10% (5)	3% (1)	4% (2)
	Decrease	12% (6)	27% (8)	24% (12)
Critical of others	Increase	22% (11)	13% (4)	6% (3)
	Decrease	14% (7)	32% (10)	28% (14)

Table 6.6 Altered self capacities (IASC) RCI results: % (*n*)

Scale	Change	6–11 Months	12–17 Months	18+ Months
Interpersonal conflicts	Increase	8% (4)	6% (2)	4% (2)
	Decrease	15% (8)	12% (4)	16% (8)
Idealisation-disillusionment	Increase	8% (4)	6% (2)	2% (1)
	Decrease	13% (7)	18% (6)	14% (7)
Abandonment concerns	Increase	2% (1)	6% (2)	2% (1)
	Decrease	6% (3)	9% (3)	4% (2)
Identity impairment	Increase	6% (3)	0% (0)	4% (2)
	Decrease	11% (6)	15% (5)	22% (11)
Self-awareness	Increase	4% (2)	0% (0)	4% (2)
	Decrease	9% (5)	9% (3)	16% (8)
Identity diffusion	Increase	11% (6)	6% (2)	6% (3)
	Decrease	13% (7)	21% (7)	22% (11)
Susceptibility to influence	Increase	13% (7)	12% (4)	2% (1)
	Decrease	21% (11)	21% (7)	25% (12)
Affect dysregulation	Increase	4% (2)	3% (1)	0% (0)
	Decrease	8% (4)	6% (2)	16% (8)
Affect instability	Increase	8% (4)	3% (1)	2% (1)
	Decrease	4% (2)	6% (2)	12% (6)
Affect skill deficits	Increase	4% (2)	9% (3)	0% (0)
	Decrease	20% (11)	15% (5)	22% (11)
Tension reduction activities	Increase	4% (2)	6% (2)	4% (2)
	Decrease	8% (4)	12% (4)	20% (10)

Increase or a *Decrease*. As prior literature has suggested that 18 months' residency potentially represents an optimal participation period for the effecting of therapeutic benefits, a view that has achieved some empirical support in the results reported in this chapter thus far, all residents who achieved 18 months' or longer participation in the programme were subsumed into a single category. This ensured that the sample groupings employed in the RCI analyses were sufficiently large so as not to unnecessarily limit the representativeness of the samples and the power of the testing being applied.

Overall, there is evidence of movement in the residents however long they remained in the TC. Generally speaking, a period of 18 months or greater appears to result in a larger proportion of TC residents achieving improvement in their interpersonal functioning. In comparison to the other assessment intervals, smaller proportions of the longer-term residents showed negative changes in their likelihood to engage in coercive or hostile activities, while increases in caring behaviours and outgoingness were proportionally more frequent.

Looking more closely at the earlier participation lengths, over half the participants who dropped out after six months were also observed to engage in less dominant and coercive behaviours, but they conversely also showed a notably high deterioration in their display of nurturant, gregarious and compliant behaviours. This latter point may point to difficulties in adjusting to the therapy environment, and so could possibly reflect approach/avoidance aspects of early therapeutic engagement.

During the 12–17-month period, a greater proportion of residents showed increases in hostility levels, coupled with a decrease in compliance and nurturance. This may be indicative of ruptures and tensions within the community, and potentially may offer insight into the reasons behind participants' subsequent departure or exclusion from the therapy programme.

In terms of self-esteem, generally there was an improvement across all dosage groups. Overall, the highest proportion of residents enhancing their self-esteem was evidenced by those experiencing the longest period in the TC, but this is only a modest increase over those remaining in the TC for up to 18 months.

There was relatively little movement with respect to guilt attribution, although there was a modest shift in seeking mental status as the locus of blame. The actual numbers who achieved any statistically meaningful change on this measure, however, are particularly small, so caution is required in drawing any inferences.

Hostility also showed movement, and overall it tended to be those in the longer dosage period who proportionately indicated greatest decrease. In terms of criticism of others, however, there was also proportionately considerable movement at the 12–17-month period. The smallest proportion demonstrating change was in the group with the shortest stay in the TC. This pattern seems consistent with respect to measures of altered capacities.

Conclusions

The most consistent improvements amongst residents appear to be in terms of enhanced self-esteem, decreased hostility, and reduced difficulties with identity impairments and affect regulation. Such progress was particularly evident for residents who remained in therapy for 18 months, with even further benefits evidenced by the 24-month mark. However, even though some measures do show continued, if moderate, improvement across this additional six months of residency, inferences about the changes have to be limited, since they lacked statistical significance. Nonetheless, the changes identified were in a continuing positive direction.

Individual-level analyses of the participants' progress on the self-esteem assessment showed a more discernible impact of the intervention. Just over a quarter of the residents who participated for between 6 and 11 months demonstrated significant improvement in general self-esteem and in the social aspects of this construct. Increasingly greater proportions of residents showed such improvements as their length of time in the intervention increased. Accordingly, residents who completed 18 months or more showed the greatest level of change, with almost 50% of such participants showing significant growth in overall self-esteem. The findings established here bear notable similarity to what has previously been found at Grendon, again using a combination of group and individual-level analyses (Shuker and Newton, 2008).

Actual behaviour as measured by the TC staff observer-rated CIRCLE showed considerable variation across assessment points, with changes occurring in both pro- and antisocial directions. A noteworthy pattern was the drop in caring and sociable behaviour occurring in early therapy drop-outs, and an increase in these from the participating residents who completed 18 months of therapy or longer. This was most strongly evidenced in the idiographic change analyses, and underlines the correspondence between longer therapy lengths and better therapeutic outcomes.

For the 6–11 month group, over half of the participants were perceived by prison staff to have significantly decreased in dominance, gregariousness and nurturance. These RCI analyses also uncovered changes in the 12–17 month participation group, which were less apparent in the results that emerged from the more traditional group-level analyses. Just over 40% of the participants who dropped out between 12 and 17 months showed a significant reduction in dominant behaviour, although almost 20% showed a corresponding increase in this type of interaction style. Over a quarter of these same participants were reported as being less hostile, but, conversely, almost half of the remaining group members showed an increase in this characteristic. Concurrently with these changes, staff also noted that over half of the participants in this grouping became less compliant in this time. Of the 18 month + group, a large proportion showed significant change in desired directions on the interpersonal behaviour scales of the CIRCLE, such as the 46% who were less coercive by 18 months or the 37% who were more caring or nurturant towards their fellow residents. However, a number of other residents simultaneously showed deterioration in their behaviour according to this staff-rated measure: 25% showed an increase in hostility, while 35% were less compliant. Moreover, many failed to show any significant change. However, the percentages showing statistically meaningful progress in the current study are greater than found in previous work examining the impact of TC residency on interpersonal functioning. Shuker and Newberry (2010), for example, found that 77% of patients sampled from Grendon failed to achieve statistically significant change on the Person's Relating to Others' Questionnaire-3 (Birtchnell, Hammond, Horn, & DeJong, 2007). Their focus was on an overall test of interrelatedness, however, so individual-level changes in specific aspects of interpersonal functioning were not examined as in the present work.

Attitudes and action towards change as assessed by the URICA measure are more difficult to interpret, but broadly point to an increase in what the "Stages of Change" model deems preliminary thinking about change (precontemplation). Nonetheless, it appears that movement onto the subsequent stages does not occur, and, in fact, there is some evidence that such cognitions and actions regarding change are inclined to decrease during residents' time in the TC, indicating a resistance to change. Given the therapeutic progress evidenced on other measures, it is unclear whether the insights provided by the URICA imply that such changes are not reflected holistically or whether this "Stages of Change" assessment lacks sensitivity to change in this context.

Little change was also demonstrated on the measure of blame attribution, the only exception in the group-level analyses being a significant increase in feelings of guilt in the participants who left after a year's participation. This increase occurred during their first six months in the community, but was reversed in the subsequent six months prior to their final assessment at 12 months. The idiographic analyses verified the absence of either positive or negative change in blame attribution shown by the majority of residents across their time in the TC. The only progress of any note detected by the RCI analyses of this measure was on its *Mental* scale, with the results on this scale demonstrating that a subset of participants across all sample groupings were less inclined to attribute their offending behaviour to psychological factors beyond their control, i.e. to mental processes.

Participants' HDHQ data measuring aspects of hostility were also subjected to idiographic analyses, and this established that, of the change occurring in self-reported hostility in the 6–11 months group, the largest proportion was for residents who showed an increase in critical attitudes towards others.

Of the prisoners who participated for between 12 and 17 months, more positive changes in self-reported hostile feelings occurred, with a third of this sample feeling less overall hostility by the one-year mark than they had at baseline. The self-rated HDHQ results for the 18+ group demonstrated an even more positive picture, with a greater proportion of such prisoners reporting a drop in hostile cognitions than reporting an increase on all scales and subscales on the measure. Previous applications of the HDHQ measure in TC settings have similarly found it to indicate positive therapeutic outcomes (Genders and Player, 1995; Newton, 1998). The results of the current study offer further clarity on the longitudinal patterns that precede and culminate in these outcomes.

The IASC measure offers an even more novel insight, as there is little reported usage of this measure in a TC context. For residents who discontinued participation prior to the completion of 18 months' residency, the group-level data pointed to a lack of therapeutic progress in addressing identity or affect difficulties. A different picture emerged with participants of a longer residency, as these showed a much wider variety of significant improvements in the dysfunctions assessed by the IASC, such as emotional control impairments and self-awareness. When these data were subjected to the RCI techniques, a subset of the shorter-stay residents were found to have achieved some benefits from the TC intervention. The strongest improvements for these participants were in the area of the affect skills deficit for the 6–11 months group (20% improved vs. 4% who deteriorated) and in terms of identity diffusion for the 12–17 months group (21% improved vs. 6% who deteriorated). A more comprehensive pattern of change was shown by the longer-term residency group, however. For this 18 month+ group, a greater proportion of residents showed improvements across different subscales on this measure, indicating a wider diversity of therapeutic achievements across different aspects of interpersonal relating (e.g. susceptibility to influence and affect skills deficits).

In summary, this chapter has shown that the completion of 18 months or more in the intervention ensures the most benefits across the broadest forms of psychological functioning. Previous research has found similar lengths of residency to be of relevance to other indicators of therapeutic outcomes, particularly post-discharge recidivism risk (Cullen, 1993, 1997). The impact of the TC intervention on reoffending rates will be picked up again in Chapter 11, but for now it is worth noting that the impact of residency length in the TC offers a potential link between these different outcome indicators. Analyses of more short-term residents of the TC did uncover some changes, but such changes were fewer in number. Where changes were identifiable in these shorter-term residents, they commonly reflected movement away from clinically desirable characteristics, for example nurturance, or demonstrated a reversal of previous clinical achievements, such as changes in blame attribution. This psychological regression may be indicative of why such residents are likely to leave or be made to leave prior to the later stages of the therapy programme. Subsequent chapters in this book will explore drop-out issues in more detail and will examine the long-term impacts of TC residency to determine whether any progress achieved during prisoners' time in the community has meaningful, lasting impact on the prisoners and their offending lifestyles.

Chapter annex

Table 6a.1   Ethnic background of the participating residents

Ethnicity	n	%
White – British	192	76.8
White – Irish	1	0.4
White – Other background	10	4
Black – Caribbean	17	6.8
Black – African	3	1.2
Black – Other background	11	4.4
Asian – Pakistani	3	1.2
Asian – Other background	3	1.2
Mixed – White and black Caribbean	2	0.8
Mixed – Other background	3	1.2
Unknown	5	2.0

Table 6a.2   Marital status of the participating residents

Status	n	%
Single	148	59.2
Married	25	10
Relationship/cohabiting	33	13.2
Divorced/separated	30	12
Widowed	6	2.4
Unknown	8	3.2

Table 6a.3   Index offence types[3]

Type	n	%
Violent	103	41.2
Sexual	19	7.6
Burglary	28	11.2
Robbery	69	27.6
Theft	1	0.4

Criminal damage	6	2.4
Fraud	0	0
Drug	13	5.2
Motoring	0	0
Other	11	4.4

Table 6a.4 Nature of preconvictions[4]

Type	n	%
Violent	152	60.8
Sexual	31	12.4
Burglary	101	40.4
Robbery	77	30.8
Theft	125	50
Fraud	35	14
Criminal damage	79	31.6
Drug	64	25.6
Motoring	54	21.6
Other	83	33.2

Table 6a.5 Residency lengths for research participants

Length of residency	n	%
0–5 months	52	20.8
6–11 months	47	18.8
12–17 months	29	11.6
18–23 months	32	12.8
24 months+	90	36

Table 6a.6 Reason for leaving TC

Reason	n	%
n/a, still in therapy	39	15.6
De-selected	48	19.2
48 hr	72	28.8
End of therapy	19	7.6
Released	23	9.2
Progressive move	11	4.4
Medical hold	1	.4
Failed assessment	29	11.6
Unknown	8	3.2

7

Experiential Perspectives from within the TC: The Focus Groups

Introduction

This chapter describes how we acquired and made sense of residents' perspectives and experiences of psychological and behavioural change during their time in the TC. We will start by outlining our rationale for using a focus group methodology and then describe how we went about setting up, conducting and analysing the discussion groups. We will then give a detailed description of our findings and reflect on how they compare with previous studies that have used experiential perspectives of prison TC residents.

Understanding the processes of change can help to explain why interventions are successful for some and not for others. This helps create and maintain responsive treatment programmes. We are not the first to acknowledge the need to examine the process of offender change (see, e.g., Day et al., 2006). We were of the view that repeat focus groups with the same cohort would shed some light on potential change catalysts, the methods and strategies used by individuals to engender *and* maintain change, the process of psychological relapse or regression, and the way in which change impacts on the individual's life.

We were also of the view that "in-therapy" indicators of positive psychological change have an important role to play in evaluating the effectiveness of a prison TC. As we have discussed, a decrease in reoffending is only *one* of the expected objectives of a prison TC.

As we reflected upon in the Introduction, service-user or consumer perspectives are an essential part of an evaluation. The client's theory of change (i.e. the client's ideas about problem aetiology and resolution) is commonly recognised as providing a route to enhanced outcome (Duncan and Moynihan, 1994; Hubble et al., 1999). A literature review commissioned by the National Institute for Mental Health in England (NIMHE) concluded that service users and workers often have very different perspectives about service provision (Glasby et al., 2003, p. 5).

Qualitative treatment evaluations are rare, especially within the field of forensic psychology. One of the few studies that have been conducted used retrospective interviews with prisoners who had completed a cognitive skills programme to gain an understanding of "'what works' in practise" (Clarke et al., 2004, p. 1). The researchers found that prisoners' motivation to change was a key catalyst for successful programme participation, whereas a perceived lack of institutional support for programmes was not. Experiential perspectives have been researched in residents of HMP Grendon TC, and these findings are discussed in detail later in the chapter alongside our own results.

Setting up, conducting and analysing

Setting up

Overall 16 focus groups, involving 40 residents, were conducted in each of the four TCs over a two-year period. Residents had to have spent a specified time in therapy, so that the focus groups represented four time points: 6 months or less in therapy; 6–12 months; 12–18 months; 18–24 months. This was done so that potential psychological change over time could be captured.

Focus group residents were between 22 and 57 years of age, with an average age of 34 years. Group composition changed over the research period. Twenty-five residents were "repeat" focus group members and the others joined the groups at various instances during the two years when original focus group residents declined to take part any more or had left the TC.

Conducting

As mentioned in Chapter 4, one researcher acted as facilitator and one as note-writing observer. A low facilitator involvement and a non-directive approach were employed so that residents' subjective views and experiences remained at the forefront (Stewart and Shamdasani, 1990; Millward, 2000). The groups comprised five to eight residents, lasted between 60 and 90 minutes and were tape-recorded and then transcribed verbatim.

Analysing

Interpretative Phenomenological Analysis (IPA) (Smith, 1996a, b; Smith et al., 1999) was used to analysis the transcripts in order to gain an "insider's perspective" (Conrad, 1987). The analysis is "phenomenological" as it involves detailed examination of the individual's world and it is "interpretative" because it recognises the dynamic and engaged role of the researcher as interpreter. The transcripts were analysed separately for each TC because each operated as an independent community. The transcripts were also analysed in chronological fashion, starting with the first focus group undertaken (six months or less in therapy) and finishing with the last focus group (18–24 months in therapy).

The first stage of analysis involved a detailed, line-by-line examination of each focus group transcript, leading to a comprehensive set of themes represented by key words or "abstract theme titles" (Smith et al., 1999, p. 221). Preliminary exploration of relationships or connections between the theme titles was then undertaken, allowing a clustering of themes. These theme clusters were kept "grounded" by re-examining residents' words in the transcripts and making use of direct quotations from the transcripts. Once these stages were completed for each transcript across the different time phases for each TC, the theme clusters were amalgamated using diagrams to capture relationships and connections. This led to an emergent "master list of themes" describing the change process for a particular TC. In line with guidelines for qualitative research, credibility checks of the evolving analysis were undertaken by a second researcher, who independently examined the detailed coding and clustering of themes (see Elliott, Fischer and Rennie, 1999).

Findings

TC A

Presented in Figure 7.1 are the main themes from the focus group discussion with residents from TC A who had experienced six months or less time in therapy.

Analysis indicated a link between interpersonal problems (such as discord with staff, discord with sexual offenders and fakers in therapy) and residents' perception that they needed to "look after number one", as described in the theme entitled "put self-first". Findings also suggested a lack of group cohesion and weak therapeutic alliances between members of the community at this early stage in therapy. In this way, it was not surprising that residents described their time in therapy as "difficult and daunting" and questioned the TC's efficacy.

Figure 7.2 shows the main themes that describe the 6–12-month phase of therapy for residents of TCA.

Some TC A residents reported that self-appraisal prompted doubt and questioning, whereas others felt it led to important realisations. We interpreted that this time in therapy was mostly characterised by therapeutic engagement, but also continued struggle in the form of confusion and uncertainty, which led some residents to therapeutic withdrawal. In comparison to time one, it was noticeable that some residents were trying to understand their offending behaviour and reported burgeoning therapeutic relationships with staff and other residents. Analysis was in keeping with previous research that has found that, if clients were positive about one type of relationship, they tended to be positive about them all (Johnson et al., 2005).

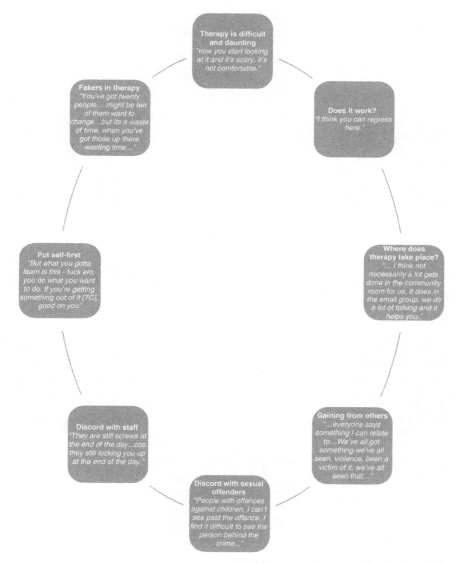

Figure 7.1 TC A six months and less in therapy

The main themes arising out of the transcripts for TCA residents who had experienced 12–18 months' time in therapy are summarised in Figure 7.3.

At this later stage in therapy, TC A residents recognised that they still had more therapeutic work to do or "unfinished business"; some viewed therapy as a lifelong commitment. However, most residents referred to persistent

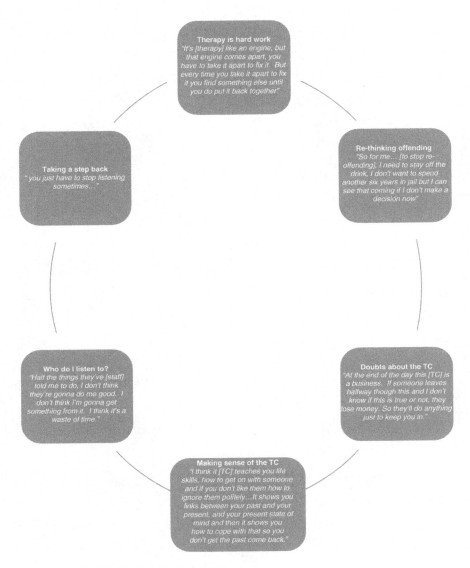

Figure 7.2   TC A 6–12 months in therapy

difficulties and potential therapeutic obstructions, such as fraught relationships with staff and other residents, and doubts about the ability of a TC
regime to operate within a prison setting. The researchers interpreted these
problems as therapeutic ruptures which are considered necessary catalysts for
change. However, research has found that a strong early alliance is needed
for ruptures in relationships to be beneficial because the key aspect of the

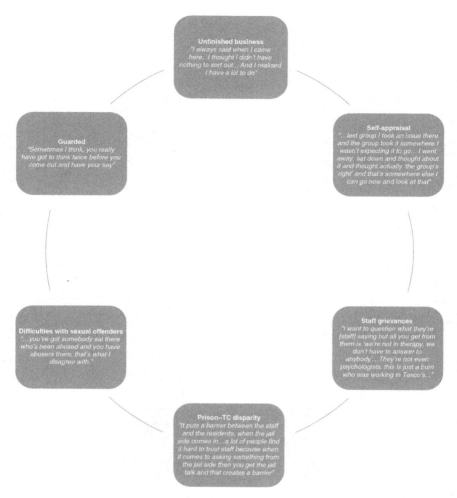

Figure 7.3   TC A 12–18 months in therapy

client experiencing ruptures during therapy is their resolution (Clarkson, 1995).

Figure 7.4 summarises the main themes emergent in the final focus group discussion with TCA residents who had experienced 18–24 months in therapy.

Most residents described a "turbulent community" which seemed to be brought about by "disingenuous residents", leading to "resident-resident dissonance" and "wanting more from staff". For two of the residents in the focus group, such problems (or ruptures) were experienced as difficult, but not impossible, to overcome. These residents described how they wanted to use the

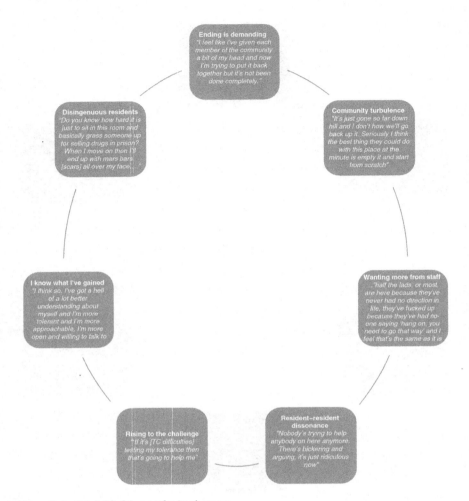

Figure 7.4   TC A 18–24 months in therapy

community turbulence and its problematic relationships to try out the skills that they felt they had acquired. Therefore, for a minority of residents, this final phase of therapy was characterised as a positive experience and a true test. Overall, however, most residents reported impaired relationships and a subjugated community that represented too large a hurdle to overcome, and described disengaging from therapy as a result.

TC A: Therapeutic process over two years

It seemed to us that the process of change over a two-year period for TC A residents looked like this:

Uncertainty and suspicion
↓
To engage or withdraw?
↓
Interpersonal conflict
↓
Therapeutic impasse versus therapeutic success

Emergent in the analysis of the focus groups for this TC was that an overall failure to establish trusting therapeutic relationships with staff and residents prevented the majority of focus group residents from reaching a stage in therapy at which they could describe themselves as having "completed" therapy. It was interesting to note that therapeutic impasse was characterised not only by poor member–member and member–staff therapeutic alliances but by a strong contextual backdrop of a community in dire straits, suggesting that the community alliance is an equally important alliance type. Positively, two residents reported that the community troubles facilitated further therapeutic development as they represented a challenge from which they could learn.

TC B

Figure 7.5 summarises the main themes to emerge from the focus group discussion with TC B residents after six months or less in therapy.

TC B residents recognised the challenging nature of the TC but held the view that they were able to learn new ways and help one another, lending support to the idea that the TC is a living–learning environment. Residents reported burgeoning therapeutic alliances with one another, suggesting that member–member alliances could be easier to come by. However, in parallel with findings from TC A, this early phase of therapy was characterised by residents' doubts and concerns about the TC, themselves and their future. An emerging tension concerned those residents perceived as not engaging meaningfully in the TC and an unwillingness to confront them, as this would be breaking the "criminal code". This is not a surprising finding, as research has identified that offenders are unlikely to report others' transgressions after only a short time in therapy (Stephenson and Scarpitti, 1968).

Figure 7.6 summarises the main themes to emerge from the focus group discussion with TC B residents who had experienced 6–12 months in therapy.

It was apparent to researchers that residents' concerns about how the TC was being operated (felt tension between TC and prison ethos) and staff behaviour combined to produce two opposing positions. The first was disengagement and the second was that such challenges could be overcome and learnt from.

Figure 7.5 TC B six months or less in therapy

We noted that this phase of "make or break" occurred earlier for TC B residents as compared with TC A residents.

The main themes to emerge from discussions with TC B residents who had experienced 12–18 months in therapy could not be transcribed and analysed due to problems with the tape recordings. Figure 7.7 shows the main themes to emerge from discussions with TC B residents who had experienced 18–24 months in the TC.

Collectively, the themes demonstrated a "weighing up" process. For example, residents spoke about difficulties within the community, but also about why the community was so important to them; they demonstrated insight into their progress and the ways in which the TC had helped them, but they also mentioned their ongoing personal struggles; when thinking about approaching the end of their time in the TC, residents reported apprehension but also optimism. However, residents reported that they could perceive the issue of

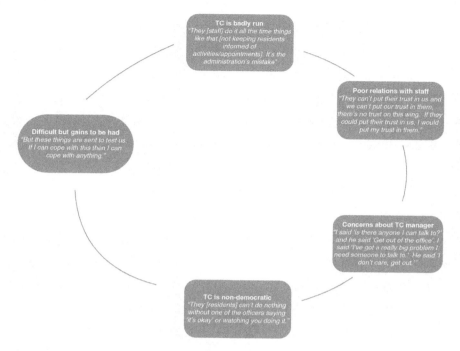

Figure 7.6   TC B 6–12 months in therapy

insincere peers in only one way: unwillingness to confront these individuals, as it would be breaking a criminal convention. The perceived damage caused by insincere residents seemed to be linked to community and individual struggles.

TC B: Therapeutic process over two years

The process of change over a two-year period for TC B residents took the following shape:

Caution and consideration
↓
Make or break
↓
Taking stock

Initially TC B residents seemed plagued by mistrust of the process, "phoney" residents and staff. Similarly to TC A, there was confusion over the role of staff,

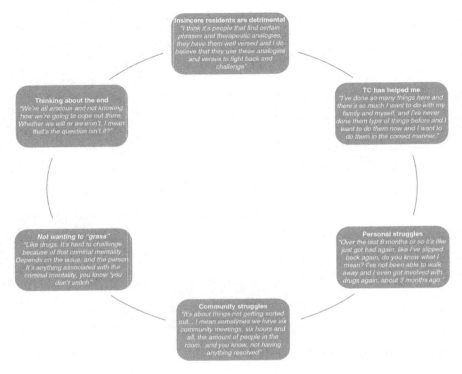

Figure 7.7 TC B 18–24 months in therapy

on the one hand residents wanting staff to "give direction" and on the other hand not wanting staff to "take control". However, despite plenty of community difficulties and an early phase of therapy that involved a general worsening (Jones, 1997), most residents reported positive changes, particularly during the latter stages of therapy, whereby they described what seemed to be a period of consolidation (Genders and Player, 1995). It seemed that early alliances were built between community members which grounded residents during more challenging times.

TC C

Figure 7.8 shows the main themes to come from analysis of focus groups with residents who had experienced six months or less time in therapy.

TC C residents described this early phase of therapy as difficult, particularly in terms of dealing with previously unleashed emotions, and, as found with TC A and TC B residents, they reported their fears and mistrust of others and the therapeutic process. However, TC C residents did recognise the importance of their small therapy groups, suggesting the formation of early member–member

Figure 7.8　TC C six months or less in therapy

therapeutic alliances, and they also seemed to acknowledge their feelings and understand aspects of their criminal behaviour. Figure 7.9 lists the main themes to emerge from the focus group with TC C residents who had spent 6–12 months in therapy.

Encouragingly, this phase in therapy was mainly characterised by therapeutic engagement. The immersion in therapy involved personal difficulties (dealing with emotions) and community struggles (disunited because of rule-breaking residents) as well as more positive aspects, such as support from small groups. Whilst residents were unable to confront peers whom they perceived as "fakers", they realised that this was not the best way forward. Absent from this phase of therapy were the concerns and doubts residents expressed during their first six months in therapy. Figure 7.10 lists the main themes emergent from discussions with TC C residents who had experienced between a year and 18 months in therapy.

Many of the focus group discussions centred upon residents' concerns about the "TC organisation", the impact of "apathetic residents" remaining in the TC (for particularly long periods of time) and "problems with staff".

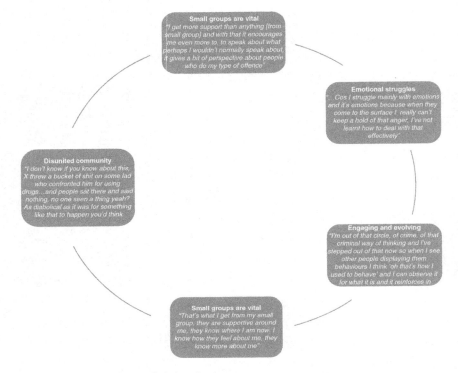

Figure 7.9   TC C 6–12 months' time in therapy

From their discussions it would seem that these issues combined to create a particularly difficult time for the community residents. Conversely, however, and as researchers observed in the other TCs, some residents reported that they were still able to gain from the TC by facing presenting difficulties. Figure 7.11 lists the principal themes to arise out of the discussions with residents from TC C who had experienced 18–24 months in therapy.

This final stage of therapy for TC C residents was difficult. Residents reported that the community was not functioning well at all, although one participant did report that his small therapy groups were still working well. His therapeutic alliances with his small group members seemed strong enough to overcome the wider community problems. For the majority of residents, relationships with staff members were seen as characterised by conflict, mistrust and disdain, suggesting that already fragile alliances had worsened. Residents also described the negative impact that others on the unit who were not genuinely committed to change had on those residents who were.

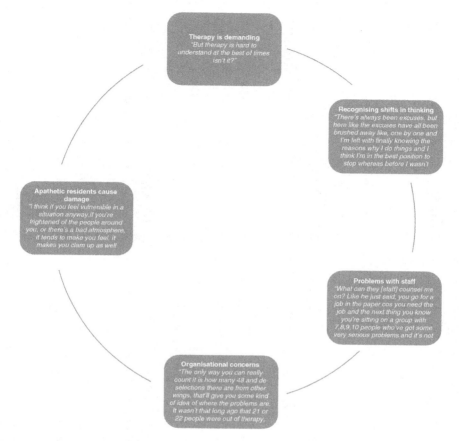

Figure 7.10   TC C 12–18 months' time in therapy

TC C: Therapeutic process over two years

The process of change over a two-year period for TC C residents looked like this:

Doubt and fear
↓
Rising to the challenge
↓
Struggle with adversity
↓
Community hopelessness

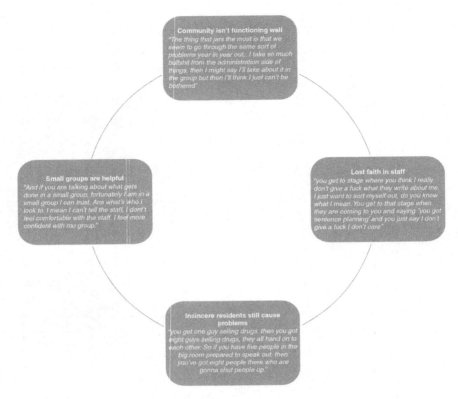

Figure 7.11   TC C 18–24 months' time in therapy

As expected, the process begins with a cautious, fearful approach, in the literature referred to as "acclimatisation" (Genders and Player, 1995) and "contemplation" (Prochaska et al., 1992). This is later replaced by therapeutic engagement and a determined attitude to overcome challenges and adversity. However, the process draws to a close in community hopelessness. It seemed to the researchers as if the challenges posed were just too much for the community to deal with. As was observed in other focus groups, a minority of individuals seemed able to prosper in the face of adversity as they had strong small group alliances to bolster them.

TC D

Figure 7.12 lists the main themes emergent from discussions with TC D residents who had experienced six months or less time in therapy.

In keeping with the other TCs' early therapy experiences, TC D residents expressed concerns about therapy staff, the therapeutic process itself, aspects of the community and its functioning, and future resettlement plans. Yet they

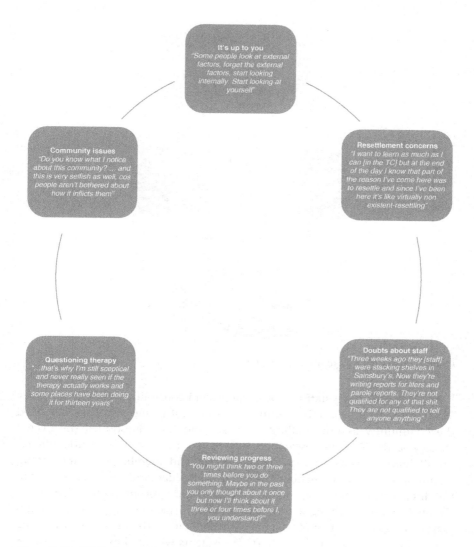

Figure 7.12 TC D six months or less time in therapy

also seemed connected to a sense of self-development. For example, residents recognised the way in which they had to be self-motivated and self-accountable in order to gain from the TC experience, and they also appreciated, albeit cautiously, the therapeutic steps they had made so far. Concerns about the dual role of staff as therapist and prison officer, an issue highlighted consistently by other residents from other TCs, were also apparent. Figure 7.13 lists the main themes emergent from discussions with TC D residents who had experienced 6–12 months in therapy.

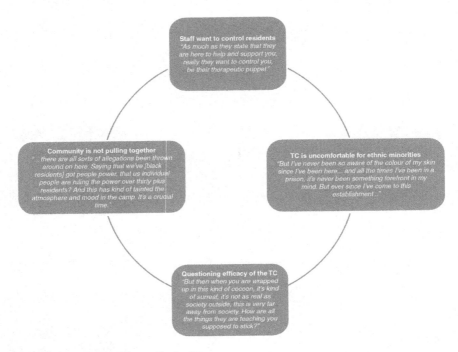

Figure 7.13   TC D 6–12 months in therapy

Residents described staff as authoritarian and controlling; in particular they felt that their needs as ethnic minorities were not being met. They described the community as not "pulling together" and they questioned the overall efficacy of the TC. The researchers interpreted a lack of therapeutic alliance on all levels – individual (member–member and member–staff) and group (community) – and a consequent lack of trust. Residents advised one another in the discussion to stop worrying about others and concentrate on themselves. Group cohesion is thought to be paramount in facilitating positive psychological change (Yalom, 1995). Figure 7.14 summarises the main themes arising out of the discussion group with TC D residents who had experienced 12–18 months in therapy.

This phase of treatment for TC D residents was characterised by opposing perceptions and experiences. On the one hand, residents described the positive therapeutic steps they had made and recognised the need and value of therapeutic alliances with other residents. On the other hand, they questioned the process of therapy and the effectiveness of the TC and also considered that honesty was not necessarily the best approach. Consistent over time were reported poor relations with staff, confirming that this type of alliance is particularly difficult to establish. In contrast, Genders and Player (1995) identified that this

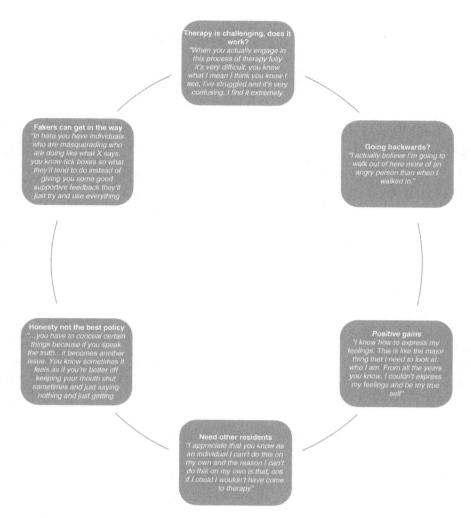

Figure 7.14   TC D 12–18 months in therapy

time in the TC was one of "consolidation", in which residents were most likely to make a stand against illicit activities and be markedly in favour of officers' contributions in therapy groups.

The main themes emergent from discussions with TC D residents who had spent 18–24 months in therapy are listed in Figure 7.15.

Overall, residents described this final phase of therapy as a change for the better. Previously reported fraught relations with staff and other residents had been resolved. Instead, residents talked about their strong therapeutic alliances

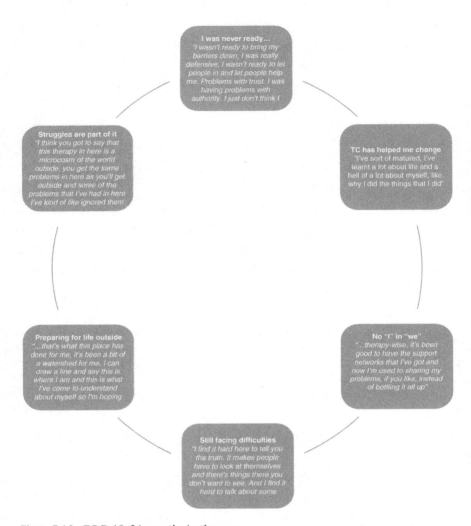

Figure 7.15   TC D 18–24 months in therapy

with others and "preparing for life outside", reflecting a readiness to move on from the TC, expected at this time. We thought that this stance reflected a maintenance stage of change needed for relapse prevention (Prochaska et al., 1992).

TC D: Therapeutic process over two years

The process of change over a two-year period for TC D residents seemed to look like this:

Dubious and tentative

↓

"It isn't helping"

↓

To endure or not?

↓

Survival of the fittest

What is particularly interesting about the therapeutic process in TC D was that it took 18–24 months for residents to fully realise therapeutic benefits. Up until this point residents remained cautious and mistrustful of the process and of others, particularly staff members. Therefore the task of building trusting therapeutic relationships can take longer than anticipated, on the basis of previous dosage research, for some. It was interesting to compare this process with TC A and TC C, as both describe a final phase characterised by community breakdown. These communities appeared to have immersed themselves earlier (6–12 months) only for relationships to break down at a later point, while TC D and TC B remained tentative throughout the first 18 months in the TC, only for their therapeutic achievements to be recognised at a much later date (after 18–24 months).

Results summary

We summarise the key findings from our focus groups in Box 7.1.

Box 7.1   Key findings from the focus groups

Each TC had its own therapeutic pathway, although there were some key commonalities.

Across all TCs, the first six months of therapy were characterised by questioning, doubt and "settling in".

TC B and TC D residents continued to doubt and question the TC until 18 months had passed. From 18 to 24 months these residents reported a striking shift in thinking, which involved fusing the therapeutic gains that they had made and looking forward to a more positive life upon leaving the TC.

TC A and TC C described engaging in therapy meaningfully by 6–12 months. However, significant ruptures in therapeutic alliances (between residents and between residents and staff) were irreparable and led to community breakdown by 18–24 months.

Box 7.1   (Continued)

The TC experience was described as a challenging experience by all residents. Although some viewed challenge as an ongoing "part of the process", others disengaged as a result of it.

Consistent across all TCs was a reluctance to confront residents deemed as "faking therapy". Seen as "grassing", this allegiance to the "criminal code" weakened the community alliance.

Most residents expressed concerns about the tension between democracy and the assumptions of security, order and control associated with prison and felt that this impacted negatively upon therapy.

Conclusion

Studies conducted at HMP Grendon TC since the mid-1980s have repeatedly identified a treatment "dosage effect" (Cullen, 1992, 1994; Genders and Player, 1995; Marshall, 1997; Messina et al., 2000; Taylor, 2000). TC graduates released after 12–18 months of therapy have lower reconviction rates (particularly for violence) than those released before this period. Other positive outcomes include reductions in drug use and positive changes in personality, hostility and locus of control measures. These findings go some way towards tackling what has been described by Hollin (2001) as an area that is not only lacking empirical evidence but is difficult to convert into practice, mainly because of time constraints relating to sentencing and/or community orders.

Early process research at Grendon TC (Gunn et al., 1978) identified that reductions in anxiety, tension, depression, hostility and antagonism towards others, especially authority figures, and increases in self-esteem and self-confidence about social interactions are indicators of therapeutic effect. The findings were replicated 17 years later, with men additionally reporting that changes were attributed to their small therapy groups (Gunn and Robertson, 1987). Since these findings, a relationship between attributional processes and engagement in therapy has also been identified by Gudjonsson (1990), who found that those engaged in group work experienced increased levels of guilt and decreased external blame attributions when compared with new arrivals. Our focus group findings are consistent with these earlier findings.

Also, Jones (1997) found a pattern of deterioration during the initial stages of TC, with improvement then occurring in the later stages. He found this change to be running in parallel with a perception of self as being aggressive (increasingly aggressive during the initial stages of therapy and less aggressive during the later stages). Jones thus proposed that confronting core criminogenic beliefs about the self and others induced a degree of cognitive dissonance, accompanied by a deterioration in self-esteem. Jones maintained that at this point in the therapeutic process an individual could *either* develop self-esteem enhancement strategies (and incorporate the value system that came with these strategies) *or* resort to old self-esteem strategies (e.g. various types of offending behaviour), thereby reinforcing the criminogenic value system. He speculated that this process increases resistance to, and disillusionment with, the therapeutic process itself, "now construed as painful and ineffectual and perhaps even punitive" (1997, p. 125). This model describes our findings accurately, with a clear distinction between residents resorting to old strategies and familiar criminal values and some residents developing self-esteem strategies in response to the challenging therapeutic process.

Genders and Player (1995) conducted semi-structured interviews with just over a hundred Grendon TC residents in their study of "Therapeutic Achievements". Residents were divided into three groups by time spent in therapy (less than 6 months; 6–12 months; and 12 months or longer). The researchers found evidence of positive therapeutic development by marked differences between the groups. Amongst residents who had been in therapy for six months or less, nearly all reported their perception of their problems had changed, and all but one reported discovering new problems and realising that their difficulties were more complicated than previously judged. They also reported a clear reduction in alienation (although this did not continue to lessen over time). The "them and us" division between staff and residents continued to decrease over time, most noticeably in those who had been in the TC for over 12 months.

During six months to one year in therapy, Genders and Player (1995) found that men were more likely to see their problems as emanating from close relationship problems (as opposed to drug and alcohol problems, for example). Compared with other groups, a distinctly higher proportion of men in the 6–12 months group reported an increase in self-confidence, improved communication and socialisation skills, and improved tolerance of other people. Interestingly, they did not find any increase in these areas in residents of longer than a year. Our findings differ, in that some residents reported significant turning points in the latter stages of therapy.

Genders and Player (1995) also found that men who had been in therapy for over a year were more likely to "stand out against the crowd...to assume personal responsibility" (p. 113), particularly in view of illicit activities such as drug supply, and were in favour of officers listening and contributing to group therapy. This is an interesting finding, as it challenges previous thinking that prison programmes can reinforce criminal behaviours and thought patterns from the presence of the prison ethos and other prisoners (e.g. Skett, 1995). Overall, we did not find that residents were willing to report the transgressions of fellow residents, as they did not feel safe enough.

Genders and Player (1995) conclude that the first six months in therapy are defined by a settling-in period or an "acclimatisation" process (whereby traditional prison culture is pulled apart and replaced with the new traditions); the period between 6 and 12 months is a process of "resocialisation" (adjusting modes of social relations, reviewing social skills and consequently gaining more from relationships, especially with authority figures); and the period after 12 months is characterised by a "consolidation" phase (achievements are consolidated alongside an increase in confidence and trust in staff and movement towards greater social responsibility). Genders and Player (1995) reported that their empirically derived stages of therapeutic development were implicit throughout staff observations of residents.

Through their observations of staff practice, the researchers noted that residents were allowed to some extent "to sit-back and observe the community at work" when they first arrived. This was followed by a stage in which "the men are expected to engage in a process of high therapeutic activity", whilst the final stage was characterised "by an expectation that inmates will embark on a process of detachment... and prepare for eventual flight from the nest" (p. 119). Although it does seem that the first two phases conceptually correspond with one another, "consolidation" (from resident interviews) and "detachment" (from staff observations) seem to be describing different processes. Our findings confirm that *some* residents embarked upon consolidation during the final stages of therapy, but others detached in a negative way because they had not formed strong attachments in the earlier phases of therapy.

Therefore, our research confirms that there are four possible pathways: (a) remaining the same (plateau), (b) continued improvement (progress), (c) improvement followed by decline (regress) or (d) deterioration.

8
Attachments: The Multiple Sorting Task Procedure

Introduction

Much research attention has been given to sexual offenders, who mostly have been found to have insecure attachments (Ward et al., 1995, 1996; Lyn and Burton, 2004, 2005; Simons, Wurtele and Durham, 2008). This chapter will begin by summarising attachment theory and explain its link to criminality. Next we describe the way in which TC residents' attachments to people were assessed through the Multiple Card Sorting Procedure. We chose this method because it allows the card sorter to provide their own categories and concepts, and we were able to engage the TC residents in this task, which was repeated several times. In this way we were able to explore psychological change with residents. Critical to the TC experience are the forming of relationships and the manner in which they are perceived and negotiated by residents. Our findings from the card sorts enabled us to track change of individuals, and the versatility of the method also allowed us to examine shifts in attachment style of the group. The chapter will present the advantages and draw attention to the limitations of this approach in working with residents to monitor change.

We adopted the Bartholomew and Horowitz (1991) four-category model of attachment, which, as mentioned in the introductory chapter, describes four types: "secure", "preoccupied (ambivalent)", "dismissing (avoidant)" and "fearful (avoidant)", providing the research team with a firm theoretical base.

In addition, we develop ideas discussed in Chapter 3 about place attachment and use a sorting task to bring to the surface feelings about places of significance to residents.

Attachment styles

The model of attachment we opted for is summarised in Figure 8.1. This has been validated using a variety of measures of attachment styles, self-concept and interpersonal functioning (Bartholomew and Horowitz, 1991) and has

Self (dependence)

Positive   Negative

| | Positive | Secure
Comfortable with
intimacy and autonomy | Preoccupied
Preoccupied with
relationships |
| Others
(Avoidance) | Negative | Dismissing
Dismissing of intimacy
counter-dependent | Fearful
Fearful of intimacy
–socially avoidant |

Figure 8.1   Model of adult attachment (adapted from Bartholomew and Horowitz, 1991)

been successfully used to classify offenders' attachment style (e.g. Ward et al., 1996). Within this model there are positive and negative aspects of "self" and of "others". "Self" corresponds to the level of dependence on others while "other" corresponds to an avoidance of others (Bartholomew and Horowitz, 1991). In an originating study, they found that around half ($n = 146$) of a sample of male (47%) and female (57%) undergraduates were classified as secure. Of the male undergraduates, 15% were fearful, 10% preoccupied and 18% dismissive. Of the women, 21% were fearful, 14% preoccupied and 18% dismissive.

Studies have found that people with a preoccupied attachment style tend to focus on their own needs and feelings rather than others (Shaver, 1994) and have high rates of relationship breakdowns (Hazan and Shaver, 1987). Dismissive individuals are less inclined to engage in therapeutic relationships (Van Ijzendoorn et al., 1997), and dismissive and fearful attachment styles, both being avoidance based, are generally associated with a pessimistic view of relationships (Hazan and Shaver, 1987) and minimal self-disclosure (Mikulincer and Nachshon, 1991).

Attachment styles of offenders

Smallbone and Dadds (1998) found that all sex offenders in their study reported significantly less secure maternal, paternal and adult attachments compared with non-offenders, thereby supporting the idea that insecure childhood attachment patterns can persist into adulthood. Ward et al. (1996) found that 69% of rapists and 78–82% of child sex offenders rated their attachments as insecure. A more recent American study (Simons et al., 2008) found an even higher rate of insecure attachment (94%) in a mixed group of sex offenders.

Ward and colleagues (1996), using the Bartholomew and Horowitz model, established more nuanced differences, in that child sex offenders were mostly preoccupied and fearful whilst rapists and violent offenders were mainly dismissive. Ten years later similar findings were reported in a Canadian sample (Stirpe, Abracen Stermac & Wilson, 2006). Interestingly, child molesters also presenting with a schizoid personality disorder seemed inclined to isolate themselves from others and retreat from relationships (Bogaerts, Vanheule and Desmet 2006).

However, other research suggests that, actually, all offenders are likely to have insecure attachments (Ward et al., 1996; Smallbone and Dadds, 1998; Baker and Beech, 2004; Ross and Pfäfflin, 2007). Baker and Beech (2004), for example, did not find any attachment differences between sexual and violent offenders.

A round-up of studies indicates that 64% of violent offenders had insecure attachments (Ross and Pfäfflin, 2007), and most of a sample of domestic violence offenders had fearful attachments (Dutton et al., 1994). A link has been established between violent psychopathic behaviour and dismissive attachment, probably reflecting a tendency to view others in a hostile and disapproving way (Bartholomew and Horowitz, 1991; Frodi, Dernevik, Sepa, Philipson and Bragesjo, 2001).

We can be confident that the research literature by and large confirms that sexual and violent offenders have high rates of insecure attachment styles reflecting some sort of disruption or disadvantage in key relationships in the early stages of life. A lack in early family attachment has been related to delinquency (Canter, 1982), as has conflict between parents (McCord, 1979, 1983; Emery and O'Leary, 1982), and parental absence has been implicated in later criminal behaviour (Hoffman, 1971).

Having established that secure attachment is a valuable psychological resource and that we can use insecure attachments to help understand offending behaviour (Ward et al., 1996), improving the strength of constructive bonds with others is an important goal of psychological interventions with offenders. In their appraisal of "what works in reducing reoffending" literature, Sapouna, Bisset and Conlon (2011) conclude that "Strong attachments trigger the motivation to change because they provide emotional support, the prospect of new social roles and models of prosocial behaviour" (p. 40). Healy (2012) provides us with some evidence. In a study following up 73 Irish probationers, the formation of strong social bonds with parents, partners and children was the most frequently given reason for changing. A number of other studies confirm that factors associated with sustained desistance from reoffending (which is generally taken to mean two or more years) include strengthening social relationships and developing new social networks (Liebrich, 1993; Maruna, 2001; Farrall et al., 2010; Healy, 2012; Caverley and Farrall, 2011). What seems to be important is the improvement in the quality of offenders' attachments to those in their immediate social circles, so that they are more likely to want to live up to the expectations of others and sustain a crime-free lifestyle.

Strong family bonds have been found to encourage desistance by providing structure to offenders' lives, with its informal monitoring and support. Interestingly, offenders report that being trusted by significant others and the wider social network is a strong motivating factor for sustained desistance from crime (Caverley and Farrall, 2011).

Tying these findings together, how does this relate to therapy in a TC? A TC aims to create a secure base using the therapeutic alliance(s), yet, insecurely attached offenders often lack empathy (Fonagy, 1999) and dismissively attached offenders might be particularly resistant to treatment (Van Ijzendoorn et al., 1997). However there are some promising findings. Fonagy et al. (1996) looked at treatment outcome amongst psychiatric patients ($n = 82$) and found that 93% of dismissive patients, 41% of preoccupied patients and 33% of secure patients did improve. Lawson et al. (2006) also found a significant increase in secure attachment from pre- to post-treatment in partner-violent men.

The Multiple Card Sorting Task Procedure

There are several ways of assessing adult attachment styles. One of the most widely used, the Adult Attachment Interview (AAI; Main, Kaplan and Cassidy, 1985), has been criticised because it is unable to fully classify forensic populations (Van Ijzendoorn et al., 1997). Hazan and Shaver's (1987) Three Attachment Style measure was found to be a relatively "crude measure" (Ireland and Powers, 2004, p. 310) with only modest reliability. Most self-report measures have been criticised because they can only measure conscious attitudes to relationships (West and George, 1999). Another problem with a forensic population is that offenders are prone to giving distorted, socially desirable answers for a variety of reasons, often connected to difficulties with self-insight, avoidance of negative repercussions and fears about being judged negatively (Smallbone and Dadds, 1998; Tan & Grace, 2008)). Appreciating these problems, we decided to use the Multiple Card Sorting Procedure (MCSP) to explore the attachments in offenders in the TC.

The MCSP is a fairly straightforward process. Participants are asked to sort a set of cards depicting some target of interest into different categories based on their perceived similarities and differences. Theoretically it has its foundations in Personal Construct Theory (PCT; Kelly, 1955), which considered how people make sense of the world around them. Kelly suggested that all individuals actively construe and differentiate events, things and people in their world and behave in ways that support their particular world view. This idea can be adapted in a clinical setting to facilitate an understanding of how the client's distinctive view of the world contributes to the development and maintenance of their offending behaviour, and, once this is understood, work on change (Houston, 1998).

The main advantage of the MCSP is that it allows the researcher to delve into the complexities of people's lives, taking fully into account the individual and the context within which they operate. This outlook is in keeping with the overall approach taken in our evaluation of HMP Dovegate TC. We also thought that it was particularly suitable because of the indirect approach to individuals' constructs, thereby making it less susceptible to the effects of social desirability on responding. The MCSP is also appealing because it involves a social interaction between researcher and participant, reflecting the co-researcher principles employed by the research team. Canter et al. (1985) provide a comprehensive technical account of the card sort method.

Exploring change through thinking about significant others

Sixty TC residents (approximately a quarter of the overall sample) agreed to take part in the MCSP every 12 months whilst resident in the TC. Their first card sort acted as a baseline and took place within residents' first four weeks in the TC, whilst they were residing in the assessment unit and prior to taking up residence in one of the four Dovegate TC units.

By way of a technical detail, of the original 60 residents, 26 were still in the TC after 12 months and repeated the card sort. Five residents who took part in the baseline card sort remained in the TC for over 24 months and took part in a third card sort. The average age of the 60 participants was 32 years and most were white British (82%) with the remainder belonging to an ethnic minority (black British, black other and Asian). Most had acquisitive or violent index offences.

Residents had been briefed about the evaluation aims and had given written informed consent to take part in the various research activities, including the MCSP. At the start of the first card sort, residents were asked to name people that they saw as present in their lives, and these were written on 5" × 3" index cards, either by the researcher or by the residents themselves. Some residents chose to use one card to represent one person (e.g. "mother"), whilst others put more than one person on one card (e.g. "parents" or "children"). No restrictions were placed on the number of people that residents chose to identify, although always included in the grid was the resident himself ("self").

Residents were then asked to sort these people into categories of their choosing with the following instructions: "Can you think of a way that will allow you to put some of these people into a particular group and others in a different group or groups?" Sometimes a further instruction was needed, such as "are some of the people that you've identified similar or different in some way?" and "might some of these cards go into one pile and other cards into a different pile(s)?" An example may help to clarify what we did. One resident reported that he "cared about his mum but not his dad" and therefore placed all the "cared about" people into one pile and all the people that "he did not care about" into a different pile. Often when residents were identifying categories, they would make changes. For instance, using the same example, whilst sorting the cards into piles the resident realised that his categories ("cared about" and "not cared about") were more complex because he "cared about some people now", he "used to care about some people but didn't at the moment" and he had "never cared about some people". We did not impose any limits on the number of categories identified or restrict the number of levels within a particular category. Participants carried on sorting their chosen cards until they said that they could not think of any more. The process was completed on a one-to-one basis with a researcher in a private room and usually took about 45 minutes. Residents got to grips with the procedure after the first attempt at sorting the cards and reported that they enjoyed the process. Many thought it was a refreshing change from the usual question and answer format.

The card sorts were recorded on the form of a grid and we assessed the relationships between the people using a Multi-Dimensional Scaling (MDS) package. MDS is particularly useful at revealing the underlying structure of data (Wilson and Hammond, 2000). We used the Guttman–Lingoes package (Lingoes and Guttman, 1973), in particular Multi Scalogram Analysis (MSA) and Smallest Space Analysis (SSA), whose technical details we describe in Chapter 4. Briefly, MSA tests the relationship that each person identified by our TC resident has to every other identified person and produces a "map" of the nominated people. SSA, on the other hand, examines the relationships between distinguishing categories.

We provide some technical information here to facilitate a reading of the results. When looking at the relationships between the nominated people, the MDS uses a "Jaccard coefficient of association", which only counts when cards get put into the same pile, thus sharing a sorting criterion, otherwise there would be a spurious level of agreement if cards were said to be similar because they did not get put into a particular pile. A visual summary of the relative weight of the similarities is calculated and presented in the form of a map of points representing the people identified by the resident. The shorter the distance between any two people, the more similar they are seen to be as a function of their appearance in the different sorting piles. Conversely, the further apart the people are in the map, the less they have in common. Analysis proceeds by identifying regions on the map which can be meaningfully interpreted. A check on the reliability of this region identification is achieved using the principles of "sensitivity" and "selectivity" (Brown and Barnett, 2000). Sensitivity refers to the way in which partitioning is able to enclose target items within a zone as a function of the overall number of target items, and selectivity refers to the exclusivity of target items being in a particular partitioned zone as a function of all items in that zone.

In keeping with our overall research approach to the evaluation, residents received feedback sessions whereby they were shown a diagram of their results, i.e. the "map". Residents reported that they enjoyed the feedback sessions and often said that they found it helpful to see and think about their relationships visually.

Case study examples of attachment styles

Michael (pseudonym)

Michael described himself as single and of white British ethnicity. At the time of baseline data collection, he was 30 years old and had served two years of his life tariff for murder. Previously he had served four prison sentences and been convicted of 22 offences, mainly of an acquisitive and violent nature. He had a history of diagnosed depression and a long record of poly-drug misuse, which included crack cocaine and heroin.

Figure 8.2 shows the people that Michael identified at baseline and how he made sense of them. He categorised the people in his life as "family" and "non-family". Within family he identified those who had "hurt him a lot" (father and brother) and those who had "hurt him a bit" (rest of family). It is interesting

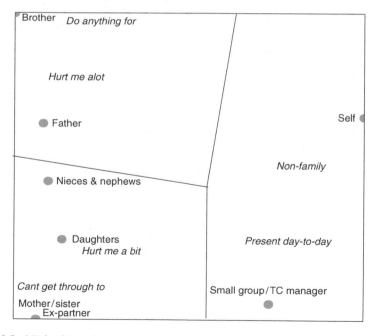

Figure 8.2 Michael's card sort at baseline

that those family members whom Michael perceived as hurting him the most are those that he would "do anything for". He also made a link between certain family members and feeling like he "could not get through to them".

Overall, our analysis suggests that Michael's family relationships are seen by him as mostly difficult and emotionally painful. At this time Michael described TC-related people in a non-emotional way, confirmed by the distance between them and his family. He placed himself closest to his small group and his TC manager, but felt that this was because he had "day-to-day" contact with them; there is little to suggest an emotional attachment with anyone in the TC. Michael made little comment about how he viewed himself ("self" card), making it somewhat difficult to classify his attachment style using Bartholomew and Horowitz's four-category model (1991), although there does appear to be a degree of fearful avoidance. Overall, findings are suggestive of a fearful attachment style.

Figure 8.3 shows that, after 12 months in therapy, Michael maintained his categorisation of "family" vs. "non-family". Noticeably different, however, is that now he described his family relationships as "supportive" and "most

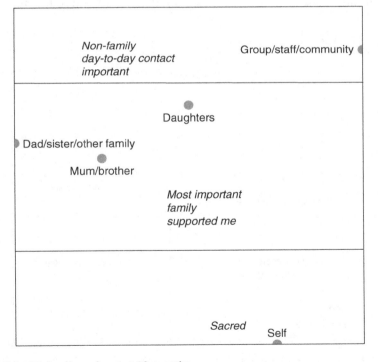

Figure 8.3   Michael's card sort at 12 months

important". The location of "self" seems consistent over time as it is detached from all other people, although, at this time, Michael reported that he saw himself as "sacred". He explained that he had learnt in therapy to put his own needs first. This could provide a rationale for the divide between himself and others (at baseline no clear explanation was given for this divide) and could suggest an improved degree of self-insight and self-esteem. Michael made sense of people in the TC in a rather matter-of-fact way by referring, as he did at baseline, to his level of "contact". That said, he differentiated between group members, staff and community (by choosing them and putting them onto separate cards) and classified them as having equal importance, perhaps reflecting a burgeoning therapeutic alliance. This is tentative because of the considerable distance between himself and TC-related people. Drawing upon Bartholomew and Horowitz's model of attachment (1991), whilst Michael describes himself as more secure in himself, there still appears to be some avoidance of others. Overall, the analysis suggests a dismissive attachment style.

Figure 8.4 shows Michael's construal systems after 24 months in the TC. It is evident that he still perceived himself as distinct from others and, as with previous assessment points, he explained that he was "most important".

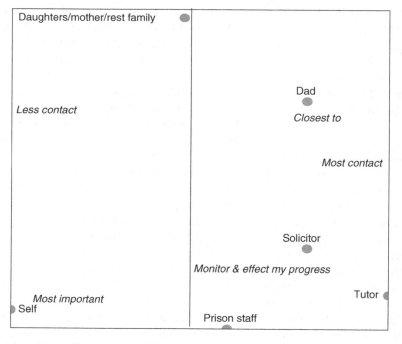

Figure 8.4 Michael's card sort at 24 months

Michael continued to report on his family relationships, but only in terms of "closeness" to his father, saying simply that he had "less contact" with other family members. It is interesting that, whilst Michael reported closeness to his father, this is not reflected in the results, as there is significant distance between "self" and "father" cards. It is also noticeable that Michael appears to have retained the same non-emotional understanding of people in the TC, simply describing TC staff as able to impact his progress by monitoring his behaviour. Markedly absent were other TC residents. It is noteworthy that, instead of his peer group, Michael chose to recognise the significance of authority figures (e.g. his solicitor and education tutor). These relationships do not seem to be characterised by a strong emotional alliance, but, rather, by the control Michael perceived these people to be having over his progress within the prison system.

Using the Bartholomew and Horowitz four-category attachment model, Michael appears to have a positive view of himself, yet experiences a distance between himself and others, suggesting a remaining discomfort with intimacy. As with the previous time point, the findings suggest a dismissive attachment style, although at this time Michael does not seem so overtly disapproving.

The results from Michael's MCSPs over a two-year period in the TC were discussed with him during his feedback sessions. At baseline, Michael's family relationships were perceived as mostly painful and characterised by communication problems. At this early time in therapy, he described TC-associated people in a non- emotional way and there was a clear divide between them and his family. Overall, the analysis suggests that Michael had a fearful attachment style at this time.

After 12 months in therapy, Michael construed his family members as more supportive and important, suggesting that he had negotiated some of the problems reported earlier, although the considerable distance between Michael and everyone else still suggests underlying avoidance. Given his positive view of himself, we suggest Michael has a dismissive attachment style.

After 24 months in the TC, Michael considered his father (who at time one was described as a person who had caused him a lot of hurt) as the closest to him, suggesting major repair in this key relationship, although the considerable distance between Michael and others, including his father, was especially evident in the results. Michael's construing of TC-related people was still rather matter-of-fact and non-emotional; a stronger emotional alliance might have been expected to be reported over time. Overall analysis suggests the continuation of a dismissive attachment style (positive view of self and dismissive of intimacy/avoidance of others).

The case study confirms an attachment style characterised by avoidance, initially a fearful type and, after time in therapy, a dismissive type. Analysis confirms the relevance of trying to improve interpersonal bonds amongst residents in the TC but also highlights the difficulties in attaining attachment-based change. Whilst this case study indicates attachment change, it suggests that, with an increase in positive feelings about himself, even after two years in therapy Michael continued to avoid others, albeit dismissively rather than fearfully. Given the links between dismissive attachment and violence, we concluded that Michael's relationships required on-going support, monitoring and further psychological intervention.

Group-level attachment-based change

As mentioned previously, of the 60 residents who completed card sorts at baseline, 26 were still in the TC after 12 months and repeated the MCSP, and further analyses were performed on their collective responses.

The categories used by participants to describe key people at the two assessment points were content analysed. Constructs that appeared to reflect aspects of attachment theory resulted in 19 themes, shown in Table 8.1.

Analysis of the attachment themes shows an increase over time in the themes "mutual relationships", "feeling close to others" and "trusting relationships", aspects that would be most associated with a secure attachment style. There is also a decrease by time 2 in the themes "pain", "communication problems" and "worrying about others' opinions", which are characteristics most associated with insecure attachment styles.

Before turning to the SSA, it is useful to briefly consider the people that residents chose to include in their card sorts at time 1 and time 2. As summarised in Table 8.2, most residents included various family members, and *siblings* were the most frequently chosen person at both time points. *Mother* was chosen less frequently than siblings over time, and *father* was only included by less than half the sample (41.6% at time 1 and 42.2% at time 2). Noteworthy differences in people chosen by residents at time 1 and time 2 include the moderate decrease in the inclusion of *peers*. *Mother* and *father* cards increase, albeit moderately, by time 2, and the largest increase by time 2 is in the *authority figure* card.

It is interesting that residents chose the card *siblings* so frequently at time 1 and time 2. The 'usual' primary attachment figures in adults are peers or a romantic partner (Hazan and Shaver, 1994). Equally interesting is that *mother* and *father* were included less often than siblings at both time points. Although Hazan and Shaver (1994) propose that attachment will be transferred from parents to peers in most adults, they also state that "parents are never completely relinquished as attachment figures" (p. 9). Therefore, the overall lack of *mother* and *father* cards is significant given the association between parental absence and/or rejection and offending behaviour (Hoffman, 1971; McCord, 1983). The largest frequency shift in cards by time 2 was an increase in the *authority figure* card. This is a positive finding, as this card represented prison TC staff for

Table 8.1 Definition and frequency of attachment themes at time 1 and time 2

Theme name	Definition	Time 1 (%)	Time 2 (%)
Mutual	Mutual or reciprocal type of relationships	8	15
Closeto	Emotionally close to one or more people	45	54
Caregi	Care-giving towards one or more people	28	27
Carere	Receives care from others	52	65
Hopes	Has hopes about relationships e.g. hoping relationship improves	28	27
Othersot	Thinking or worrying about other's opinions, particularly about himself	22	8
Abando	Feeling abandoned or neglected by others	18	19
Anger	Anger towards others	18	15
Dislik	Dislike of one or more people	23	23
Pain	Pain caused by one or more people	25	8
Comprob	Communication problems with one or more people	27	12
Unsure	Unsure and uncertain about one or more people	25	19
Noemot	Sorts the people cards with minimal/no emotion, e.g. live far away/live near; give me money/don't give me money	12	15
Alone	Feeling alone or "cut off" from one or more people	20	19
Mefirst	Need to put himself first, look after number one	7	8
Effect	Aware of the effect that behaviour has on others	22	31
Demand	Sees others as demanding and arduous	12	3.8
Trust	Trusts one or more people	13	23
Unworth	Sees one or more people as unworthy and not good enough	10	19

some offenders and suggests progression in the seeking out of pro-social attachment figures; although, as the case study showed, authority figures were seen as important because they could impact progress in prison. The decrease in the *peers* card by time 2 could be seen as encouraging, given the link between peer association and antisocial behaviour (Vitaro et al., 2000), although some of these peers would have involved fellow residents, in which case raising doubt about the presence of resident–resident therapeutic alliances.

The themes are grouped in a way that describes the four attachment styles (see Figure 8.5). Dismissive attachment is made up of the variables "no emotion", "unworthy", "demand" and "mefirst". Together they reflect a dismissive attachment style with low dependence on others and high avoidance of others

Table 8.2 Type and frequency of people chosen in the card sorts at time 1 and time 2

People type	Time 1 $n = 60$ (%)	Time 2 $n = 26$ (%)
Sibling	73.3	80.8
Peers	63.3	57.7
Mother	51.7	57.7
Children	51.7	54
Extended family	50	38.5
Father	41.6	42.3
Romantic partner	38.3	23
Authority figure	25	42.3
Ex-romantic partner	21.7	15.4
Parent	16.7	15.4
Family	11.7	7.7

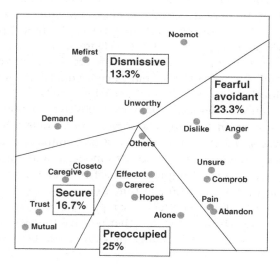

Figure 8.5 SSA attachment styles and proportions at time 1

(Bartholomew and Horowitz, 1991). The lowest proportion of residents (13.3%) was classified as dismissive. The SSA suggests that fearful-avoidance (23.3%) is characterised by the variables "dislike", "anger", "unsure", "communication problems", "pain" and abandon". Together these describe an attachment associated with high dependence and high avoidance of others (Bartholomew and Horowitz, 1991). Preoccupied attachment (25%) is made up of "alone", "hopes", "care-receiving", "others' opinions" and "effect on others", which describe high dependence on others and low avoidance of others (Bartholomew and Horowitz, 1991). Finally, secure attachment (16.7%) is defined by "close to", "care-giving", "trust" and "mutual". Combined, these reflect a positive model of self and others characterised by low avoidance and low dependence (Bartholomew and Horowitz, 1991).

Overall, 78.3% ($n = 47$) were classified as having a predominant attachment style at time 1. The sample was classified using a stringent approach in which a resident had to have proportionally twice as many variables within one attachment style when compared with all other attachment styles. Of those classified as having a predominant attachment style, 61.6% were insecure ($n = 37$ out of $n = 47$), while 21.7% ($n = 13$) of the sample had hybrid attachments which comprised multiple attachment styles.

A further test of the adequacy of the attachment model considered the correlations between the four attachments. Table 8.3 shows that attachments have no statistically significant positive relationships with one another as measured by Spearman's rho correlations. Secure and fearful attachments have a highly statistically significant negative relationship with one another, which is encouraging, as Bartholomew and Horowitz's (1991) model positions these attachment styles as absolute opposites (see Figure 8.1).

The SSA revealed an attachment structure that corresponds with Bartholomew and Horowitz's (1991) four-category model of adult attachment, and this empirical structure was reinforced by correlation analysis, which showed and absence of statically significant positive relationships between attachment styles. Given that the majority of the sample (78.3%, $n = 47$ at time 1, and 69.2%, $n = 18$ at time 2) had a predominant attachment style, results confirm Bartholomew and Horowitz's model as a useful way to classify the residents' attachments. The proportion of offenders with secure attachments (16.7% at time 1 and 34.6% at time 2) was, as expected, considerably lower than those found in non-offender samples (e.g. 47–57% in undergraduates). Support is thus given to the idea that positive therapeutic alliances are important for attachment-based change (Bowlby, 1988) because the building

Table 8.3   Spearman's rho correlations between attachment styles at time 1

	Secure	Dismissive	Fearful	Preoccupied
Secure	–			
Dismissive	−0.205	–		
Fearful	−0.467**	−0.207	–	
Preoccupied	−0.016	−0.044	0.115	–

Notes: ** $p < .01$.

of trusting, mutual relationships defined by "care-giving" and "closeness" were the features that residents used to define secure attachments.

The attachment styles derived from card sorts with those residents still participating in the TC after 12 months ($n = 26$) were examined. Here individual-level comparisons were made amongst the 26 offenders who took part in both assessment points, and these are shown in Table 8.4. The majority of the sample (69.2%, $n = 18$) at time 2 were classified as having a predominant attachment style, meaning that 30.8% ($n = 8$) had hybrid attachment styles. Although, as shown in Table 8.4, half of those with hybrid attachments ($n = 4$) at time 2 had secure attachment features, Table 8.4 also shows that more individuals had a secure attachment style by time 2: nine at time 2 compared with five at time 1. This is a promising finding and suggests that the TC can enhance interpersonal relationships for some (Cullen, 1997). Interestingly, most of the offenders classified as having secure attachment at time 2 had preoccupied and/or fearful attachments at time 1, suggesting that the TC could be particularly effective at facilitating positive attachment-based change with this group. Indeed, the proportion of individuals with fearful-avoidant attachment decreased by time 2.

There was an unexpected change from secure attachment at time 1 to insecure attachment at time 2 for three offenders. This suggests that the TC can have a negative impact on a small proportion of offenders. Alternatively, it could be that an insecure attachment style is part of the therapeutic passage for some residents. These individuals may have more "work" to do. Previous research has found that 12–18 months is the optimal treatment time for offenders in prison TCs (e.g. Marshall, 1997).

Table 8.4 also shows the overall increase in dismissive hybrid attachments by time 2. Again, this may suggest that the TC is not helpful for certain individuals or that some residents are still undergoing change at time 2. Jones (1997) found a pattern of deterioration, with improvement only occurring in the later stages of TC treatment. It may be the case that the process of feeling more secure about oneself involves, for some residents, dismissing others. This certainly seemed a likely interpretation of Michael's attachment change as represented in the case study.

Five residents did not report shifts in their attachment styles, and most of the remainder moved towards a more adaptive attachment style. Given that there are some studies that have identified differences in attachment styles between violent and sexual offenders (e.g. Ward et al., 1996), our final set of analyses considered associations between participants' index offences and attachment styles. Cross-tabulations revealed no statistical significance between the three main types of index offences (violence, sexual and acquisitive) and attachment styles, although this could be an artefact of the small numbers. Looking instead at the proportions, Table 8.5 shows that the majority of sexual offenders were

Table 8.4 Attachment change over time in the $n = 26$ residents who completed both card sorts

Resident	Time 1	Time 2
1	Secure/fearful	Dismissive/preoccupied
2	Secure/fearful	Secure
3	Preoccupied/fearful/dismissive	Secure
4	**Fearful**	**Fearful**
5	Preoccupied	Dismissive/secure
6	Fearful	Preoccupied/secure
7	Preoccupied/fearful	Secure
8	**Secure**	**Secure**
9	Fearful	Preoccupied
10	Fearful	Secure
11	Secure	Preoccupied
12	**Secure**	**Secure**
13	Preoccupied	Secure/preoccupied
14	Preoccupied	Secure
15	Fearful	Secure
16	**Preoccupied**	**Preoccupied**
17	Secure	Dismissive
18	Dismissive	Preoccupied/fearful/secure
19	Preoccupied	Dismissive
20	Dismissive	Preoccupied
21	Fearful	Secure
22	Preoccupied	Dismissive/preoccupied
23	Preoccupied	Preoccupied/fearful/dismissive
24	Secure/preoccupied	Preoccupied
25	Secure	Preoccupied
26	**Preoccupied/fearful**	**Preoccupied/fearful**

preoccupied at time 1 and had hybrid attachments by time 2. There appears a fairly even spread of dismissive attachments across offender types, although at time 2 there is an increase in the number of violent offenders being classified as dismissive, although violent offenders also had lower fearful and preoccupied attachments and a higher rate of secure attachment rates by time 2. Table 8.5 also shows the relatively high proportion of acquisitive offenders classified with fearful-avoidant attachment at time 1 and secure or preoccupied by time 2.

The finding that the majority of sexual offenders were preoccupied at time 1 supports some of the previous research findings (e.g. Ward et al., 1996; Stirpe et al., 2006). By time 2 sexual offenders had hybrid rather than pure attachments, suggesting that they may have more attachment-based change to undertake. The results are encouraging, though, because of the tendency of some sex offenders to isolate themselves from others (Bogaerts et al., 2006),

Table 8.5   Associations between index offence and attachment styles at time 1 and time 2

Index offence	Secure		Dismissive		Fearful		Preoccupied	
	Time 1	Time 2	Time 1	Time 2	Time 1	Time 2	Time 1	Time 2
Violence	22%	30%	11%	20%	17%	10%	22%	20%
Sexual	14%	0	14%	0	14%	0	57%	0
Acquisitive	16%	27%	13%	0	29%	9%	16%	45%

and suggests that the TC approach is able to keep up its principles of social inclusion even amongst fearful-avoidant individuals.

There was a fairly even spread of dismissive attachments across offender types, and the current findings do not reflect a link between dismissive attachment and violent offending (Frodi et al., 2001) or fearful attachment and violence (Dutton et al., 1994; Van Ijzendoorn et al., 1997). That said, at time 2 there was an unanticipated increase in the number of violent offenders classified as dismissive, suggesting that this group might be particularly resistant to treatment (Van Ijzendoorn et al., 1997). A relatively high proportion of acquisitive offenders had fearful-avoidant attachments. This differs from Ward et al.'s (1996) findings, as their "non-violent/non-sexual" group of offenders were relatively spread across the attachment styles: dismissive ($n = 11$), secure ($n = 10$), fearful ($n = 7$) and preoccupied ($n = 2$). The current study also found that the acquisitive group were more preoccupied or secure as a result of therapy. It may not necessarily be undesirable for an offender to be preoccupied. Preoccupation could include thinking about the ways in which offending behaviour had detrimentally impacted upon others.

Place attachment

Fifty-nine residents completed the place card sorts, which comprised cards with the following labels: Dovegate TC, First prison, Home (now), Holiday place, School, Scene of first crime, Police Station, Home grew up in, In the Park, Alone in cell.

Findings

Time 1 (baseline, i.e. whilst in the ARU)

The structural model in Figure 8.6 illustrates the average relationships between the settings as indicated in the residents' sorts.

What is apparent is the distance between Dovegate TC and all the other places. Encouragingly, this might suggest that participants view the TC as unique, even at baseline. We might interpret this as suggesting that Dovegate

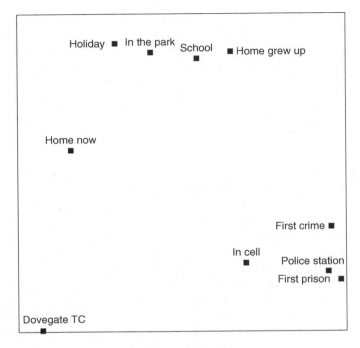

Figure 8.6 COSPA item plot of "place" sorts at baseline

TC lacks place attachment because our research participants had only recently relocated there. Also, the cluster of items relating to crime-associated places is nearer to Dovegate TC than early attachment places, which might imply either that Dovegate TC is simply thought of as another but different criminal justice system (CJS) association, or that it is a place where reflection about crime-related places is coming to the surface and there is a degree of separation between these. Thus, there appear to be two underlying dimensions to the way in which our TC residents thought about places: those related to the CJS and those that were not, and a time dimension, that is, the present and the past.

Being in a cell, first crime, police station and *first prison* are close together, meaning that these places were construed very similarly. That they are associated with the past is suggestive of a sense of moving on and a desire to leave these places behind. The item *alone in cell* is not judged by the same criteria as Dovegate TC. Perhaps this is due to the social milieu.

Theoretically these findings make sense. Giuliani (2003) summarises that it is not unusual to construe places in terms of positivity/negativity and time, that is, current/past/future:

We have all experienced some form of affective bond, either positive or negative, pleasant or unpleasant, with some place or other – a place that can be related to our current or past experiences, sometimes to the future. (p. 137)

At baseline residents did not distinguish any places as related to their future, as gleaned from the criteria by which they distinguished between places. This is perhaps reflective of the short time spent in the TC.

The COSPA analysis also produces a fit index which denotes the degree of stress in shaping each participant's sorting data to the two-dimensional item model. The fit of individuals' sorts to the map representing the whole ranged between a low of 0.016 and a high of 0.987 (the higher the index, the better the fit), with an average of 0.58, which is an acceptable degree of stress.

Time 2 (after 12 months of therapy)

Figure 8.7 shows the collective analysis of the place sorts. *Dovegate TC* is still situated separately from all the other places, confirming that it is still seen as a unique place after 12 months in therapy. In comparison with the baseline plot, it can be seen that *in cell* is now in closer proximity to *Dovegate TC*. This could be interpreted as a positive finding, as residents are encouraged within the TC to view their cells, referred to as "rooms" in a positive manner, as places of contemplation and choice rather than being "bang-up".

One major difference between this and the time 1 construal of places is that participants view the TC in the *non CJS* space. We determine this from the

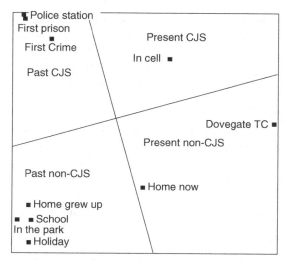

Figure 8.7 Partitioning COSPA item plot of "place" sorts at 12 months

location of the card representing the TC in the sorts. In this case the TC was not placed in a sort reflecting CJS places. This is a positive finding, and confirms the initial indications that the TC is perceived by residents as distinct from other crime-related places, such as first prison and police station, and is indicative of a positive place attachment.

The same underlying past/present distinction between places exists in the data at time 2, although being in a cell is now incorporated into their present living circumstances. Home was now more often than previously placed with the TC in the various sorts. Perhaps this represents an emergence of some acknowledgement of hopes and aspirations in terms of *future* places, that is, "home", which might be expected as a result of time spent in therapy.

The degree of stress, as measured by a delta score, ranged from 0.014 to 0.912 with an average of 0.454. Despite the smaller sample size ($n = 26$) at this second analytic time point, the stress index remains similar to the baseline time point and its larger sample size ($n = 59$).

Conclusions

This analysis confirmed Bartholomew and Horowitz's (1991) model of adult attachment as a useful way to classify residents' attachment styles. As anticipated, prior to engaging in Dovegate TC the sample reported insecure attachments, and attachment-based change was apparent in the 26 offenders who completed 12 months in the TC. Although this was a small sample, there was a notable increase in secure attachment styles and a decrease in fearful avoidance after 12 months in therapy. This is an impressive finding, given the difficulties associated with treating insecurely attached offenders (Fonagy, 1999), and suggests that the TC is place in which some residents can strengthen their interpersonal attachments (Cullen, 1997).

Analysis of index type and attachment style revealed some positive attachment-based change across all groups, although it would be useful for future research to further examine the acquisitive group by implementing a larger sample size, especially as these types of offenders have such high rates of reoffending. Findings support the idea that sexual offenders are likely to be preoccupied (Ward et al., 1996), although the current study was not able to differentiate between child sex offenders and rapists because of the small sample size. Treatment providers might find it useful to consider behaviours associated with a dismissing style of attachment because of its increase over time in the TC amongst violent offenders, for example, by being aware of and working with those who are inclined to avoid self-disclosure (Mikulincer and Nachshon, 1991) or those who are particularly pessimistic about relationships (Hazan and Shaver, 1987). It may be, as has already been hypothesised, that a dismissive attachment style emerges during therapy alongside an increase in self-esteem as "a step in the right direction" but clearly signifies the need for further psychological change.

It would be useful for future research to also consider attachment-based change over a longer period of time with a larger sample size because of the high levels of drop-out from the TC. There were some, most notably sexual offenders at time 2, who had hybrid attachments, which could indicate that they were still in the process of changing. Equally so for the preoccupied residents with acquisitive offences at time 2. Those residents who reported change from a secure to an insecure attachment style after 12 months in therapy could change further, although it could be that these groups may be unable to attain a completely secure attachment style. Future longitudinal research could try to answer these questions and consider if there is a connection between a secure attachment style and sustained desistance from offending (Sapouna et al., 2011).

For all participants taking part in this strand of the research, the TC is perceived as a highly unique place, at baseline *and* after 12 months in therapy. In particular, the TC is not seen as similar to other crime-related places such as previous prisons. Significantly, at time 2, participants construe the TC as a non-crime place.

Over time participants view their cells (or "rooms") within the TC as significant and as a place that characterises the here and now. Consistent over time were the underlying distinctions between cards based on time (*past* vs. *present*) and crime (*criminal justice system* vs. *non-criminal justice system*).

Findings support aspects of place attachment theory that suggest (a) place attachments can operate at an individual, group and community level and (b) place attachment can decline when needs are no longer met (Shumaker and Taylor, 1983).

9

After the TC: Post-Residency Questionnaire, Interviews and Psychometrics

Introduction

Our second major set of research questions focused on life back in mainstream prison after having been in Dovegate TC. For this part of the research, we were interested in what the process of change looked and felt like for the men themselves. We wanted to inquire into the experiences of TC residents who had either dropped out or been required to leave as well as those who had completed at least 18 months of therapy. Interestingly, a Grendon study examined the TC residents' perspective looking at premature leavers, but did so relatively soon after the decision was made to leave and by means of exit interviews (Sullivan, 2011). We decided to give former Dovegate residents some time for reflection before asking them about their time in the TC because, as well as obtaining their assessment of the positives and negatives of their therapeutic exposure, we wanted to gain some understanding of how they reintegrated into mainstream prison, which was the destination of most of our leavers.

There were several sources of evidence available to us for examining the post-Dovegate experiences: our psychometric data, analysed by Darragh O'Neill, a follow-up questionnaire of leavers collected by Amelie Bobsien[1] and detailed interviews with former residents undertaken by Rosemary Simmonds.[2]

The premature leavers

As explained in Chapter 4, there are two types of premature "leavers": those who were de-selected from the TC for some rule infraction or behavioural problems and those who chose to leave. We were able to gain some insights into the reasons people chose to leave the TC early from our interviews with ex-residents once they had returned to mainstream prisons and from a questionnaire sent to 57 premature leavers. We present the results of the interviews first and then describe our questionnaire results.

The interviews

A number of themes were discernible from the analysis of the interview material from those who left therapy early. Simmonds (2008) classified these as sex offending; insincerity; drug taking; institutional issues; and staff issues. What follows is a brief exposition together with extracts from the ex-residents interviews to elucidate the five themes.

Sex offending

Two aspects of sex offending that were cited as problematic: being bullied or intimidated as a sex offender, and not being able to cope with sex offenders in the TC. Both were nominated as reasons for leaving. Besides experiencing extremely negative reactions from other residents to their crimes, it seems that sex offenders were particularly targeted for bullying and intimidation. As one sex offender ex-resident explained:

> I found it very difficult on there. There wasn't very many sex offenders on there and as soon as I went onto the wing I told them I was a sex offender and I had a mixed reaction from people. A lot of people were ignoring me completely, some would just give you dirty looks, snide comments...Before I even got onto the group, a lot of them were complaining about having me on the group. They were asking staff if they could change groups and they weren't happy with me being on there. When I did actually get onto a group and started talking about my crimes, people would shout and swear at me and leave the room. They weren't very happy so I found it quite difficult.

He left after six months. Ex-residents with a history of sex offending reported that they felt unsupported, and threatened by other non-sex offender residents to the point where they became isolated, anxious and afraid for their physical safety:

> when I got to Dovegate I was asked what I was there for and explained that I was in for a sexual crime and automatically that got all the residents' backs' up and I've come across death threats and opposition all the time with the community itself. When we'd go to our little meetings and that everybody is lovey dovey. Lovey dovey in the setting where people can be seen and assessed but when I was in my cell, that's when people used to come up and say like "you've been a bit of a...I'm going to come and slit your throat" and stuff, that type of thing.

These extracts highlight two important points: first, some sex offenders experience the TC as an unsafe place for them because they believe they will be the victim of a serious physical attack; second, peer group therapy is only effective when participants are supportive of one another. Feeling unsupported and insecure works against the building of trusting relationships and forming strong therapeutic alliances, which are the key building blocks for successful therapy.

Non-sex offenders who left the TC at an early stage often gave the presence of sex offenders as one of their main reasons for leaving. They intimated their sense of moral superiority over sex offenders, who they suggested undermined constructive interaction and therapeutic progress. One early-leaving resident said:

> [The TC] wasn't how I thought it would be, I used to go into groups and all and I'd been in groups about five months... There's a dude in the corner who's a prolific paedophile and he's trying to judge me [saying] "you're just a fucking junkie" and I say "tell you what mate, you mess with your fucking kids – I can walk out and be accepted in society when I leave, you'll be known as fucking sex offender." He sits there judging me and voting me off....

The excerpt illustrates not only a hierarchy of criminal activity where sex offenders are placed at the bottom but also the outrage felt at being in a situation where a sex offender could "judge" the resident as well as have the power to vote him out of the TC. In trying to understand the function that such criminal hierarchies may have for residents in the early stages of therapy, it seems by accepting parity with a sex offender is tantamount to removing the resident's main or possibly only source of positive self-esteem. Take this contrasting statement by a longer-stay resident (18 months) and how he managed to break down his prejudices about sex offenders when he was in the TC:

> once I got onto the main TC, as painful as it was for me to go through me own stuff, but also listening through a small group of paedophiles, you can see, I don't really agree with what they've done, not at all. I think it's despicable. But listening to what they went through as kids, sort of things and as horrible as this is to admit to myself, I can see similarities between my life and their life. The only difference is that I chose drugs, and not to become an abuser, you know. Don't get me wrong, I didn't have none as my best mate, but after 3 or 4 months on main TC, I accepted them for the people they was, or what they are, not for the people that they was. If you understand what I mean.

This resident was able to identify with and accept some common ground with sex offenders by acknowledging that they shared negative childhood experiences. Through understanding that the roots of criminal behaviours were similar, even though the crimes were not, the longer stayers gained an insight that the early leavers were not able to achieve.

For non-sex offenders in the TC, accepting sex offenders as equals is in itself an important process for the residents, as it encapsulates some key therapeutic goals, such as: rejecting criminal codes, taking responsibility for their own crimes and effects on victims, capacity to empathise and recognising the need for pro-social behaviour.

Insincerity of other TC residents

Some early leavers said they left the TC because they felt disillusioned by other residents who were not taking therapy seriously:

> it's just the wrong environment because for me to really appreciate therapy and embrace the positiveness from it and gain all I can from it, I need to be in a different environment. Not where I'm seeing a guy that seems really sincere, while I'm in the group and then when we leave the group he's basically telling me it's all a load of bollocks. That is . . . that's thrown me off balance now because, I've just given him a load of admiration and respect for what he's just done in the group but now he's left, that's gone by one comment. You see what I'm saying? He's been talking for a whole hour and he's got my respect and he's left and ten minutes later one comment has taken it all away . . . Therapy can't work for you like that.

To more fully understand the behaviours of residents who are reported as having insincere motivations for the TC, we made use of the concept of "passing" (Furnham and Bochner, 1986). This term has been used in race relations to describe how some migrants or stigmatized groups have assimilated to an alien culture or dominant social group to the extent that they can "pass" for British, American, white or whatever is deemed important in the context. This concept links to further literature on psychological reactions to unfamiliar environments and to the process of "culture learning", which may prove relevant to issues of commitment for the TC residents. Culture learning is based on a social skills model that draws a distinction between skills and values.

It would seem plausible that the less sincere residents are acting like sojourners, being instrumentally motivated and learning selected aspects of the TC in order to "pass", and that what is learnt will not effect a permanent change in the participant, although it will allow him to acquire the skills to construct a therapy mask whilst retaining a criminal identity. The presence of those who put on a good therapy "performance" and then behaved very differently on the "landings" was linked to the quality of relationships between residents and staff (therapeutic alliances). "Passing" and "sojourning" were associated with early exit, as these residents could not sustain the motivation to continue.

Drug taking

Drug taking in the TC not only perpetuates criminal codes and values but also affects residents' experiences of therapy, as the following resident explained:

> the TC at the time was going downhill and there were a lot of people taking drugs and the meetings were getting hijacked by people talking about drugs and that and I was kind of getting fed up with that...

One participant expressed the view that TC staff did not challenge drug taking enough or provide sufficient support for residents with a drug-related criminal history. He stated:

> Yeah because I don't feel the support was there from the staff, they were aware of what was going on and everything and it is all in my sentence planning thing, in me life sentence planning thing, reports and that, so they were aware of it but you know they did nothing to alleviate it or challenge the other people, you know what I mean?

The selling and taking of drugs was a community rule infraction and would most likely lead to being required to leave Dovegate.

But acceptance and then resisting drug taking becomes a breakthrough issue, not dissimilar to the insights about sex offending, as one of Bobsien's ex residents expounded.

> "You come in here, the smackhead that is ignorant of other people's feelings... but as time goes on you gradually start to feel things like other people. You start to feel guilty about what you've done something wrong in the community, because you usually confront people in the community if you are doing something wrong like taking drugs, its against the constitution. It hurts a lot when you are sitting there and then you are tempted to take more drugs... but in all I think that self-awareness is the biggest thing in here".

Institutional issues

Issues of de-categorisation and completing sentence plans were also given as reasons for leaving by interviewees. The following excerpt typifies this problem:

> I was on the main prison first of all in Dovegate and before I went I was due for a category review. Before I went over to the TC I checked that the category review was still going on and I was told yes it would still go ahead exactly the same as it would on the main prison. I did my time on the assessment wing

and I was told all through that it would still go ahead exactly the same and when I got onto the proper wing and they told me it wasn't the case, exactly the opposite and they informed me that I would have to serve at least 18 months if not 2 years before I would get recategorisation... then I wouldn't get the opportunity for a D Cat and resettlement, which I always said in my sentence plan was my main target to get to a Cat D jail, get a job and get myself working before my release... every time I challenged or questioned anything there I got exactly the same response "what is more important your problem or the therapy?" and to be honest the category is more important to me.

This would-be resident found himself caught in having to make a choice between therapy or a resettlement programme at a Cat D prison; ideally he should have been able to benefit from both, as they would have helped him in different but complementary ways. Although it is important for residents to be motivated for therapy because they want to change, it is also important to remember that prisoners are part of a penal system that includes sentence plans with courses that have to be completed, such as Enhanced Thinking Skills (ETS), which is not available in the TC. The following participant talked about his reason for leaving the TC as follows:

Because... I mean, I was making good progress, for the first time in my life, like, in almost, what, 27 years, first people had recommended an inpatient stay in a therapeutic community, and, um, finally I was able to access that... So I had the opportunity to go to Dovegate and the fact that there was no SOTP [Sex Offender Treatment Programme] there was just a very, very difficult decision for me, but I had to complete that SOTP to stand any chance of progression, really. I couldn't help my... risk factors reduced until I finished my SOTP, and obviously that was preventing my progress.

This ex-resident could not access a sex offender treatment programme in the TC that was part of his sentence plan. As this course would be of some benefit to him both on a therapeutic level and in helping his sentence progression, the participant made a rational decision to leave the TC.

Staff issues

Although staff at the TC were often praised by ex-residents, some interviewees said high staff turnover and lack of staff training or limited life experiences were their reason for leaving the TC. Participants referred to staff as having previously worked at "Tesco's" or "Asda", invoking the image of well-meaning but untrained 'amateurs' who found themselves out of their depth working in a difficult therapeutic context. Having a high staff turnover was also thought to have had a negative effect on therapeutic alliances and residents' progress in therapy.

Commenting on staff turnover and insufficient training/life experience, the following resident said:

> there was only 3 original staff from when I started. So you know they was coming and going all the time, so you never felt settled in your group because you know you always had someone new. They were quite young some of them and there was a couple of them on our wing and you know it looked like they were fresh out of school, to be honest you know. You do look at them and think "what can he tell me"?

High staff turnover, inexperienced staff and inconsistent approaches to the role of a group facilitator seem to have marred this resident's experience of therapy. Cullen and MacKenzie (2011) do comment on staffing problems and periods of apparent "chaos" amongst staff, so this ex-resident's comment raises a legitimate issue. It was also an issue mentioned in HM Prison Inspectorate reports, so there was some reality to these complaints; they should not simply be dismissed as "projection" whereby residents sought to blame others rather than deal with their problems, although it would also be fair to say there was a certain amount of projection.

Questionnaire data

Data to address the question of the TC legacy for those leaving came from a sample of 60 residents who had left the TC (Bobsien, 2004). The majority of those taking part in this survey (57) were premature leavers. The average time all questionnaire respondents had spent in the community was nine months, although this covered quite a span, 1–17 months. Of the premature leavers, 29 were de-selected and 28 made their own decision to leave. The analysis presented here is on those leaving prematurely.

Bobsien wished to establish the ex-residents overall reflections on being in Dovegate. The open-ended responses were analysed by creating a master list of the comments they provided. Over half, 57%, said they had benefited from their time in the TC and just under half (49%) said they had made some specific positive gains. About a fifth (26%) said their experiences had been negative and 33% said they had made no gains.

The questionnaires were further analysed by means of an Multi-dimensional Scalogram Analysis (MSA). Profiles of the ex-residents' reflections were coded. Twenty-five distinct profiles were found, i.e. several residents were coded as having an identical pattern of responses. The MSA showing the profiles is presented in Figure 9.1, which also shows the broad partitioning that distinguishes between types of residents. The MSA statistic provides an overall map of all

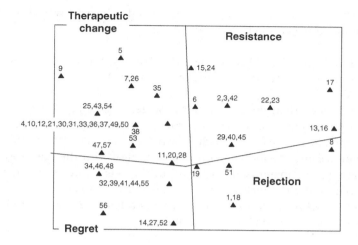

Figure 9.1 MSA of premature leavers (the numbers represent a questionnaire respondent) taken from Bobsien (2008)

respondents in terms of the similarities and differences between their pattern of responses and the list of reflections they had itemised in their questionnaire return. The more similar their responses, the closer together the points representing them are in the MSA. Thereafter, separate maps are produced indicating the presence or absence of each itemised response derived from the questionnaires. By overlaying these, we can indicate which set of affirmative responses (indicating those reflections mentioned by the ex-residents) characterises clusters of these former residents. Collectively after overlaying all the response maps, the MSA could be defined by four broad regions, described as: some degree of change (44%); resistance to change (25%); regretful (22%); and rejecting (9%).

The rejection region contained both ex-residents who were de-selected and those who chose to leave. They indicated that the TC had left no impact on them, they experienced no gains and that they left due to a failure to deal with their problems. This appears to have left rather a negative impression on these former residents. It would seem that, in order to protect themselves, these individuals, rather than looking at their own behaviour (i.e. what had led to their de-selection or withdrawal), tended to project blame on to the other residents.

Within the resistance region, the majority of cases were de-selected (12 out of 14), whilst the other two left by the 48-hour procedure. Ex-residents who fell into this region mentioned being "misunderstood" by their fellow TC residents. This implies that they may have made a fair attempt at opening up and engaging with the therapeutic process; however, this was not handled well by the community. As one de-selected resident said, whilst he was liked by some in the group, others thought he "took liberties", and so

> I used to fly off when I heard what others were saying but that was cos they didn't understand what was going on in my head.

This could mean that, during the initial stages of change, if the community is unable to "manage" a resident's particular problems, support for the "difficult" individual is likely to break down and may result in some form of acting out because the individual is unable to deal with the pressures exerted by the group. The majority of cases within this region are de-selected, which is the community's choice to dispel individuals who cannot be contained. The residents who felt misunderstood often also felt over-analysed, which was something they found difficult to handle:

> Because I didn't know how to handle the TC... I was led into a false sense of security and analysed too much for everything I did or said and when I opened up all my old wounds I was shipped out with no help to put myself back together...

or they simply could not deal with issues that came to the surface:

> I opened up a door in my life that had been closed for a number of years... and I couldn't sit in my small group and talk about the details and how I feel.

All of the cases within the regret region reported that they left the TC because of a failure to deal with their problems. However, they all also reported that they had gained something from the TC experience. By internalising the reason for leaving, it may be that with hindsight the residents can recognise the potential for the positive impact that the TC could have had. As one individual explained, it seems "easy" to put in the 48-hour notice. In particular, the first days in the TC are likely to be unsettling, disorienting and challenging, and settling in to this new environment may be difficult:

> I didn't give myself the chance to settle down in the TC. I put my hours in and by the time it ran out it was too late. I was transferred back here and have regretted leaving the TC ever since.

The therapeutic change region contained 10 profiles representing 26 cases and was approximately evenly split in terms of the de-selected and 48-hour leavers. Half of the de-selected residents reported that their reason for leaving was failure to adhere to TC rules, as did two of the 48-hour leavers. For the remaining former residents, eight reported that they found the TC too challenging. Overall, this region can be conceptualised as the one in which the majority of ex-residents had experienced some form of change but for various reasons had not been able to cope with, or be coped with by, other members of the group. De-selected individuals were more likely to provide an external attribution, explaining their leaving as related to factors in the therapeutic environment, whereas residents who chose to leave seem to have internally orientated attributions, explaining their leaving in terms of their own avoidance of the environment.

The responses given by the men in the four quadrants of the MSA are listed in Table 9.1. (after Bobsien, 2004).

There were four responses that statistically significantly differentiated the de-selected from the 48-hour leavers: more of the former stated they had not adhered to the TC rules, had felt misunderstood and had made no gains.

Table 9.1 Open-ended responses from premature leavers about their Dovegate experiences

Therapeutic change	Regret	Rejection	Resistance
Able to deal with difficulties	Lack of help adjusting	Over-analysed	Mainstream prison is easier
Improved behaviour	Difficulty fitting in	No gains	Failure to deal with problems
Increase in positive feelings	Current environment seems harsher	Uncomfortable experience	Increased defences
Increase in awareness of self and others	Regrets about leaving	Negative experience	No improvement
Gained something		Staff issues	Non-acceptance of others
Challenging experience		Frustrating	Not adhering to the rules
Feeling vulnerable		No help	
Greater tolerance		Others' pressure (backstabbing, etc.)	
Being more determined		Not given a chance and non-acceptance	
Ability to control emotion		Felt misunderstood	
Able to avoid violence		Opened up old wounds	
Remain drug-free			

A greater proportion of the latter stated that the TC had been challenging. The implicit assumption is that those who do not finish the programme are treatment failures, or, putting this another way, only those who graduated from the treatment programme will have experienced positive benefits. Positive TC therapeutic impacts reported by these early leavers included increased awareness (47%) and improved behaviour (33%), whilst gains included greater tolerance (9%), ability to control emotions (10.5%), ability to avoid violence (7%), being more determined (5%) and remaining drug-free (3.5%). It seems plausible that tangible gains are more difficult to achieve, hence their lower frequency, but also these are the potentially crime-reducing behaviours, i.e. addressing criminogenic need. This mirrors the TC approach, in which initially treatment sets out to explore general psychological difficulties and only thereafter does the treatment focus shift towards exploring residents' criminogenic needs (Shine and Morris, 2000). Most of these former residents had less than the optimal 18 months in the TC, and possibly the TC process had yet to address their criminogenic needs.

In terms of the more negative experiences, it could be that this is a real reflection of the staff difficulties at an institutional level, for example, staff training issues or turnover. Alternatively, it is possible that the ex-residents made assumptions about therapy and the therapeutic milieu that do not fit the TC model. TC staff aim to work "alongside" the TC member (Barnes et al., 1997; Griffiths and Hinshelwood, 1997), so care is not provided in the traditional sense, but, rather, in helping the individual to become a carer for himself. If the person cannot make this transition, it might be easier to project any difficulties on shortcomings of the TC and its institutional arrangements.

Psychometric indicators

For residents who had dropped out at the very initial stages of therapy, i.e. between baseline and five months, some positive changes were still observable. There were notable decreases in passive aggression levels (CPAI). Another measure of aggression, the Ramas Anger Assessment Profile (RAAP), also showed that high proportions of these ex-residents showed significant decreases, particularly in terms of self-reported assaultative behaviours. In terms of clinically significant shifts, only control of anger, as assessed by the RAAP, and relatedly in the internalisation of general Locus of Control of Behaviour (LCB), represented movements into or within score ranges expected from non-offending populations.

The ex-residents who remained in therapy for between 6 and 11 months were more likely than the earlier drop-outs to show changes in their propensity to report offending-supportive cognitions (PICTS-4 Psychological Inventory of Criminal Thinking Styles, version 4), primarily reflecting a decrease in such thinking styles. Anger, as assessed by both the RAAP and CPAI, showed some change. The *Control* of anger indicator on the RAAP showed more clinically meaningful change than was the case with the earlier drop-outs, with 40% of the participating sample showing statistically significant change into or within normal ranges. The *Consequence* and *Attitude* scales also showed clinical improvement, albeit in much smaller proportions of the sample. The internalisation of the *Locus of Control of Behaviour* showed improvement in this group of former residents.

Residents who made it through to one year of therapy but left before reaching the important 18 months of participation showed similar patterns of change to the earlier drop-outs. Although no change was evident on the locus of control measure (Locus of Control Behaviour (LCB)), there was evidence amongst some of these longer-surviving residents of a decrease in criminal thinking styles (PICTS-4). Not all sub-scales on the RAAP showed significant change, but almost all that did were in a positive direction, reflecting a decrease in anger and related issues. However, none of these statistically significant changes represented clinically meaningful improvements. Box 9.1 summarises the key findings related to premature leavers.

Box 9.1   Key findings related to early leavers

- Four conceptually distinct reflections were identified:
  therapeutic change, regret, resistance and rejection
- *Therapeutic changes* were reported by many early leavers, challenging the notion that only those who adhere to and graduate from the full-term TC achieve therapeutic gains.
- Few early leavers reported singular *gains* which were criminogenic in nature, but the longer the stay the more likely these are to be addressed.
- Problems with staff as a reason for leaving was interpreted as a possible "lack of fit" between expectations of therapy and the reality of the TC or a possible reflection of actual problems with staff, such as lack of training.
- De-selected residents showed more resistance involving an apparent inability to deal with the processes of the TC and externalised their blame attributions, whereas the resistance of residents who asked to leave (48-hour group) was manifest by expressions of regret and taking responsibility for departure by acknowledging avoidance of their problems.
- Some sustainability of therapeutic gains was demonstrable through the psychometric evidence, particularly controlling anger.

TC graduates

The therapeutic spiral

This analysis is drawn from Simmonds' (2008) post-Dovegate interviews with 30 Dovegate residents who had remained in therapy for at least 18 months. These interviews took place after they had been discharged from Dovegate and returned to mainstream prisons. In piecing together these reported experiences, there were three interlocking clusters and milestones of achievement that seemed to allow the resident to make progress. In constructing this model, it appeared that, rather than linear, it was a circular process; although a spiral might be a better way to describe what seemed to be happening, i.e. a resident might achieve a certain degree of insight by working his way through these stages and, with that heightened awareness, move through the cycle again, so that there was a forward propulsion to gaining deeper self-knowledge and acquisition of resources to deal with issues. The diagram in Figure 9.2 illustrates this. The darker boxes are indicative of therapeutic processes and the smaller boxes therapeutic gains.

Learning to talk and forming a strong therapeutic alliance

Initiating self disclosure, accessing emotions and gaining a level of self awareness is difficult, especially for people not used to talking about or accessing their feelings and whose emotional vocabulary may be limited. The following excerpt illustrates what this can feel like:

> disclosing to other people caused me a hell of a lot of grief inside myself but it also generated a strength through the care and warmth of people in the therapeutic community.

This resident explained how painful it was to disclose his abuse in the group and how he managed to cope with that trauma and became stronger through the support he received in his TC. In a peer group TC, trust is one of the essential ingredients for building strong therapeutic alliances, as explained by the following resident:

> at first you haven't really got the confidence to speak in front of the group. When you go in a room and there is forty people it is hard to talk about yourself in front of so many people, especially when you don't know them. So you have got to build up a trust first before you bring certain important things about yourself or your family to everyone else but as time goes on and you see other people doing it, you gain their trust, even though at times it does get abused you can say certain things in a group and then outside a group or inside a group someone might try and throw that back at you and try to hurt you.

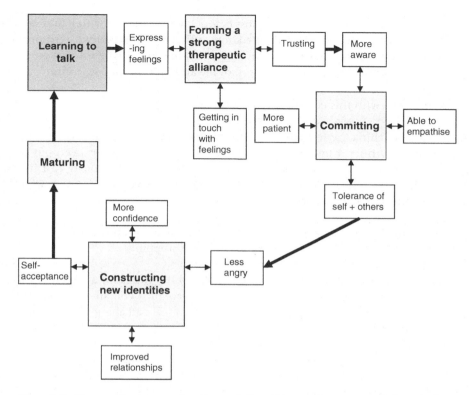

Figure 9.2 The residents' construction of the therapeutic process (adapted from Simmonds, 2008)

Bordin (1979, p. 110) draws attention to how the therapeutic alliance is "the ingredient that enables the client to engage in therapy and to persevere through its difficult stages." Difficulties in forming a therapeutic alliance may disrupt this cycle of accessing and exposing emotions and trust-building. As the resident increases emotional exposure he gains a level of self-knowledge and awareness. This is often revealed through how he perceives others see him. Failure to manage the process of revealing a damaged self often led residents to exit the community, as seen in this following extract from a resident who left after six months:

> To be honest, I think at the time I were still finding the sentence hard because I were immature as well, I didn't have a good head on my shoulders and I'd been abused in my childhood – physically and sexually. Now it were easy for me to talk about the physical abuse, coz it were from my father, yeah? I struggled with the sexual abuse because it were from a male care-worker and

I'd never told anyone before and just before I left I come out with it and said that I'd been abused and I didn't know... that were "unknown territory" if you will and my head were all over... I didn't know where I was going with... and that and it all got on top of me and I found it easier to run.

Contrast this with this comment from a therapy stayer

Actually I think my feelings and emotions and that... I have a real problem with everything. I understand it now, but only because it has been put to me bluntly. You're just nothing if you've got no feelings, you re just like a robot you just don't care about other people 'cos you don't know what you're feeling like yourself.

As residents become more aware of why they engaged in criminal behaviour, their insights enable them to make choices about stopping

"I was in on the drug culture and all of that. I do things for acceptance off people I respected... so when you become aware of it you are able to break the cycle, you're able to go 'alright I'll do this, I feel bad about it and I don't need to do it and you can stop"

For therapy to work, access to emotions and a strong, supportive therapeutic alliance are critical if the resident is to gain insights into the why of their offending. By and large, this tended to develop within the first six months of therapy, when there was relatively little measurable change (as revealed through the psychometric measures) but the ground work was being established for either progression or premature exit.

As one of Bobsien's research participants said

"Its hard to know how it works... you start to feel more confident... its kinda weird 'cos things like fit into place... its little things that click into place. You can point out things that you are aware of about yourself and that you see in other people that they might not see about themselves, so you can say 'Hey look we've got the same things in common and I found out that this was the reason why I do this. What's your reason why you do it?."

Another commented

"When you first come on the wing... it seems negative... that you are dealing with feelings dealing with emotions and now it's a positive thing. I mean there are still some people here now that think you're talking shite if you talk about your feelings but in time the'll see because it's easier to slag someone off for speaking your feelings than it is to speak about your own in the early stages."

Commitment

"For therapeutic communities, the commitment vote is the ultimate therapeutic tool" (Cullen and Miller, 2010, p. 39). This was the mechanism at Dovegate whereby residents could be put on notice that they needed to change or be excluded from therapy. Underpinning commitment was motivation to continue or exit. Studies on the role of motivation in programme retention have emphasized the interaction between motivation and treatment process. Melnick et al. (2001, p634) argue that "motivation is correlated with more favourable perceptions of counsellor competence and support from peers". Their proposed model of programme participation was based on a feedback loop between motivation and treatment process in which "higher motivation leads to greater participation, participation leads to progress, and progress sustains higher motivation" (p. 635). One resident illustrates this loop:

> Yeah definitely, probably half the people there [thought they would do therapy to help their sentence plan]. When I first went there that was why I went there. I didn't have the right intentions when I went in there, if I was to tell the truth but after a while you kind of get into it.

This suggests that instrumental forms of motivation can be changed by participation in therapy. This resident stayed in therapy for 18 months.

However, it is important to remember that one of the aims of the TC is to dismantle the values, beliefs and behaviours that constitute a criminal identity so that positive change can take place. If residents are managing two identities in the TC, therapeutic and criminal, it is more difficult for that change to take place.

Residents who engaged with the therapeutic process articulated a new-found sense of others and an ability to empathise:

> I don't think I thought about it really you know, I know that I created a victim but that is all I thought about I never thought about the victim's side or even my side. It never entered my mind really and then I started getting into things and I started to realise what damage I had done...I have just found out more about myself you know I didn't create one victim, I created a load of victims and I learnt that, which I never thought about before, not only my family, but my victim's family, all the way down the line.

The gateway to the next therapeutic milestone seemed to be an increased tolerance. By connecting with their own feelings and by being enabled to take the perspectives of others, residents learnt how to be less judgemental and more accepting, again another indicator of more positive attachment style, as the following extracts illustrate:

> I learned how to tolerate people that I don't really get on with or people that I do not usually associate myself with.

> I learnt to be a lot more tolerant of people in TC. Both the staff and residents but I'd already made that decision that I had to change...

Constructing new identities and maturing

As time in therapy increased, so too did self-confidence, and, when this was associated with a measure of self-acceptance, residents seemed able to let the mask slip and don a new identity.

> Before going into therapy you know I had a lot of that mask thing because you know I spent a lot of time in dispersal prisons but since then I don't think I wear a mask and this is me and that's it. I don't feel like I need to wear a mask, now I look back I didn't need to wear one at that time either but I didn't know then what I know now. You know I think I get on better with people now than I did before because when you wear the mask people don't really know you, they are just assuming things about yer. I think it has allowed me to see that being meself is better for me than going around pretending that I am something I am not and putting silly acts on.

The extract above tells a story of someone who has changed his coping strategy from a performance approach to one based on being himself. The resident now appears to have the confidence to act in a way that is consistent with who he is and what his values are. The resident also comments that being "true to himself" has helped him relate to others, which is one of the goals of therapy in the TC.

In the following exchange another resident explained why some prisoners find it hard to drop their masks and be themselves:

> Ex-Resident: ... well it is about image and people have a certain image and it takes a long time for them to drop that image, some of them do it and some of them don't.
> RSr: Is that like wearing a mask?
> Ex-Resident: Yes, it is hard to completely drop it because you are making yourself vulnerable in front of everybody and shows people what is the real you.

This extract also draws attention to how divulging personal fears and weaknesses can feel very uncomfortable. In the TC, residents are encouraged to "reveal themselves" in a supportive and caring environment made more possible when the therapeutic alliance is strong and therapeutic milieu is positive. With the support of these therapeutic processes, residents can learn that being themselves is OK as long as they are honest and are motivated to understand and control their offending behaviour. When therapeutic alliances are working well and a resident is motivated to change, revealing vulnerabilities can lead to self-acceptance and the confidence to "be oneself".

Bearing these points in mind, one ex-resident reflected how therapeutic processes had affected his beliefs about the merits of being true to himself, saying:

> In therapy it's about your own efforts and it's about seeing other people change and wanting that for yourself as well and at the end of the day when you are sitting on groups and listening to people. At the end of the day we all want the same anyway. We don't want to walk around with these masks on, we want to be ourselves and be comfortable with who we are.

Learning to recognise and accept oneself is a key part of personal and socio-emotional growth. Having the strength and confidence to drop the posturing in exchange for reconstructing a "good" self is a mark of success at this stage in the therapeutic spiral.

Managing anger is also part of the process:

> Hardest thing I've ever done in my life. To be honest though I think if they were easy they wouldn't be worth doing. I think, um, I'm amazed within myself how clued-up I've got and how I can hold a conversation, how I can identify with people and everything. A whole lot of things. And that's all through therapy. Honestly, when I come in I were a 21 year old, imma- ture...and anger...I were probably the angriest person on earth, in my opinion [laughs]. But now I don't feel angry.

Increased levels of self-awareness and self-confidence also helped residents to adopt more assertive styles of interaction, rather than overly passive or aggressive approaches, as illustrated in the following excerpts:

> It's like if I've got a disagreement with someone on the wing and there was a confrontation between us I've got to sort that out there and then because if I don't sort it out I know what it's going to be, it's going to eat me up so I've got to deal with it. As soon as a problem arises now I deal with it, whereas before I wouldn't and it'd build up and then weeks would go past and then one and then another one and then another one and before you know it boom...you open up and you explode. But now I deal with a problem as it

arises, I'm not saying it's perfect but it gives me peace of mind, you know what I mean, and that's the way I deal with things.

This resident gives a neat summary of the kinds of personal changes that can occur and identifies some of the processes involved.

I mean, in a nutshell you become more of a balanced person. You see, trauma is corrosive, and for me therapy was... it enables you to bring every-thing together... you do grow in confidence, you do grow in awareness, you do grow in sort of, intellectual ability, understanding ability, you know, recognising all of the things that will bring you down, masks, cognitive distortions, all these aspects.

When asked to reflect on changes that might have been made, there was evi-dence of a developing maturity and a realisation of growth that had enabled the resident to recognise positive changes.

I've never felt like this, the way I've felt I mean I've had my ups and I've had my downs but I'm forty-two years of age now, my parents are old age pensioners, you know I'm seeing my nieces and my nephews, they're all growing up and I ain't there. But you know, its just like I said before, there's a time in your life when you've got to say enough is enough and regardless of what people say... I'm never going to portray myself as being some kind of an angel because I'm far from it, but I'm going to try my damned hardest to, you know, to not return back to another prison. I've been doing this for twenty-seven years, I've had enough. There's a time in your life when you say "enough's enough" and that time in my life has come and I've had enough.

Interestingly, there is supportive evidence from the psychometric data that demonstrates positive change by residents completing at the 18-month stage of therapy. On almost every scale many of these former residents showed improve-ments on their baseline scores by the six-month post-TC follow-up assessment, particularly in terms of drops in criminal thinking styles (PICTS-4) and the varied forms of aggression tested (RAAP and CPAI). Other changes are also apparent, such as in interpersonal functioning, as assessed by the Chart of Inter-personal Reaction in Closed Living Environments (CIRCLE). For the residents who reach either 12- or 18-month points in therapy, there are, furthermore, common indications of desistance in propensity to adopt offending-supportive cognitions or to poorly handle feelings of anger. This is an interesting contrast to the early drop-outs, who seemed to make less progress on their criminogenic needs.

Reintegration strategies

Many participants reported a sense of shock on returning to a mainstream prison and found reintegration hard.

> It were bit like a lunatic asylum when I come back here [*mainstream prison*], seriously, everyone was running around at five million miles an hour just chasing up and down, grafting and wanting to buy stuff, sell stuff, swap stuff. It were just like being in a main street somewhere in a city centre somewhere, seriously it was all too much it was all Speedy Gonzales for me it was all too much, it were happening too fast. Everyone is in your face and running off and in and out, whereas at Dovegate it was really relaxed, everyone was all right and ambled about and you went for your work and you come back, you did your groups, your time out, you relaxed and you know all that type of thing but it wasn't like that at all when I come back here. And it were a dirty depressing place when I come back you know they put me in this cell with four really big spiders on the roof and all lights off and gloomy it were like going back to dungeon days before you get strung or hung or something. It weren't good.

One of the key elements of their experiences centred on "talking", a central plank of the TC process. Some residents completing therapy missed the conversations they had had in the TC, whilst others reported being able to use improved communication skills in mainstream prisons to seek help for themselves when needed. This help seeking behaviour is an integral part of forming positive attachments (see discussion in the previous chapter). Furthermore, the typical topics of conversation between prisoners in a mainstream prison were focused on "how many" ... robberies, fights and sexual conquests they had had. As Simmons (2008, p.66) says: "This kind of 'one-upmanship' discursive strategy is indicative of a macho prison culture where manliness is associated with aggressive domination, power and virility that can be coercive and hierarchical in nature". This is opposite to the egalitarian notions of a democratic TC and its focus on dealing with emotional content.

Being transferred from a TC to a mainstream prison can be a stressful experience for many prisoners (Sullivan, 2011). Our Dovegate graduates seem to use several reintegration strategies, which Simmons (2008) suggested is either a performance approach to reintegration or a value-consistent approach. Some try to retain their Dovegate identity outwardly and to be congruent with their TC acquired interior sense of self. Others also retain an interior identity but adopt a false persona in order to fit in with the mainstream prison culture. Table 9.2 provides some detailed examples of the strategies adopted.

Ex-residents claiming that they did not put on a performance on returning to mainstream prisons, preferring to "be themselves", seemed to have a few more

Table 9.2 Re-integration strategies adopted by ex-residents (adapted from Simmons, 2008)

Strategy	Commentary	Example
Performing	Some participants were able to manage reintegration into a mainstream prison by calling upon their previous experience of "how to perform" in some mainstream cultures. Ex-residents know how to "do" mainstream by wearing a false persona, even if they did not feel this reflected the way they now wanted to think or behave.	*[I]n mainstream prisons, umm, they kind of look at a place like Dovegate as a place where mainly sex offenders and stuff go. So I was a bit wary when I come to a normal prison and they say "where have you come from?" and you say "Dovegate" they assume straight away... and you have kind of got to come onto the wing with a bit of a swagger about you and then they don't..., be cause sex offenders are very quiet and they stay out of the way and they kind of walk along the wing with their heads bowed towards the floor and like and you can tell straight away if someone has come from Dovegate and they are like that, pretty much you know what they are in for... (Participant 63: 12-month assessment in TC)*
Masking	Mainstream prison culture was less predictable and more violent than TC culture. Under these circumstances the wearing of a mainstream prison "mask" seems to serve a protective function.	*That's exactly what it is, it's safe isn't it, on a community you don't need that because it is a community but when you are mixing with the rest of prison as well you have got to have two faces.*
Therapeuton	Being able to recognise the kind of maladaptive thinking and behaviour that could be addressed through therapy but being in an environment where these cannot be addressed in a positive way. Indeed, sense of identity is compromised by this experience.	*I come here as a "therapeuton", as they like to call us, and you're very therapy orientated, you spot everybody's mistakes, you know where everybody's going wrong, and you try to help everybody... Because you've got the answers, you know what's wrong. And then you sort of have to go back down to their level. And I think coming back down to that level, it's very difficult for most people to sort of maintain the therapeutic sort of stance, in an environment where it's sort of skulduggery, thuggery and buggery and people projecting their hurt and pain, and you find yourself back in a negative, very negative environment, from what was a really positive environment. And that's very hard to bear. That's very hard to bear.*

Sustaining a Dovegate identity	Some residents did seem able to sustain the identity work they achieved in Dovegate. Others found this more difficult.	*I suppose here … No I don't believe I do wear a mask here. I think I'm quite the person I am, really. I don't pretend to be anything I'm not. I am who I am.* *When I come back here I struggled quite a lot. I struggled with, erm, criminal mentality, you know, because I'd managed to break that kind of thing … I really did struggle coming back to all this skulduggery … all the drugs, all the deceit. It did do my head in, quite literally.*

problems in the early stages of reintegration because they tended to act according to internal values rather than social expectations. These men appeared to be more self-confident and assertive than the performance men and less influenced by a desire to relate back into macho constructions of masculinity.

Positive changes attributed to TC involvement

When talking about their experiences of reintegration to mainstream prisons, in the interviews, quite often ex-residents realised that they had changed through re-encountering their pre-Dovegate TC selves.

I left here [present mainstream prison] to come to Dovegate originally, so soon as I come back there is still the same people here "have you got any drugs, have you got em"? and they were all asking me this type of question and I looked at meself and said "I don't want that at the moment" and I looked at meself and thought "that was me" before I went to Dovegate.

Many ex-TC residents spoke about specific as well as general changes they felt they had made as a result of being in Dovegate TC. The most frequently mentioned changes were: improved communication skills, increased self-confidence, more tolerance of others, decreased anger, increased victim awareness/empathy and improved ability to trust others. Other changes included: improved relationships with family members, abstinence from drugs or alcohol (where this had been a problem) and increased levels of maturity. Table 9.3 provides some examples.

Sustaining positive change in a mainstream prison

Ex-residents who talked about having made positive changes in Dovegate TC also spoke about how they were managing to maintain these in a mainstream environment. They reported asking staff for help (help-seeking behaviour), being cautious about who they mixed with in prison (more discerning in their associates), keeping focused on improving their circumstances by doing courses

Table 9.3   Examples of positive changes (adapted from Simmons, 2008)

Experiences	Example
Expressing feelings	*My sort of thing is, I will feel a bit depressed, I'd go for a drink and think I've been for a drink now, I'm drunk, let's go and burgle a house, I'd burgle one house and before I know it I've done a hundred within a space of a month and then I'm out of control but I think I've gained enough insight into my behaviour to, kind of, before it gets to that stage, if I ever get to that stage again that is and even, I might not think like that again, but I know what I've got to do, if I start feeling down and depressed, I've got to go to my probation team or my support network and say "This is how I'm feeling and these are the feelings I got before, before I got into trouble last time." And I've got to tell them how I'm feeling, that's gonna work for me, everybody's different but I think what's gonna work for me is talking and saying this is how I feel . . .*
Asking for help	*That's what I found so bizarre, when you want help ask for help. I was struggling to ask for help. If I had got a problem I wouldn't even sit down with a counsellor. But what I do now . . . if I . . . I deal with a situation . . . if something arises I deal with that problem there and then . . .*
Ability to listen	*Yeah what I have tended to do is listen more and I was a bit more supportive to people and you know talk them out of dealing with their problems in a stupid way and give them different options to look at and give them different ideas of how to go about solving something*

and planning for their release, helping other prisoners with problems where appropriate, nurturing improved family relationships, and pursuing religious and spiritual activities (pro-social activities).

The issue of drugs was a very strong theme throughout the interviews with ex-TC residents, and one of the biggest stumbling blocks for men returning to mainstream prisons appeared to be the "abundance" of drugs available and the pressure to become involved in a drugs culture.

Some ex-residents spoke about how relationships with family members had improved since going to the TC and how focusing on nurturing these improvements had helped them sustain positive changes generally. The following ex-resident talked about how a traumatic event in his family had given him the motivation to sustain change. He reflected:

I can only speak for myself, you know, and this has been a rocky road for me, this whole thing. My sister was only 35 when she died and I found it really hard. A couple of years back, I just, I would've reacted totally different to the way I'm reacting now. Whereas I'm thinking about the family, I'm thinking about the kids, you know, I can cope, I can feel, I can understand that she's gone and she's not coming back. But I've got a family there that fell apart and they need someone there to support them, and that's it, that's the role that I'm taking…That's what Dovegate's given me, it's given me an inner strength. Well, I've given it myself basically.

In the excerpt above this ex-resident talks about how he plans to support his dead sister's children when he is released from prison. He claims that he is now able to think about the welfare of others and is strong enough to cope with a supportive role in relation to his sister's family.

Another ex-resident talked about the positive changes that had taken place for him within a broader context of family relationships. He said:

It [Dovegate TC] has made me think a lot more, it has made me like…I had a lot of problems with me family and that and my mother and that and our relationships weren't too clever so now I can talk to them about it, think about me own feelings and talk to me family and things like that errh it has made me think about the consequences more errh that is really it, I have got a lot more patience, a lot more tolerance for people, me aims and goals are a lot different now errh I am more realistic about things, I don't really want to get involved in the same kind of stuff that I used to.

This excerpt paints a picture of someone who has used his time in Dovegate TC to understand his background and himself.

Some former residents spoke about maintaining therapeutic change in terms of their personal identity, illustrated by the following example:

I could have "dissolved". But I didn't. My morals are still present, I still do believe that people should respect each other, treat each other how they wish to be treated. But, I don't try and push that onto other people. That's up to them. What I learnt at Dovegate, I still hold, I've still got. Adamantly, I've sharpened my tools so I can go on a different approach, sort of thing. But my morals are still the same.

In this extract the interviewee talks about therapeutically informed beliefs, values and morals as constituting the core of his identity. He appears confident in his beliefs and to have the ability to adapt to prison life without compromising his deeper values.

We have summarised the key findings in relation to the therapy completers in Box 9.2. This indicates that ingredients of success are strong therapeutic alliance, strong staff support and a strong internal motivation to change.

Box 9.2 Key findings related to therapy completers

- Successful participants seemed to develop a deeper understanding about the reality of therapy than shorter stay residents. Although they acknowledged that support was available in the TC, successful participants concluded that therapy was essentially a lonely and difficult journey, that only they could take.
- Key to successfully engaging therapy is a strong therapeutic alliance, both in therapy groups and in the TC milieu. Factors that undermine and weaken alliances may contribute to early drop out rates, impede the therapeutic progress of residents and may also impact negatively on the mental health of men who are not supported adequately in therapy, when disclosing traumatic life events.
- TC staff are a vital ingredient in the formation of attachments and therapeutic alliances. Improvements in staff retention through better recruitment, training and remuneration should provide improved continuity in attachment relationships that is often missing from the early lives of residents and is so important for improving the socioemotional development of men in therapy.
- Returning to mainstream prisons was experienced as a shock by most participants. It was often at this point that men realized how much they had changed and this surprised some interviewees; not being able to 'talk' like they did in the TC was one of the main issues cited in the interviews. From the analysis of personal transformations that participants attributed to the TC, it can be seen that talking was the key to a number of personal changes.
- On re-integration to mainstream prisons successful and longer stay participants seemed to have gained a different sense of personal and social identity. Longer stay ex-residents participants also seemed to have gained the confidence to be themselves and act according to their values, rather than adopting a mainstream prison mask.

Conclusion

By valuing participants' accounts of their own experiences, feelings and meaning-making and by treating them as lay "experts" in the TC experience, the interviews elicited some valuable insights about the relationships between institutional, (inter)personal and therapeutic processes, criminal values and therapeutic change, the quality of motivation and the reality of therapy, and how these factors coalesce with each individual resident in their journey through the TC and back into mainstream prison.

Issues of concern about the TC, such as insincere residents, sex offenders, lax selection procedures, bullying, drugs, TC staff turnover and issues of sentence progression, were shared by the majority of ex-residents and *should not* be totally attributed to therapeutic problems (such as negative transference). More help and support are needed for residents with a history of substance abuse/addiction issues, and sex offenders would also benefit from some extra support, perhaps in the form of a sex offender treatment programme. As many residents have to complete offending-related courses as part of their sentence plans, such as those addressing substance abuse and sexual crimes, the provision of these courses may help to retain residents who would otherwise leave the TC.

Admitting unsuitable men to the TC works against the formation of strong therapeutic alliances, and the presence of insincerely motivated men seems to demoralize residents who are taking therapy seriously. Improved selection procedures could help to better target men who are likely to benefit from therapy whilst improving drop-out rates and continuity of attachments in the TC.

Finally, a participant sums up the TC experience as follows:

You know in the old days when you got the knights and they fight the dragons, right. We are all the knights and we're going down the forest and all of a sudden someone is sending the dragons in ... and its grabbed hold of a few of us and had a struggle with a few others before that. That's the kind of way I see it. The certain issues are the dragons and they're delving between us trying to break us up. I think the forest is growing stronger now and we're all sort of fighting them off. But we still get a few dodgy knights with big swords stabbing each other in the back so the dragons got an easier meal . . . . But a lot of people help each other and give each other a pat on the back and saying to someone 'well done' so they give them the courage to do it again. Some of us have got strong enough to say 'Now listen we don't want your dragons' so the dragons have to go and find somewhere else that is weak. Your mood changes day to day, I mean like today is a pretty shite day because we've had all these meetings and there was all sorts of rubbish being chucked about when the dodgy knights are avoiding the real issues so another day is wonderful, everyone is getting on with each other and you feel wow this is good why can't it be like this all the time?

10
Back in the Outside World: Case Studies of Former Residents on Release

Introduction

We followed up ex-residents after release from prison and who were in the care of the Probation Service to gain their reflections on their Dovegate experiences. Participants in this part of the study were approached and agreed to be interviewed by Emily Cahalane.[1] What follows is a summary of her findings and commentary and includes extracts from six of the interviews she conducted. Pseudonyms are used and some details redacted to preserve the anonymity of the participants.

Emily drew on the psychometric data that had been previously collected on these former Dovegate residents by the research team. She conducted a further administration of a selection of these tests as part of her data collection. Space precludes giving a detailed account of all the measures, so here we provide a descriptive account of the insights offered by these former residents in their interviews. The full data are available in Cahalane (2006). The ex-resident's current probation officer conducted an additional Chart of Interpersonal Reactions in Closed Living Environments (CIRCLE) assessment and these results are presented alongside the CIRCLE data collected whilst the person was in Dovegate. File data were consulted in order to provide some background information about the former resident.

Bill's story

I've been in and out of prison since the age of 14 so you know, prison was just a regular thing. It got to the stage where it was just a way of life. It weren't no big drama going to prison. Going to prison at the age of 14, in a detention centre, like a boot camp, where it was like army training and it was really strict. I come out there at 14 and I felt society owed me somat. Coming out of that detention centre it was like I'd lost something. They'd took something off me; my youth or something. I just felt society owed me and that led me to committing crime.

186

Once I got this four and a half year sentence I decided I wasn't going to sit back like every other sentence I'd done and take it, you know I was going to get something out of it and that's what led me to Dovegate. I'd reached the stage where I had to do whatever, I needed to do to, you know, to change. You've got to hit that rock bottom, for me I had to for it to work. I was prepared to do anything to straighten my life out, to change my thought patterns and everything.

Box 10.1   Bill

Bill is white, 38 years old and British. His file stated that he has one daughter; however, during the interview he also mentioned having a son. He is divorced from the mother of his children and currently lives with his girlfriend. Offending commenced at an early age with his first conviction at 14, when he was sent to a detention centre. The index offence leading to the sentence which brought him to Dovegate was attempted kidnap and affray, for which he was sentenced to four years and six months. Bill has 32 recorded preconvictions, including several for assault, affray, ABH, GBH, theft, drug offences, weapon offences, arson and resisting arrest. His education was limited, leaving school at 15 years with no qualifications. However, in prison he has received Oxford, Cambridge and Royal Society of Arts (OCR) English Literature, Computer skills and Business Studies. He has a history of unstable employment, and has not held a regular job since he was 16 when he was made redundant. He has experienced bouts of depression since the age of 15. When sentenced Bill attempted suicide and consequently spent four weeks in a psychiatric unit and was prescribed anti-depressants for three months. Bill experienced extensive physical abuse in childhood and felt caught in the middle of a violent relationship between his parents. Substance misuse has been a large part of Bill's life: alcohol use from 14 years old, the file reported Bill as a heroin user, cocaine for the past ten years and glue from 14. Bill spent 20 months in Dovegate TC and was transferred to an addiction centre before his ultimate release.

In prison I'd mainly worked on the crime which was, well definitely for me and I think a big percentage of the prison, was that it ain't just about crime, it's about drugs as well. There's no point half doing the job you know, just saying all right then I won't do crime no more but I'll carry on taking drugs. It won't work. While I was in Dovegate I was always looking ahead. It's up to you if you really want you divulge into some really traumatic experience its up to you, you don't get forced into it but the more you talk about it the more it gives you a chance to deal with it. When I first got there and they started being over friendly, I was very suspicious and it took a bit of time to get my head round that you know it is very different, its not the same as normal prison and once I had adjusted to that you know the staff were over helpful.

When I was using drugs and committing crime I was a very selfish person. I didn't care about anybody else. By the time I left Dovegate I knew it was up to me, it was my fault not others but that I could cope and not let the guilt get me down but use that knowledge to help myself.

I've progressed to getting my own flat and I've got my car, and it's going really well for me. I ain't involved in crime, I ain't getting in trouble and you know I ain't taking drugs. And that's what it comes down to what I leant there. A big part of it was what I learnt in the rehab as well. I've used them both. I couldn't have done one without the other. I'm very grateful for my time in Dovegate.

I even went back to Dovegate and did a speech in front of 40 of them. I knew them all as well. I went back about three months after I got released and it was brilliant and the talk actually gave, you know, a lot of people got a lot out of it. They knew me, they knew what I was like, a few people thought yea you'll get out and straight away you'll mess it up and be back to how you were but it gave a lot of people quite a lot of hope because you know, they lived with me for 19 months so they knew about me, they knew what I was like.

I wouldn't want to commit crime now and I was a prolific offender for years and years, but because I've been able to take that step back and take a look at myself and not being too pleased about what I saw, like about the type of crime that I'd committed and the people that I'd hurt. That was a big thing for me, to be able to take a step back and have a look at myself. Every other time I've been released from prison it's been like I've been kicked out the gates, thrown back into society and not been able to cope with no support. And because I wasn't able to cope, then I turned to drugs and then eventually the drugs have leaded to crime and then you know it's a vicious circle. [Named town] was a big problem for me, you know, I'd go back time and time again. When I was in Dovegate I could think clear and see the mistakes I had made. I could see it had been a mistake keep going back to [named town]. It's just not for me even going to [named town]

I'm 38 now. I've had enough. It was a God send that I got four and a half years because today I'm glad that I got that sentence, I really am because otherwise I still would've got a couple of years and I would've been drifting about. I definitely would still be involved with crime and taking drugs. Definitely.

Bill's precontemplation for change was high when he first went into Dovegate, and increased again prior to his release. He described prison had become "a way of life" and that it had taken his latest sentence to catalyse the desire to change. Bill went on to report his determination to stay "clean" in society and how, through his own motivation, he went to a drug rehabilitation centre. Bill indicated he was "prepared to do anything to straighten my life out". The action sub-scale on the stages of change measure was congruent with his claim of wishing to engage in active change, and he succeeded in learning to live in an environment where drugs were readily available and gain the strength to resist reverting to drug taking. In his post-release interview, he reports how much his life has changed for the better, how he is finally happy and how far crime and drugs are behind him.

Further analysis of Bill's psychometric scores showed that, by the time he left Dovegate, his internal guilt attributions had increased and external attributions decreased. Bill described in his interview how he accepted that his offending was his own fault and he could not blame his chosen lifestyle on anyone else, but that he learnt to cope with the guilt and chose to turn his life around, identifying his need for support to aid this and using the support he was offered. He not only showed a decrease in his criticism of others, but also an increase in self-criticism and guilt, which were highlighted in his own account, when he emphasised how he grew and gained respect for others, and the abhorrence he had of his past (Figure 10.1).

Bill was regarded highly by the staff at HMP Dovegate and subsequently by his probation officer. The scoring of the CIRCLE highlights this, and, despite the lack of statistically significant change, this measure does highlight Bill's compliance in Dovegate. The three main positive sub-scales, compliance, nurturance and gregariousness, are scored highly across Bill's time in Dovegate, with each of these scores nearing the maximum (maximum scores are 27, 15 and 15 consecutively). Comparatively, the negative sub-scales are scored as

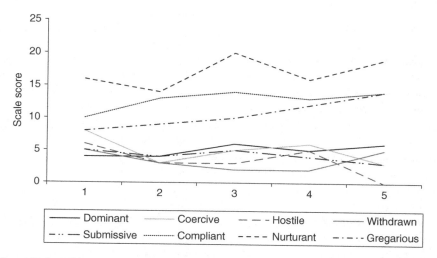

Figure 10.1   Bill's CIRCLE psychometric scores across time (baseline (1), 6 months (2), 12 months (3), 18 months (4) and a follow-up one year later (5))

low. These positive scores are supported by Bill's own account of his time at
Dovegate, disclosing his acceptance of the therapeutic community (TC) rules,
caring for others and working with staff.

Niles' story

Box 10.2   Niles

Niles is a 28-year-old, single, white British male with learning difficulties.
His first conviction was at 19 years of age and his reported number of
preconvictions is 14. He has served two previous sentences. His convictions are all drug-related. Niles' index offence was possession of Class
A drugs with intent to sell, receiving a sentence of five years and six
months. It was within this sentence that he came into contact with
Dovegate TC, being admitted after serving one year and seven months of
this sentence. He has no history of mental illness or deliberate self-harm
and has received no psychological treatment. His drug misuse history is
extensive, having abused an abundance of illicit substances throughout
his life. He currently reports no dependency. Niles spent ten months in
the TC, leaving after being de-selected. He was advised to complete an
ETS (Enhanced Thinking Skills) and R&R (Reasoning and Rehabilitation)
programme when back in mainstream prison. Niles stated that he had
undertaken and completed R&R. He has since been recalled into custody.

---

*If I did go back to jail I would like to go to a therapeutic but not Dovegate, Grendon
or something. I've done all the courses you know R&R and stuff, those courses and
they've never worked in the past so I thought well I'll go to this therapeutic. It's a good
choice, but it was the wrong choice for me. As soon as I got there it weren't working.
Some of the things you don't prepare yourself for it. When you get there and it's all
there, it's too much to handle. I was ready, I wanted to change, that's why I went there,
but after a while I just gave up. I got on with some of the residents; I didn't really get
on with any of the staff. You had to work in groups and to be truthful it was a lot of
hard work, it's not easy. At the end of the day it [the TC] made it worse, they just kept
nagging at me.*

*I kept giving it a go but in the end it was just a waste of my time – But after a bit
I just couldn't be bothered with it. You know it's just a break from jail really that's all,
and I just used it as that, as like a holiday camp. I didn't want to be there no more.
I wanna make it on my own. I don't want people breathing down my neck.*

*My plans were exactly what I went there to do, to better myself and get my D cat,
to work on getting out – an open jail, and I got that anyway, on my own, with no*

help from them. So I could've done it anyway. So I still achieved the stuff I wanted to achieve on my own. It pushed me more to do it.

I have started meeting people, but that's only one of the problems. When you get out here there are lots of things facing you. You know, I was doing a lot of drugs before and so I didn't really bother about problems but when you're not on drugs they're all hitting on you. It's hard work. I go out and stuff. Unless something proper happens soon, I could see me going back. I can't say I'll never go back to crime but I don't wanna go back.

I've never been like this, at the minute I'm a bit down so, when before I'm used to having money, I'm used to having this and that, now I'm proper struggling.

I'm in a hostel at the moment and I keep myself away from them all. I just wanted to be left alone. I wanna just do it on my own and I know there's support there if I need it. I don't like probation (Figure 10.2).

Niles' compliance with the research team was sporadic, so the available psychometric data were at base and 12 months and the post-release follow-up. His psychometric scores, his presentation at the interview and his account of his experience at Dovegate indicated he found Dovegate very difficult. He had spent ten months in the TC when he was de-selected. The data collected, including Niles' own account, suggest he had low motivation, low self-esteem and seemed to be withdrawing, and, seen in juxtaposition with his discontent with being in probation, this may have contributed to his reoffending.

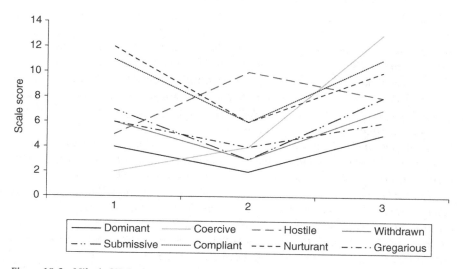

Figure 10.2 Niles' CIRCLE psychometric scores across time (baseline (1), 12 months (2) and a follow-up at one year (3))

At the beginning of his time at Dovegate, he stated he was trying to change; this was reflected in the high compliance, nurturance and gregarious scores. He complained about the lack of consideration for his needs when put in the TC with sex offenders and how this made him feel, mirrored in the increased coercive and hostility scores. Niles reported he began to withdraw from the therapy and saw it more as "a holiday camp".

Bob's story

Box 10.3   Bob

Bob is a white, British male of 23. His first offence occurred at 14 years. Much of his prolific offending occurred as a youth offender, having 80 preconvictions. His past offences have included theft, arson and violent offences. Bob has served four sentences and was serving four years and nine months for attempted robbery. He had served one year and nine months prior to his admission to Dovegate. Bob witnessed domestic violence between his parents when young. He has reports of deliberate self-harm. His extensive drug abuse includes misuse of valium, cannabis and heroin. Bob was deemed not ready for the TC wing and was sent to the High Intensity Programme. After four months, he was assessed as unsuitable to gain entry onto the main TC wing. Bob went back into mainstream prison to complete the remainder of his sentence.

There were some people there that liked me that I could relate to serving shorter sentences than me; like seven months instead of five years. Others said I was aggressive towards people and I'd take liberties. They'd put you on agenda and basically they say well why did you do that. In my world that's how it worked. As a criminal you don't grass. You don't grass and you don't stab your own colour. I've got some good pals like my dad's old mate, who support us. I like people that like who support me.

I spent half my life in prison. I can't get a job or a flat with my record. I just have to stay strong. – I'd love to do things like that (help others), but at the same time I know I'm not ready. To this day I hate to speak about it cos it's always in my head.

It was a hard experience looking at other people as well as yourself was hard; sitting there with all the nonces and that and I was only in for robbery. They were fighting for their freedom. Sometimes I just got scared. I'm just scared. I'm scared of everything. Scared. I'm scared because I've spent a lot of my life in prison. How could they judge my life; my dad, why I turned to crime and substances when their lives were so different? My dad jumped off a bridge. He basically, I don't know why he did it and I was like only 13 year old do you know what I mean. It was hard. You know when someone says to you that you're never going to see someone again, it's hard.

Maybe with counselling I would have let them get into my head. They didn't know how I saw it. They try to get you to look at your life and like ask you well how would you want to be if your dad was still alive and they want you to say it would be different but it's hard. They grained away at you. At the same time sometimes I felt they were trying to catch us out. I'd say something and they'd twist it to put it to me. I don't like people that are trying to get in my mind.

I'm trying to change man. I'm trying to change out here after spending 87 months in prison and dealing with all the heart ache from the age of seven. And from 14 to 22 locked in institutions and they expect us to get out and cope without help cos of my record. I'm not a bad person. I did it when I was a kid an emotional kid on substances. It was a vicious circle. I'd abuse substances, sell it and I got greedy and even though I had money from that I used to go out and rob people at the same time. I used to think I was invisible. I was violent, aggressive and had a weapon aye it was bad but I need help.

I don't want to do that shite anymore, but at the same time it's hard to stay strong and all my pals do it still. All my good pals are drug dealers or armed robbers or in jail. Out here, if you've always used drugs and been violent, they think you'll always be like that. You have a reputation. Now I've been released into the community and I've got nothing. I haven't got a flat, I haven't had any help off the council getting a flat, nobody helps us because of my past.

Even though I was only there for a few month and it's an 18 month programme that was enough for me. You know what I'd like to do? I'd like to go and see a member of staff at Dovegate and say look I've been in institutions most my life and I did listen to you but like, they thought I wasn't ready and that I wasn't good enough.

I'm happy sometimes but I'm not happy other times. I've got low confidence and so it's really hard. Out there it's very violent and you have to be violent, you have to be ready and I'm always ready.

Bob's self-esteem is quite low, despite a slight increase between the two times of psychometric administration. His presentation throughout the post-release interview reflected this low self-esteem. Bob showed an increase in external blame attribution, believing he turned to a life of drugs and crime due to his upbringing and trauma surrounding the death of his father. Bob's decrease in self-criticism occurred in conjunction with the increase in external blame attribution. A particularly interesting sub-scale was the urge to act out hostility, which showed an increase in the psychometric assessment and which Bob's own comments supported when he stated a desire to be violent towards others. Bob has had various interpersonal conflicts throughout his life, such as the death of his father, and lack of support for these have left him as a lonely and

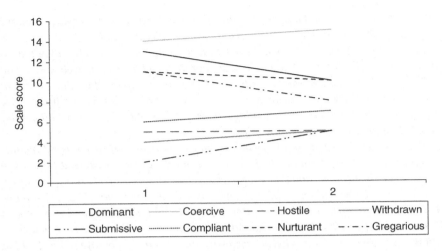

Figure 10.3   Bob's CIRCLE psychometric scores across time (base (1) and a follow-up two years later (2))

vulnerable man susceptible to influence. This has contributed to him venting his pain through other ways, such as violence (Figure 10.3).

Bob's CIRCLE scores show that the people most involved in his care concur with his own account. Bob found the TC very difficult: "It was a hard experience; looking at other people as well as yourself was hard", "How could they judge my life". The fact that Bob has not demonstrated any change (that achieved statistical significance) between time 1 (base recoding at Dovegate) and time 2 (nearly two years later in the community) suggests he was indeed resisting the therapy. He is a man suffering from low self-esteem, who has not yet grieved properly for the death of his father, and achieved minimal change through his Dovegate experience. Despite his claimed motivation to change, the psychometric evidence suggests he lacks both the self-knowledge or had the support he felt he needed to change in a positive direction.

Will's story

I think I were there for an easy ride at first you know, Dovegate sounded like a good idea, and I was in for seven years. So I thought yea I'll have a bit of that – But when I got there, after a bit, I worked harder than some and less than most – I don't fly straight don't get me wrong, I'm not the straightest guy in the planet, I don't abide by every single rule – It's given me the courage to talk to my dad about some problems I had with him and my mum, and I think if I hadn't have gone there then I don't think I would've spoke about it.

Box 10.4   Will

Will is a 30-year-old single white male with one daughter. He has had regular employment. Will's index offence was manslaughter, for which he received a sentence of seven years, serving ten months prior to the TC admission. He has received 33 preconvictions and two sentences resulting in imprisonment. These preconvictions have included theft, drug offences, robbery, burglary and harassment. His highest qualifications were GCSEs, leaving school at 16. Will has a recorded history of physical abuse in childhood. He has no recorded history of mental health treatment, but has the prognosis of antisocial personality disorder (PD) and possible borderline PD. In the past, Will has threatened deliberate self-harm. Will's drug-taking history was extensive, taking drugs since the age of 12, such as cannabis, LSD, speed, heroin and crack. Will was about to embark on the Think First Programme, a cognitive skills programme, part of the Probation service's What Works initiative. This is part of the on-going support his probation officer intends to offer Will, and whilst Will is complying his chances of gaining lower-risk supervision increase. Will was de-selected after 11 months.

Everyone is known by their first name. It's not like being in jail its like being locked up in a youth club – I had good relationships with some of the residents, I had some good pals – Some of the staff I didn't like, some were alright. It's like them was the staff and we was the crims you know what I mean? They always sat in the office and that so you never really kind of have any kind of relationship with any of the staff.

Like at the end I were like not taking any drugs and I were like trying to help others. Because I knew I were leaving and I'd sorted the things out I needed to so I thought I'd help others more. I was chatting to them a lot when I were barbering like.

I think you become more confident. In a group at first you're gonna feel like the outsider aren't you. You know there are all these cliques, cliques of people. Then I was in a clique, with a few of us, some lifers and a murderer you know a few of us. It's a clique you get in and then the more you hang around them, you become more confident you know. But yea I did become more confident.

I got kicked out didn't I. I got kicked out for selling drugs. I never actually saw the drugs; they were given me through someone else. I was asked would you pass that to someone else. I never thought nothing of it. The lad went up the next morning and grassed me up and that.

You have to put your boundaries back up [when back in regular prison]. It's completely different. You can't go to a main jail chatting therapy and what not. They'll just think you're well strange. I can get confused with other things and I think that's due to my relationship with my old man. And the fitting in process you know I still find that a lot to deal with.

I use a lot of excuses to take drugs, especially with my old man and that. There's no excuse – That's what I dealt with in Dovegate, but not consciously, learning that it were my fault, not my dad's and so I forgave him in my own way and that's how I can now talk to him.

I know that I used to blame my old man and that. I took drugs for a long time, from I was 12 till I were 27 and that, heroin for ten years and I used to blame my old man for that – My mum and dad used to have nothing to do with me. My dad used to knock me about when I were a young lad and that but then he used to buy me things after.

I think a lot of people sail other people's ships, they just leave cos they're sick of the blame. They talk so they can point the finger, they want to divert the shit away from them – The therapeutic bit it's just a name cos none of the staff really, you know you have these meetings like ten of you in a room, but none of the staff say anything to you, they don't say anything, they just sit there. They don't like, you know, I don't think, they don't help you; they leave it to all the others. So it's like sick people trying to paddle the same canoe in the same direction. You know, I expected trained staff and there isn't it's just the John Smith who used to be a dustman – How can I get advice off someone else when he's been as sick as me? Sick or on the gear and that, you know how can he help me, how can that work? He has the same defects as me, if that's the case then he's in the same shit as me, you know he's in the same position.

When you go in for the three monthly review, they'll try to tell you what you need to work on and I just thought, how the fuck do you know what I need to work on, you don't even know me, you've never even spoke to me, you've never been in my group, you don't know what I'm about.

I used to fix myself with girls when I were a bit younger. I still do sometimes, but I know that, I still suffer from low self-esteem, and I don't fix myself on drugs, I know it's still the same behaviour innit but you know it's healthier. It's like you know I don't know how to explain it, I've put down the drugs but you know I've picked up somat else. And it ain't so intense you know I still suffer from low self-esteem but I surround myself with things to fix me like friends and stuff.

It's just helped me look at things differently. Not, arghh, be a bit more realistic you know, instead of living and dreaming in some fantasy world of drugs, you know still ain't no Armani suits and BMWs but like, its not shit. So it's just been, I've just got different priorities you know what I mean? I just don't want to do it. I don't even smoke weed anymore. I go out and get pissed with my mates at the weekend and that or with my missus, but that's it. Its all good, know what I mean – I don't want to go back inside, so, I don't choose to be the person that I used to be anymore. I just don't want to be the way that I was.

There are a lot of people I don't associate with they're just scum like me.

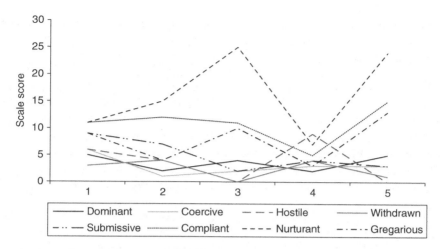

Figure 10.4 Will's CIRCLE psychometric scores across time (base (1), 6 months (2), 12 months (3), first follow-up (4) and post-release (5))

I'm not sure what keeps me clean, my offence is definitely one of them. I don't want to go back inside, so, I don't choose to be the person that I used to be anymore. I just don't want to be the way that I was. Now I don't do drugs I don't think shit like that – My friends I've got a different set of friends, people that I never hung around with and now I hang around with. Obviously when you're on the gear you only hang around with people that's on the gear (Figure 10.4).

Some changes in the CIRCLE measures were found to be statistically significant, within the sub-scales of hostility, compliance, nurturance and gregariousness.

Will's contemplation and action scores increased whilst in the TC but, on release, these scores decreased. However, by the 12-month follow-up Will's contemplation and action are again on the increase. Will reported how he still shows addictive behaviours but he also said that he has a different set of friends now, which could be evidence of the increased action to sustain chance more recently. Will found it hard immediately post-release but is now finding his feet again.

Will self-reported that he has low self-esteem, which is corroborated by the low personal self-esteem psychometric score. Will gives many reasons for this: the fact that he was bullied at school, being "kicked out" of Dovegate, and his relationship with his father. He said that hearing the sex offenders talk about their offences was difficult. Will presented defensively at points in the interview, which also supports the low self-esteem scores. He stated that he used to make excuses, blaming other people, and that now he knows it is his fault but has learnt how to cope with his guilt and move on. This is shown explicitly in his blame attribution psychometric scores: his guilt is very high across the whole research period, while his external attributions have been very low.

The change in Will's hostility was found to be clinically significant, with a decrease at 11 months, just before his de-selection. By the second visit after his release, his hostility had again reverted to the 11-month Dovegate levels. Hence, as assessed by his probation officer, Will is currently not presenting as hostile at all. His presentation at the interview corroborated this. The positive changes observed more recently were also supported by Will's own account, in which he highlights his compliance and acceptance of the decision made by Dovegate to ask him to leave, and his acceptance of others in the same position as he was in. However, throughout the interview, Will was highly critical of others.

Will has recognised and changed many areas of conflicts: resolving his relationship with his father, recognising his susceptibility to influence and moving away from his pro-criminal friends, and learning to be more patient. Despite his low self-esteem, with his high motivation to change, he has managed to turn some of these areas around.

Larry

Sixty per cent were just up for the ride. Now I could well be guilty of that, so I'm not just slagging other people off. When I got in there, it was such a nice atmosphere in there, so easy-going – The only reason I went there was because I wanted to get closer to home, the only way I could get closer to home was put down for this Dovegate and then I got it and I was made up cos my Mrs could come visit me in the same day.

Box 10.5   Larry

Larry is a 48-year-old white British male, married with three daughters: two grown up and one of school age. He has had continuous unemployment throughout his past but is currently working. Larry's first conviction was at 20 years of age. He has received 31 preconvictions and numerous sentences resulting in imprisonment. These preconvictions have included theft (majority), rape, drug offences, physical assault and weapons offences. Larry's index offence was importing class A drugs, for which he received a sentence of seven years, serving two years prior to the TC admission. Larry has a recorded history of physical abuse in childhood. He has no recorded history of mental health diagnoses or treatment, and no deliberate self-harm history. Larry's drug-taking history was extensive, but he got into drug crime later in life. Larry had a period of 26 months' residency before being released.

There was a fear; one of the main things that made me change was the fact that I'm getting old and it's took this sentence to get me to realise that. But then I realised when I got to Dovegate that I were just making excuses again. And when I got my head to thinking in a different way than I would normally. It's all new; I was looking at things in a different way I'd never done before, and that also takes it into being hard in so far as you had to express yourself in a different way as well. I wanted to change, cos well I had no option really. So it was, I wanted to change but I didn't really have a choice cos if I'd have got nicked again I were going away for life.

So in a lot of respects I think I've grown up a lot. And it takes, it's horrible for me to sit there and say to a young girl like you, I've grown up a lot, Dovegate did that for me, and I know it did. I'm still getting used to this new me, which sometimes I don't recognise and that scares me when I don't recognise its me. Sometimes I'll be honest with you, I feel like I've fucked my head up sometimes. Cos sometimes, I used to be so confident, and sometimes I'm not now, because I'm questioning everything. I suppose that's a good thing, but in some ways for me it may well be negative as well. I feel better in myself. I told you that sometimes I lost confidence and this that and the other, well I have, but in myself. The confidence rate is on a steep level, if you know, but as a person, as a man, I think that I'm more confident.

I've got two brothers on heroin and I hate, I hate, I hate the stuff and I was investing in 50 kilos of it. And when I see the lads on heroin and I see all the bad things that they've done and they tell you their life story, I helped contribute to that, whatever way I did it, I did, I know I did. I've made good living out of it. But I think the penny finally dropped that it was never the right way. Crime for me was like a buzz and it was like an adrenaline rush and you got a few quid and sometimes you got caught. The lows weren't anywhere near as much as the highs and the highs were good when they were good, you know what I mean?

I've said this before in Dovegate and I'll say it again, I think it was the hardest jail I've ever been in. Dovegate played games in my head; I have arguments in my head about what's right and what's wrong. I know what's right and what's wrong but I look at things and if I start slipping towards the wrong route then the right one comes in. But sometimes I become physically tired with it, but then at the end when I know which way I'm going, I just, I try not to worry too much.

It was in them nine months that I sort of switched, switched off a little bit and took a back seat. Well what could I do? Kick off or somat? And then get kicked out. I thought well I'll just plod on and just do it. No matter where I was gonna do it I knew I was doing the time and I was ok there, I was settled there, so I just decided to bite the bullet and do it.

You're forced to be, be concerned for everyone and look after people. They did well for us I suppose and it was stuff up here in their head, rather than like maternal things; it was looking after them, giving them someone to moan to and like talk to.

When you're with the guys at Dovegate, 90 odd %, not all of us, 90% are on the same wavelength. You all want the same things, so it's a bit easier. When you're out here, they're not. So it's, I haven't had anything to do with any of my old associates, but that's through choice.

Normally, every other sentence I've done I'd be up to no good now, I would be having my fingers into something now, but I'm not. I'm working now and it's the first time I've worked for 26 years. It's so new to me. I'm working for a week what I used to earn in five minutes. I don't want to be one of those failed statistics down the line; I want to be one of the successes (Figure 10.5).

Change in the CIRCLE coercive sub-scale between time 1 and time 6 was found to be statistically significant; however, other changes were not. Larry's account stated that he was quite dominant in Dovegate, especially when nearing the end of his time, which may account for the scores on this measure. The decrease in coercive scores was significant, and this was supported by Larry admitting "when you're there you do nothing but complain about it, you do, but I think that's because you're there and you're absorbed in it". The high scores of compliance, nurturance and gregariousness, the three more positive sub-scales, were also supported by Larry's own account; Larry complied with the refusal of parole despite feeling this was unfair, Larry mentored others while he was in the TC and the staff often sought his opinions.

Larry's University of Rhode Island Change Assessment Scale (URICA) psychometric scores were variable throughout his time at Dovegate but

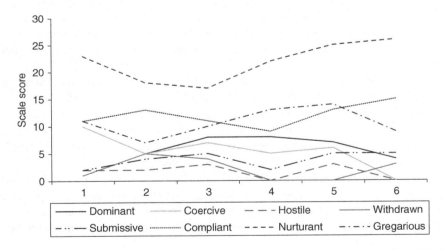

Figure 10.5   Larry's CIRCLE psychometric scores across time at HMP Dovegate (base (1), 6 months (2), 12 months (3), 18 months (4), 24 months (5) and post-release follow-up (6))

showed overall positive statistical change, and the key to this change was the high action throughout and the significant maintenance increase in the first 18 months. In his interview, he highlighted how his successes drove his motivations and also suggested that he is maintaining his changed behaviours now in the community.

Larry's social self-esteem was scored as consistently high, and this was supported by both his interview comments and his presentation at the interview; he is an able and confident communicator and has learnt skills at Dovegate in order to communicate better. However, the psychometric scores suggest that his personal and general self-esteem are comparatively low. Larry talked about this explicitly in his interview; his account suggesting that, while he learnt a lot and things were "opened up", this also caused a lot of unease: "I don't recognise its me", "I used to be so confident, and sometimes I'm not now, because I'm questioning everything".

One change was found as statistically significant; the increase in guilt between time 1 and time 2. The psychometric score also highlights an increase in the urge to act out hostility and a high critical of others score throughout, which Larry identifies in the interview as being due to the increase in his time at Dovegate and Dovegate's acceptance of referrals of people he felt were "just unsuitable".

When I was in Dovegate for a while, say 12 months, they started letting in what I thought were people that were just unsuitable, even I could see that and one thing was, they were too young. They had no intention of changing. They're full of spirit and no-one's gonna change them and they're not ready for change. Now when I come to Dovegate, you had to six months drug-free, six months adjudication-free, different jails have different criteria and until you get all that bang on the same, you're gonna get problems at Dovegate. But it can work, but it's got to be done, they've got to be cruel to be kind and say no you can't go, you can't go you don't fit the criteria, you've got to fit the criteria or you don't go. They're just bending the rules and as soon as you do that. I could see it and the staff could see it. I said to them why don't you just get them the fuck out of here? They said, oh we can't, you vote them out. Well never mind me voting them off, we're the cons and you're the officers. We could vote them off and they could stay for another six months and then whoever's voted them off, is going to get a hard time off them and then they're going to go through that much.

Overall Larry learnt a great deal from his time at Dovegate; he gained victim empathy and internalised blame, he was able to gain the motivation to change once he saw that he could succeed, and was confident even to help others. Despite his low self-esteem, he is on the right track and recognises the change within himself, also recognised by others.

Len's story

Box 10.6   Len

Len is a 39-year-old, single, black British male. Len has received 19 preconvictions, which have included theft, drug offences, burglary and public disorder. Len's index offence was burglary, for which he received a sentence of five years, serving two months prior to the TC admission. Len left school at 16, but completed two-thirds of a year at technical college and received a CSE qualification as a chef. He has no recorded history of mental health diagnoses or treatment, and no deliberate self-harm history. Len's drug-taking history is extensive; taking cannabis, heroin and crack from the age of 13. However, his file reports he was abstinent for four years and was clean on this Dovegate sentence. Len spent 20 months in Dovegate TC before being transferred to another prison, serving a further two and a half years. He then went to an open prison for eight months before release.

Some people thought it was an easy ride, well they saw it as an easy option but really sooner or later they realise it's not, they wanna go back to a mainstream prison because it's less, its stressful. I didn't go there for an easy ride, I went there cos I knew what the options, I knew what I would be facing. I knew that before I even made a decision to, but, cos at the end of the day wherever I go, I knew I would be getting out in two or three years down the line, so it wasn't a case of oh I'll go here it'll be easy for me.

I wasn't happy with, you know, with the fact that I'd spent a fair portion of my life taking drugs and in and out of prison. And I needed to break the cycle somewhere so I thought I'll try this, cos I'm sick and tired of being sick and tired. Age played a significant part; I'm not getting any younger. As you get older, as I got older, it gets harder to serve longer prison sentences.

I were more honest. I talked about stuff that affected my life, that I'd never spoke about before and I thought well I need to talk about this stuff otherwise it'll come back and still have an effect on my behaviour in the future. So you know I talked about stuff that was quite sensitive to me.

I was quite active. I wasn't gonna just sit on my arse and expect it to happen. I worked hard. I had built up some good relationships with people cos I got to know some intimate stuff about people. The mainstream system I couldn't have those kinds of relationships so I kind of, not struggled but I found that quite weird at first. Cos I come from an environment where I got close to certain individuals and I had to, kind of, get used to, kind of, being quite shallow, in, not in my thinking but in my relationships, with prisoners and other people, but the only thing was that, like after a month or two I got back on track.

For me as a black man you know, you know I'm not one to kind of go on about the colour of my skin, but we were very poorly represented, and you know its ironic that in the TC itself we were quite poorly represented so I felt like we didn't have as much of a voice as the other people.

I knew I was gaining a lot more than I was losing cos of the things that I'd lost. The most important thing of all, that changed me, was the fact that you know I've had other options you know and that I didn't have to resort back to the same behaviours that I had done for so many years. You know that was the most important thing; that I had a choice. Cos sometimes I was in the madness and I thought I had no other option.

People tend to stick with their own, subconsciously, you know, or people that they can kind of relate to. Like at that time I could relate to the black guys cos they was going through the same thing that I was going through, you know, and its how they are. Not to say that, you know, not to say that I can't have friendships with other people, white guys, cos I do have friendships with white people, with white guys, but I can't relate to them, cos I'm not white – What made me go there was my lifestyle and my behaviour over the years.

What I learnt in Dovegate was some sort of acceptance of my past. Why would I wanna be the person that I was for so many years that only cared about himself? I had to kind of get down and knuckle down deal with, and talk about and deal with and accept the painful stuff that had happened in my life. And I had to do it straight away, cos otherwise I knew I'd come back to prison – I think what happened was just meant to have happened no matter how I was brought up in life, or how my childhood and stuff was. It was just unfortunate that that's the, a path that I was put on, by whoever.

I spent a lot of time in prison, or in and out of prison, I spent nearly four years in and out of prison, four years of my life, you know, and it didn't prevent me from going back out and doing the same things – There was many things that contributed, you know, like my relationship with my mum, like my hair falling out, like you know, being brought up in an environment where crime and having to have been a fighter was quite, fighting a lot, and crime was very prevalent in my, growing up, in the area that I grew up in, my family-life wasn't that healthy, you know, all those, are contributing factors. No I can't blame that stuff in the past.

My family relationships are different, yes, but obviously time is precious and that will kind of hopefully heal whatever wounds there is. That's a kind of, a separate story cos my family have always kind of been indifferent, a lot of the pain that I suffered was within my family, so I've kind of got a different view on families, or well my family.

I was hoping to get a job while I was still in prison but that didn't happen cos you know, they said, you know, it was quite difficult being black. Prison and being black just doesn't do you any favours.

I got something from it, so why would I want to keep that all to myself. Yes others changed there, and I wanna share. I wanna share what I've learnt; I wanna share, and be unselfish to try to pass on a little bit of, whatever, whether its wisdom, or its I don't know, could be, could be crap that I'm passing on for all I know, but also it could be something positive.

This is the first time that I've come out, you know and I've not committed any crime or I've not taken any drugs for a long time. I know there's another way of life – I combat that stuff today is that, I just focus on the day that I'm living in, I just make a decision, whether its conscious or subconscious as I wake I say to myself, today I'm not using drugs.

I'm just using support, today and every day, you know I go to support groups, three or four times maybe five times a week, and I have issues that I need to talk about, and I have that platform now that I built, I have friends that I can confide in and talk about the stuff that could be affecting me, you know that might seem trivial or might seem quite normal for people that have not been into drugs. But they can relate to me, cos they are recovering addicts themselves (Figure 10.6).

Len's CIRCLE scores showed an overall positive shift: coerciveness and withdrawal decreased, and nurturance increased, although these were not statistically significant. Len's account and his presentation in the interview supported this overall movement. However, the negative change observed included the only statistically significant change: a decrease in compliance between times 2 and 3, and an increase in hostility and dominance. Len stated that people found him threatening but he explained that this was just the way he and his black friends communicated; however, he acknowledged that others have in the past

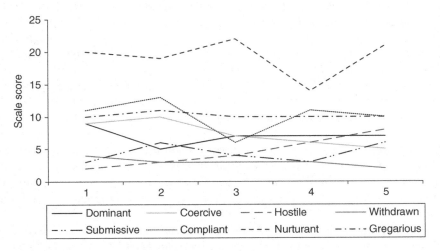

Figure 10.6 Len's CIRCLE psychometric scores across time (base (1), 6 months (2), 12 months (3), 18 months (4) and post-release follow-up (5))

found this intimidating. In the interview, his presentation did not come across aggressively.

Overall, Len seemed to have been grateful for his time at HMP Dovegate and stated that he had definitely changed for the better. His psychometric scores also show this overall positive change. Len has high motivation and has acknowledged his own culpability for his criminal lifestyle. Although gaining more control of his life, Len still has low self-esteem, which, when he feels discriminated against, can catalyse hostility. Len has the ability to maintain the changes made with support and turn his life around.

Len's social self-esteem was moderately high throughout his time at Dovegate, and this was supported both by his own account, stating that he managed to build up some good relationships, learning the importance of communication, and by his presentation at the interview, where he was able to communicate well to the interviewer (Emily). His psychometric scores paint a picture of a man with good general self-esteem but low personal self-esteem and confidence, often resorting to defensive strategies. Len's account in the interview supported this where he acknowledged when he felt discriminated against he could come across as an aggressive black man. Len's scores on the Hostility and Direction of Hostility Questionnaire (HDHQ) psychometric show that, despite the lack of statistical change, overall his hostility had decreased by the 18-month administration. Len's interview highlighted some of his self critical feelings and also the criticism he felt towards others.

Summary

Bill, Will, Larry and Len are deemed to have changed, whilst Bob and Niles remained more resistant to change. The former were characterised as having high motivation to change, had internalised blame and had positive evaluations from others involved in their care, all supported by their own insights made during their post-release interviews. Bob and Niles showed more negative patterns and both were de-selected from Dovegate. Bob attributed blame externally and revealed a profile of a vulnerable man in need of support. Niles had psychometric scores suggesting an internal attribution of blame; however, in the interview he attributed blame externally. There was also evidence for Niles that he had low motivation and a negative scoring on his psychometric data. He was subsequently recalled to prison.

Will's profile indicated clinically significant negative changes i.e. a decrease in maintenance of change in the URICA, and there was also a decrease in the positive sub-scales of the CIRCLE. These were observed post-release from Dovegate. This negativity could be explained as a regression subsequent to Will's return to mainstream prison following his discharge from Dovegate. His interview supports this hypothesis: "You have to put your boundaries back up. It's completely different. You can't go to a main jail chatting therapy and what not. They'll just think you're well strange."

Larry admitted he came to Dovegate for reasons other than wanting to change ("the only reason I went there was because I wanted to get closer to home and the only way I could get closer to home was put down for this Dovegate and then I got it and I was made up 'cause my Missis could come visit me in the same day"). Conversely, Bob's motivation to change was high ("I'm trying to change man. I'm trying to change out here after spending 87 months in prison and dealing with all the heart ache from the age of seven. And from 14 to 22 locked in institutions and they expect us to get out and cope without help 'cos of my record". Whilst Larry had the potential and capacity to change, Bob seemed unable to use the TC appropriately.

Research has found diminishing effects if residents are sent back to mainstream prison following their time at the TC, as opposed to being released straight into the community, as this demoralises them (Wexler et al., 1999; Cullen et al., 1997a, pp. 161–179). This detrimental effect was accentuated by Larry in his interview ("the lads in Dovegate that were on drugs, when they go from there to another jail, the chances are they will use drugs again, so the chances are all the good work they done in Dovegate will become undone"). The two deemed as "unchanged" were transferred to mainstream prisons after de-selection. However, two of the four changed also went to mainstream prison post-Dovegate (Will and Len). A distinction between those who "changed" and those who did not was that the changed participants both verbalized the fact they were clean from drug abuse when they left Dovegate, which was lacking in the interviews with Bob and Niles. All participants had extensive drug abuse histories dating back as far as age 12, but the two who were unchanged were still using drugs when interviewed.

A concept brought up by the residents themselves was age. Both Larry and Len commented on how their age played a significant part in their motivations to change. The demographics of the ex-residents were considered to see whether they could explain the differences between these two classes of ex-resident, in the light of the work of Farrington et al. (1986) and criminogenic risks. Index offence (IO) and sentence length were observed as irrelevant, as the two "unchanged" participants (Bob and Niles) had similar sentences and index offences to others in the "changed" group. Number of preconvictions varied, with Niles and Bob having the two extremes of 14 and 80, respectively. The age at first conviction could not offer an explanation either. Only two of the six ex-residents, represented in both the "changed" and "unchanged" groups, had no record of physical abuse in their childhood; however, this may have been due to a lack of disclosure rather than an absence of abuse in life. Three of the residents who had changed were responsible for a child, which may have had an effect, and Will was one of these, which could be one of the factors supporting his change despite other things being against him. All participants had left school by the age of 16, but the ones who had "changed" had all received some form of education and qualification either recently or in prison.

Another possible explanation is highlighted by Gocke, who stated that those without motivation to change "divert attention away from themselves, their actions and motivations by an obsession with the way that they had been treated whilst being processed through the criminal justice system" (Gocke, 1991, p. 1). In fact, the two deemed as "unchanged" both talked about the unjust manner in which they were treated (also highlighted by their high coercive scores) and avoided speaking about certain things in the first person, diverting attention away from themselves: "They grained away at you. At the same time sometimes I felt they were trying to catch us out. I'd say something and they'd twist it to put it to me" [Bob]; "before you know it you start shoplifting don't you for the beer, and it just on and on and it's the pressure and to look cool" [Niles].

11
Getting It: A Quantification of Long-Term Outcomes

"You've got it, Stephen...you've nearly got it, Emma...yes, Neville, you've definitely got it..." I never seemed to get it. It's the story of my life. I'm trying so hard to get it I'm in danger of contracting mercury poisoning. It doesn't seem to matter how hard I try: I become so desperate that I eventually take to faking...Then eventually, one lesson, just when I am least expecting to, I hear her say the words I'm aching to hear: That's it Michael, you've got it.

Michael Simkins' autobiography "What's My Motivation?" (2003 pp. 40–41)

Introduction

The above extract is an account from Michael Simkins of his experience as a RADA student trying to learn expressive movement by conveying the sensation of beads of mercury travelling up and down various limbs. Success in doing so seemed to elude him until, almost unconsciously, and through his own perseverance and the guidance of his tutor, he eventually got it and it was an awakening experience. This is a nice example of both succeeding in something that is difficult and elusive, which then opens up other possibilities, and the combination of one's own motivation supported by tutored assistance. There is something of this intangible quality and combination of effort that resonates with the TC residents' experiences. It also accords with Roland Woodward's experience in trying to explain the possibilities and potential of the TC and what it can achieve to the prison organisation that houses it. He writes:

I have lost count of how often I have inwardly thought "oh no, I've got to explain this all over again. Don't they ever learn"? It is at this point that I recall the counsel of one of the first group therapist I worked with in a TC. Whilst complaining in frustration about the fact that people took so long to "get it" he calmly said "Its good practice for raising children. You just have to keep saying the same thing until they understand it.

(Woodward, 2007)

So, in this chapter, we try and pin down post-residency outcomes more tangibly using our quantitative assessments. This chapter then explores the sustainability of the TC's impact as residents moved back into mainstream prison and eventually progressed beyond the prison environment, returning to the outside world. We examine this progression using our "hard" data – the psychometric measurement, adjudication records and reconviction rates. This exploration is broadened towards its conclusion as we investigate the implications of these results for the wider prison system by showing how representative the TC residents are of that wider population of incarcerated offenders.

Throughout this book, we have striven to emphasise the need to bear both process and outcome in mind. This chapter offers us an opportunity to explore these in the longer term.

Lasting psychological change? Post-TC psychometric results

The psychometric measures used to explore therapeutic processes during the prisoners' time in the community offer a useful means of determining the psychological impact of their residency once they had moved on to other settings. They provide an informative addition to the qualitative findings established through post-residency interviews (see Chapter 10) and, importantly, they enable us to gauge whether the cognitive and behavioural changes already identified during the residents' time in the community can be meaningfully related to these residents' pattern of functioning and interpersonal interaction as they move back into the wider prison system, and ultimately into the community.

Characteristics of the psychometric follow-up sample

Quantitative data collection continued once residents left the TC and moved elsewhere in the prison system. These assessments continued at six-monthly intervals, although the dispersed nature of this sample across differing prison and community contexts made recruitment more difficult. In total, 60 former residents participated in follow-up psychometric assessments, of whom 47 offered data within an appropriate six-month window for inclusion in subsequent follow-up analyses. Attempts were made to secure longer-term follow-up assessments, but tracking and access difficulties meant that insufficient numbers were obtained for appropriate analysis. Table 11.1 offers a breakdown of the number of former residents assessed within this six-month interval, distinguishing them according to their length of time in the TC.

Table 11.1 Six-month post-TC assessment: Sample size by residency length

Length of within-TC participation	n
0–5 months	12
6–11 months	17
12–17 months	7
18–23 months	9
24 months+	2
Total	47

The follow-up sample had an average age of 32.4 (SD = 7.3) at their baseline assessment, almost exactly the same as the mean for the overall sample of TC residents. The ethnicity of the follow-up sample was quite representative of the overall sample, with the most frequent ethnicity being white British (76.8% of the follow-up sample). In comparison to the overall sample, this post-TC sub-group included slightly fewer participants with a violent index offence ($n = 20$, i.e. 33.3%) and more with drug offences ($n = 6$, i.e. 10%). All other offences were represented in approximately the same proportions as with the overall sample. In terms of the follow-up sample's history of criminal offending, they served on average 5.1 (SD = 4.4) prior sentences and held 20.2 (SD = 16.1) previous convictions. The proportional representation of the types of preconvictions was again very similar to that seen in the overall study sample.

To comprehensively explore the change shown by residents after they leave the TC, a broader battery of psychometrics was used than had been employed in the within-TC follow-ups. The primary psychometric tests used previously to assess residents during their time in the TC were supplemented with a further five measures to obtain a more detailed insight into the outcome of therapy on residents' psychological and behavioural functioning. These assessments had been administered as part of the baseline testing when residents first entered the TC, thus enabling a pre–post-therapy comparison. The full battery used at the post-TC stage is listed in Box 11.1.

Box 11.1   Battery of follow-up psychometrics

- Revised Gudjonsson Blame Attribution Inventory (GBAI-R)
- Culture-Free Self Esteem Inventory 2 (CFSEI-2)
- Chart of Interpersonal Reactions in Closed Living Environments (CIRCLE)
- Hostility and Direction of Hostility Questionnaire (HDHQ)
- Inventory of Altered Self Capacities (IASC)
- University of Rhode Island Change Assessment Scale (URICA)

- Cork Estrangement Scale (CES)
- Cork Passive Aggression Inventory (CPAI)
- Locus of Control of Behaviour (LCB)
- Psychological Inventory of Criminal Thinking Styles, version 4 (PICTS-4)
- RAAP Anger Assessment Profile (RAAP)

Sustainability of change: The post-TC psychometric results

A series of Wilcoxon signed-rank tests were conducted on the data to explore the significance of change that occurred once participants left the TC. For the primary psychometrics that had been used in the within-TC follow-ups, their final assessment within the TC was compared with the subsequent assessment conducted six months after their departure.

First, we looked at the same measures as had been used to evaluate the TC residents during their time in the intervention. This offered an insight into the sustainability of earlier patterns of change. In most cases, the scores achieved by former TC residents in their post-residency follow-up assessments indicated an overall trend towards improved functioning. Increased overall self-esteem was observable in responses on CFSEI-2. A number of scales on the HDHQ conversely showed statistically significant decreases in overall feelings of hostility, but also specifically in terms of tendencies to criticise others or to self-isolate. Some scales on the IASC demonstrated trends towards continued improvement of self-identity and social skills, but these fell short of being statistically significant. All of these scales were reliant on the former residents' self-perception, however, and so it is interesting to see how they were reflected in the observer-rated CIRCLE measure. Indeed, many of the scales comprising that measure showed clinically desirable and statistically significant changes in interpersonal functioning. Residents were seen to interact more pro-socially and be less coercive of others. In terms of blame attribution, the post-TC scores on the GBAI-R indicated greater levels of guilt but also greater attribution of blame to external or mental health sources. These latter trends were not statistically significant. All of the significant results are reported in Box 11.2.[1]

Box 11.2 Significant changes from end of therapy to six months post-therapy

- CFSEI
  - Total: mean difference $= +3.29$, $z = 2.51$, $p = .012$
- HDHQ
  - Total Hostility: mean difference $= -4.38$, $z = 2.99$, $p = .003$

Box 11.2   (Continued)

- Criticism of Others: mean difference $= -1.2$, $z = 2.89$, $p = .004$
- Intropunitiveness: mean difference $= -1.97$, $z = 2.63$, $p = .009$
- CIRCLE
  - Coercive: mean difference $= -9.35$, $z = 3.98$, $p < .001$
  - Withdrawn: mean difference $= -3.97$, $z = 2.82$, $p = .005$
  - Compliant: mean difference $= +4.87$, $z = 3.24$, $p = .001$
  - Nurturant: mean difference $= +8.56$, $z = 3.06$, $p = .002$

Whilst it was possible to examine how change continued from the final assessment during TC residency with the psychometrics used in the within-TC test battery, there were additional measures administered only at baseline and at follow-up. In other words, the change explored with these measures was between their baseline scores on entry to the TC and their six-month post-TC assessment scores. These measures also demonstrated change in the clinically positive direction of the scales.

Statistically significant decreases were identified in passive aggression as reported on the CPAI, whilst responses on the RAAP measure similarly demonstrated a reduction in feelings of anger and less sensitivity to provocation. Significant decreases in criminal thinking styles were demonstrated across all sub-scales on the PICTS-4. There was a slight decrease in estrangement as measured on the CES, although this was not statistically significant. A summary of the notable results for all of these measures is provided in Box 11.3. Overall, the results indicate that the sample as a whole showed positive changes between their baseline assessments at the beginning of their residency and their follow-up assessment post-departure from the community.

Box 11.3   Additional significant changes from baseline to six months post-therapy

- CPAI
  - Passive Aggression: mean difference $= -7.55$, $z = 2.69$, $p = .007$
  - Resistance to Demands: mean difference $= -3.09$, $z = 2.25$, $p = .025$
  - Aggressive Impulse: mean difference $= -4.5$, $z = 2.72$, $p = .007$

- RAAP
  - Anger Control: mean difference $= 3.42$, $z = 2.71$, $p = .007$

- Duration: mean difference $= -3.71$, $z = 2.82$, $p = .005$
- Provocation: mean difference $= -2.58$, $z = 2.78$, $p = .005$

- PICTS-4
  - Mollification: mean difference $= -2.56$, $z = 3.41$, $p = .001$
  - Cutoff: mean difference $= -3.89$, $z = 3.11$, $p = .002$
  - Entitlement: mean difference $= -2.13$, $z = 2.44$, $p = .015$
  - Power Orientation: mean difference $= -3.5$, $z = 3.56$, $p = .000$
  - Sentimental: mean difference $= -2.12$, $z = 2.73$, $p = .006$
  - Superoptimism: mean difference $= -2.09$, $z = 2.33$, $p = .020$
  - Cognitive Indolence: mean difference $= -3.34$, $z = 3.14$, $p = .002$
  - Discontinuity: mean difference $= -3.19$, $z = 3.15$, $p = .002$

As with the analysis of change demonstrated by residents *during* their stay in the TC, it is important to account for residency length of stay when analysing the post-departure data. However, grouping respondents according to their length of therapy participation results in samples of insufficient size for group-level analysis. Consequently, an alternative approach has been adopted for exploring the relationship between TC residency length and these psychometric outcomes, this method being the Reliable Change Index (RCI; Jacobson & Truax, 1991; O'Neill, 2010). This provides an idiographic perspective in that it assesses change at the individual participant level, and it is thus applicable with the smaller sample sizes available for this analysis. It is only applicable, however, with measures for which there is sufficient normative information available for generating the required thresholds of statistically meaningful change on that measure. Tabulations of these RCI results are provided in the appendix for the psychometric measures for which the necessary normative information was available. These idiographic analyses offer a simple means of exploring whether the length of stay in the community has a role in the patterns of psychological and behavioural change occurring post-therapy.

It must be acknowledged that, although such idiographic methods of analysis are appropriate, the numbers remain small, and so caution is needed in drawing any broad inferences. However, a number of useful points of note are evident in the results. Looking at the sample when grouped according to residency length, all such groups have a higher proportion of prisoners who experienced increased overall self-esteem (CFSEI-2). There was a trend amongst former residents to demonstrate significant improvements in their interpersonal functioning (CIRCLE), again regardless of the former residents' time in the TC. This is perhaps most strongly reflected in the increase in compliance that occurred in the six months post-therapy scores of former residents across the groups of differing residency length. More surprisingly, the earlier leavers were most likely to self-report decreases in their hostility (HDHQ) levels post-therapy.

Less clear patterns of change were evident on the IASC and GBAI-R. Whilst this could be perceived as a stalling in the influence of the TC, the absence of change could also be interpreted as demonstrating that there is no deterioration in what progress was achieved on these constructs during the residents' time within the TC. A full list of these results is provided in the appendix. The unusual pattern of results, when compared with the earlier within-TC results, must, however, be interpreted in the light of the greater error of estimation that small sample sizes can introduce.

In addition to idiographic change from the end of therapy to the post-therapy follow-up, we can also look at the role of residency length in the former residents' longitudinal change using the other psychometric measures for which only baseline and follow-up data were available. For residents who had dropped out at the very initial stages of therapy, between baseline and five months, some positive changes were observable, including decreases in passive aggression levels (CPAI) and feelings of anger (RAAP) as well as an internalisation of the residents' sense of control (LCB). These changes were typically reflected to a similar extent by the longer-term residents, i.e. those who completed more than 18 months' therapy. Moreover, these longer-term residents showed a wider range of changes. This included, for example, their propensity to report offending-supportive cognitions (PICTS-4), with the changes from baseline to follow-up in longer-term residents primarily showing a decrease in such thinking styles.

Summarising the post-TC psychometric results

These post-TC assessments provide us with some understanding of the ongoing development of former TC residents as they move beyond the TC. The sample sizes available for these analyses were smaller than was the case with the within-TC analyses. With the residents moving to different locations and settings (be that prison or community), there were increased difficulties in tracking and engaging them. Important data have been accrued nonetheless, and these have shown that the therapy participants show patterns of improved functioning, psychologically and behaviourally, as they reintegrate into other contexts. Improvement in self-esteem is particularly evident in the follow-up analyses of residents once they have moved out of the TC. For each grouping of participants, the CFSEI repeatedly reflects further clinically meaningful improvement, at least for some participants. Other changes are also apparent, such as in interpersonal functioning as assessed by the CIRCLE. For the residents who reach either 12- or 18-month points in therapy, there are, furthermore, common indications of improvement in propensity to adopt offending-supportive cognitions or to poorly handle feelings of anger.

In terms of elaborating on the findings of this set of idiographic analyses, it would be of clear benefit in future work to further clarify which residents demonstrate significant change over time and the longer-term stability of these changes. Such inquiry could feed into the refinement of admission criteria for TC applicants, as well as the adaptation of the therapy programme itself to address issues relevant to those residents who fail to make notable and long-lasting progress during their time in the TC.

Exploring the TC's impact on reconviction rates

Although psychometric results offer a meaningful and detailed insight into the therapeutic efficacy of the TC, recidivism rates remain a key focus in outcome research with prison populations. Indeed, one of the underlying core aims of prison-based TCs is to lower the rates of reoffending in those who take part in them. Recognising this fact, we investigated the reconviction data for former TC residents who had been released back into the community.

To provide some context, the expected impact of prison treatment programmes on recidivism is a reduction of around 10 percentage points, according to McGuire (2002). Notable variability in the exact figure continues to be shown in this work, however. For example, the reconviction rate for offenders who participated in an Enhanced Thinking Styles programme was lower than for the matched comparison group, showing an initial 2.5% reduction in reconviction likelihood (Cann et al., 2003). The advantage gained by the intervention seemed to wane with time and inter-group differences disappeared.

The results from reconviction studies of prison TCs have also been mixed. In an early HMP Grendon TC study, Newton (1971) compared reconviction rates of TC residents with a matched sample from HMP Oxford and found no significant differences. Similar disappointing results were obtained by Robertson and Gunn (1987) in their ten-year follow-up study of Grendon graduates. However, subsequent recent research from Grendon TC yielded more positive results. Marshall (1997) and Taylor (2000) both found that prisoners who had remained on a waiting list for entry to the TC ended up with more reconvictions than a general prison sample. The researchers considered that this was due to Grendon selecting higher-risk offenders. Importantly, the prisoners who succeeded in gaining entry to Grendon ended up eventually with fewer reconvictions than those who remained on the waiting list. The Grendon graduates had a four-year reconviction rate of 60% in comparison to a rate of 65% in the waiting list group (Marshall, 1997).

A number of factors have been associated with recidivism, including preconvictions (Kershaw et al., 1999; Cuppleditch & Evans, 2005). Studies have also highlighted treatment dosage as an important factor, with this research indicating that programme completers tend to have a lower reconviction rate than non-completers. Research has shown that this is true even when differences in baseline risk are taken into account (Stewart-Ong et al., 2004). More recently, Hollin and colleagues (2008) found that the completion of a community-based offender treatment programme had a positive effect on reconviction, but the converse was true of early leavers from the programme. With regard to treatment dosage in prison TCs specifically, researchers have consistently identified that the TC intervention is most effective after 18 months (Cullen, 1993; Marshall, 1997; Taylor, 2000).

Methodological issues

Of the 250 TC residents taking part in this evaluation, 156 (62.4% of the sample) were serving the same prison sentence as before their participation in the TC, and therefore had not had the "opportunity" to offend in the community. The remaining 94 (37.6% of the sample) had been released into the community, however, and these comprised the sample upon which the majority of the present analysis is conducted.

The reconviction data were collected within Dovegate TC using the Inmate Information System (IIS), the central database used by the UK prison service. The IIS records all reoffences resulting in a guilty court conviction. Therefore, reconviction here is defined as a rearrest for an offence that leads to a court hearing resulting in a guilty verdict. The dates of reconvictions and, where identified, the nature of reconvictions were collected alongside other relevant variables (mode of release, passage of time post-release, length of TC residency, age and criminal history).

Findings

Of the 94 participants who had been released into the community at the time of data collection, 45 had reoffended, giving a reconviction rate of 47.9%. There was very little difference between this reconvicted group, who had spent an average of 19.26 (SD = 11.26) months in the community, and the non-reconviction group ($n = 49$), who had spent 18.43 (SD = 11.7) months in the community. The majority of participants who reoffended did so once ($n = 24$) or twice ($n = 19$) during the research period. As a result of their reoffending, the reoffending participants served 67 new prison sentences between them. There was no statistically significant association between reconviction rates of those participants released directly into the community ($n = 25$) and those who returned to the mainstream prison system prior to release into the community ($n = 69$; χ^2 (1, $n = 94$) = 0.00, $p = .98$).

Table 11.2   Time in months prior to first reconviction

Reconviction period	*n*	%
Less than 1 months	12	26.7
Less than 2 months	14	31.1
3–5 months	6	13.3
6–12 months	8	17.8
12–24 months	3	6.7
24 months or longer	2	4.4

Time prior to reoffending ranged from two weeks to 44 months. Of those who did reoffend, a large majority (87.5%) were reconvicted within a year of release from prison. Table 11.2 gives more detail about the pattern of reconvictions across time by considering the number of months prior to first reoffence. It can be seen that the majority of prisoners were reconvicted within two months.

To examine the influence of the reason for departure from the TC, the sample was broken down into the 22 participants who failed Dovegate TC assessment and the 72 participants who passed the assessment and therefore took part in the primary stages of the TC intervention. A series of *t*-tests identified no differences in background characteristics between the two groups, and logistic regression found that no background characteristics could predict membership of the failed-assessment group (i.e. those participants who failed TC assessment procedures and did not make it onto a TC), suggesting that the failed-assessment group comprised a useful comparison group. The failed-assessment group reoffended more quickly than the successful assessment group, and this difference (4.4 months) was statistically significant ($t(40) = -2.164$, $p = .03$). The failed-assessment group also committed a slightly higher number of reoffences (1.7 compared with 1.63) and served more post-TC prison sentences (1.5 compared with 1.37), although these differences were not statistically significant. Surprisingly, however, the failed-assessment group had an overall lower reconviction rate (36%) than the passed-assessment group (51.4%), although, when subjected to Fisher's exact testing, this was not a significant finding (χ^2 (1, $n = 94$), $p = .161$).

The time residents spent in the TC, as a measure of treatment dosage, was also considered. The reoffenders spent less time in therapy (13.5 months; SD $= 8.5$) than the non-reoffenders (14.61 months; SD $= 10.5$), although this difference was not statistically significant (t (92) $= -5.34$, $p = .6$). However, when participants were allocated more broadly into two groups "less than 18 months residency" and "18 months or more residency", this dosage effect was more evident. As shown in Figure 11.1, just over 70% ($n = 34$) of all reoffences were committed by those who had experienced 17 months or less in the TC, whereas

Figure 11.1   Proportion of reconvictions by < or > 18 months of TC residency

Table 11.3   Criminal history characteristics of reoffenders and non-reoffenders: Part I

Criminal history characteristics	Released reoffenders	Released non-reoffenders	Mean difference
No. of previous prison sentences	6.92 (SD = 6.3)	4.81 (SD = 4.3)	2.11
No. of preconvictions	20.35 (SD = 19.2)	16.52 (SD = 11.9)	3.83
Age at first conviction	14.83 (SD = 2.7)	15.93 (SD = 4.3)	−1.1
Age at current conviction	29.29 (SD = 5.2)	30.67 (SD = 8.8)	−1.38

only 29% ($n = 14$) of reoffences were committed by those staying for 18 or more months. Statistical tests of difference revealed that the mean number of reconvictions was higher, although not significantly so, amongst those who experienced less than 18 months in therapy (t (46) = 2.04, $p = .05$).

The majority of those who reoffended were aged between 31 and 40 years, although logistic regression showed that age was not a statistically significant predictor of reoffending (B (1) = −.045, $p = .85$). As is shown in Table 11.3, released reoffenders had a higher mean number of previous prison sentences and preconvictions and were slightly younger at the time of their first and current conviction when compared with non-reoffenders. There were no statistically significant differences between the groups.

As shown in Table 11.4, reoffenders had moderately more burglary index offences and fewer drug-related index offences. They also had moderately

Table 11.4 Criminal history characteristics of reoffenders and non-reoffenders: Part II

	Offence type	Released reoffenders (*n = 45*)	Released non-reoffenders (*n = 49*)
Index	Violent	20%	18.4%
	Sexual	6.6%	6.1%
	Burglary	37.8%	30.6%
	Robbery	35.6%	38.8%
	Theft	8.9%	6.1%
	Criminal damage	4.4%	4.1%
	Drug	6.7%	18.4%
Preconvictions	Violent	68.9%	57.1%
	Sexual	15.6%	12.2%
	Burglary	33.3%	42.9%
	Robbery	26.7%	22.4%
	Theft	48.9%	51%
	Criminal damage	37.8%	26.5%
	Drug	28.9%	32.7%

more violent and criminal damage preconvictions, although none of these associations were statistically significant.

The final set of analyses focused on the nature of reconvictions. The nature of first reconviction was not known for 43.8% of cases. For these known cases, reoffending predominately comprised breach of licence (in 74.5% of cases) and the most prevalent type of first reconviction was absconding. There were no reports of violent reoffending, and one offender was found guilty of committing a sexual offence. Of the 24 offenders who received a second reconviction in this period, 17 (71%) of them had the nature of this additional reconviction recorded. As before, the majority of these reconvictions involved a breach of licence (66.7%), and this was predominantly due to burglary or "breaking and entering". The nature of third reconvictions (known for four out of five participants) followed a similar pattern to the second reconvictions in that it predominantly involved burglary or "breaking and entering". Finally, one former resident had a further fourth and fifth reconviction, both of which were for criminal damage.

Summary of reconviction results

Overall, the findings are encouraging. The 47.8% reconviction rate for Dovegate TC residents was significantly lower than rates found in national samples (58%, Kershaw et al., 1999; 54.5%, Ministry of Justice, May 2008). As Dovegate TC selects high-risk offenders, including those with personality disorders, the finding that its rates are lower than the national average is particularly positive. This 47.8% reconviction rate is also impressive as it reflects the expected

10% reduction in reconvictions as a result of offender treatment programmes (McGuire, 2002), which other treatment programmes have found difficult to achieve. Whilst the reader can make comparisons between Dovegate and Grendon TCs' reconviction rates, potential differences in population profiles (particularly in view of different selection procedures) make this inappropriate at the present time. We think it would be helpful to establish whether there are any differences between the two populations, by comparing census information, for example.

The finding that Dovegate TC's reoffending peaked within a few months (56%) to a year (87.5%) of release and then decreased rapidly over time was encouraging because Ministry of Justice statistics (May 2008) showed that national male reoffending rates increased over time. However, there are differences in sample sizes across these studies and a lack of matching between samples. The Ministry of Justice figures did not distinguish between those offenders who received any psychological treatment and those who did not.

The Dovegate TC failed-assessment group reoffended more quickly than the passed-assessment group, and had a slightly higher number of reoffences and post-TC prison sentences, giving some support to the idea that offender programme non-completers are at the highest risk of recidivism when compared with non-starters and programme completers (Hollin et al., 2008). That said, the failed-assessment group in the current sample had an overall lower reconviction rate (36%) compared with the passed-assessment group (51.4%). This finding does raise concerns for TC selection, a domain already being considered in prison TC standardisation and accreditation processes.

Dovegate reoffenders had a higher mean number of previous prison sentences and preconvictions, characteristics associated with high risk as per the OGRS (Offender Group Reconviction Scale; Copas & Marshall, 1998). Unfortunately, it was not possible to classify the current sample using OGRS as not all of the information required to calculate risk was available. Future researchers would benefit from looking at the nature and prevalence of personality disorders (PD) in this population, given the association between PD and reconviction (Taylor, 2000). Another interesting finding was that those who spent less time in therapy were more likely to reoffend: just over 70% of all reconvictions were committed by those who had experienced 17 months or less in the TC, while this figure fell to 29% for those staying for 18 or more months. Also, those who spent 17 months or less in the TC had a higher rate of reoffending. These findings offer some support to the idea that optimum treatment "dosage" time in a prison TC is 18 months or more (Marshall, 1997; Taylor, 2000) and provide an interesting development concerning treatment effect and rate of reoffending that requires more research attention.

The recidivists were most likely to be aged between 31 and 40 years. This was an unexpected finding, as it is the 18–25 year age group amongst males who are most likely to reoffend (Ministry of Justice, May 2008). However the average age of the current sample (both recidivists and non-recidivists) was 29.7 (SD = 7.51), suggesting that the TC population is typically characterised by an older set of individuals, which makes the likely age of reconviction less unusual.

The nature of participants' reconvictions and their frequency of occurrence were not reported on the IIS in all cases, so that results and their interpretation are restricted by relatively small sample sizes. Most reconvictions were for breaches of licence (in 74.5% of first reoffences) and were likely to involve absconding. There were no reports of violent reoffending, and only one offender was found guilty of committing a sexual offence. The lack of violent offending was particularly striking as 69% of the sample had a history of violent offending. A particular problem with the IIS was some of the terms used to define the nature of reconvictions, for example the unclear probation classification of "poor behaviour". Another shortcoming of the IIS was that it only provided information on reoffences which led to a conviction. It did not provide details of those who had reoffended but not yet been convicted.

Drawing together these findings, Box 11.4 summarises the likely profile of a Dovegate TC recidivist.

Box 11.4   Profile of Dovegate TC reoffender

- He is likely to have served more previous prison sentences than non-reoffenders, an original offence of burglary and a higher number of preconvictions, especially for violence and criminal damage.
- He is likely to reoffend within two months of release and almost certainly within a year.
- He is likely to have served less than 18 months in the TC.
- He is likely to be within the age category of 31–40 years.
- It is likely that he will end up back in prison for a breach of licence conditions, which may be in the form of absconding.

This analysis was reliant on a small sample size of ex-TC residents who had been released into the community. Also, the study did not have its own comparison group, nor did it randomly allocate offenders to treatment or no-treatment conditions. Instead, we made comparisons using previously published reconviction data so as to contextualise the findings, but these comparisons come with a caution because of differences in sample characteristics. Another shortcoming is the four-year reconviction time span. Taylor (2000), using the same Grendon TC sample as Marshall (1997), found a higher reconviction rate within a seven-year period (rising from 60% at four years to 66% at seven) and Cann et al. (2003) found that the impact of cognitive-behavioural prison programmes faded over time. Together, these findings suggest an increase in offending longer term, which needs to be addressed with longer-term research. There would be benefit in considering seven and ten-year reconviction rates using this Dovegate TC sample. This will only be achieved in the fullness of time.

Adjudication data: Prison rule violations as an outcome measure

Whilst the reconviction data provided a means of exploring the TC's impact on important behavioural indices, they cannot fully capture this type of outcome for former TC residents still awaiting release into the community. Antisocial behaviours within the mainstream prison system are often dealt with via in-house disciplinary hearings and sanctioning rather than via the standard court system. This process and the resultant censures, known as adjudications, offer a useful means of gauging a prisoner's level of disruptiveness and frequency of rule violation and so offer an outcome indicator in a similar vein to the reconviction data.

Although adjudications tend to not be used within the TC itself, it is possible to use a prisoner's adjudication history from before and after his time in the intervention to establish whether there is a change in adjudication frequency. Consequently, details of TC residents' adjudications one year prior to and one year after being in the TC were collected. The average number of adjudications pre-TC was 1.73, and post-TC was 1.66. When the sample is broken down by length of time spent in the TC, the biggest change was observed in the prisoners who completed 18–23 months in therapy. These also had the lowest post-TC adjudication rate overall (pre-TC: $M = 1.47$; post-TC: $M = 0.58$). This change was statistically significant (see Table 11.5). The only other residency length group to show noteworthy change was the group who completed 24 or more months in the TC, although the drop in their observed adjudication rate fell just short of the probability cutoff used in determining statistical significance.

Table 11.5 Wilcoxon signed ranks test analysis of adjudication data

Length of participation	z	p
0–5 months	−.45	.656
6–11 months	−1.21	.226
12–17 months	−.23	.816
18–23 months	−2.28	.023
24 months+	−1.90	.058

Contextualising the results: Comparing TC residents and the wider prison population

As highlighted in the introduction to the reconviction analyses, previous work at Grendon has established that the TC sample differed in important ways from the population of the wider prison system. This has implications for how treatment outcomes, and specifically recidivism rates, are interpreted. With this in mind, the final section of this chapter aims to establish how the TC sample from Dovegate recruited for the current evaluation differs from putatively comparable samples of offenders within the prison system.

To obtain context for the TC outcomes already described, the TC residents who completed 18 or months of therapy ("Completers") were compared with the following samples:

- offenders held in mainstream prison settings (i.e. a standard "Comparison" sample),
- prisoners who unsuccessfully sought access to the TC but were rejected ("Unsuitable"), and
- prisoners who were admitted to the TC but left in the early stages of the programme ("Early Leavers").

The sample size and demographic characteristics of each of these groups are documented in Table 11.6.

The only significant differences in these fields were in terms of prior substance abuse, with the Early Leavers having the greatest history of drug use and the TC Completers having the highest rate of prior alcohol misuse. Some significant differences between the groups were also observed in terms of criminal history (see Table 11.7). The Comparison sample had the latest age of first and current convictions, and the Early Leavers and Completers all had notably more prior offences on their records. Figure 11.2 shows that the Comparison sample differed notably from the other groups in terms of the type of offence for which they were currently serving a sentence. They were statistically significantly more likely to have committed a sexual or drug-related offence, and less likely to be serving a sentence for violent offending.

Comparing the groups: Psychometric findings

The demographic characteristics and criminal histories of the different samples as discussed above have shown that the TC applicants and admissions tend to differ in important ways from prisoners recruited from a general prison environment. The groups were additionally compared in terms of baseline psychometric results to explore whether differences could also be identified in terms of their behavioural and psychological functioning. Box 11.5 lists the

Table 11.6 Demographic characteristics of the samples

	Comparison	Unsuitable	Early leavers	Completers	Sig.
Total count (*n*)	56	59	131	60	
Age (mean)	38	33	32	33	No
Marital status (%)	61 Single	56 Single	55 Single	58 Single	No
	19 Married	17 Divorced	15 Cohabiting	18 Married	
Ethnicity/ nationality (%)	75 White British	75 White British	71 White British	76 White British	No
Employed ever (%)	75	68	61	65	No
Employment stability (%)	46 Stable	10 Stable	14 Stable	15 Stable	No
	21 Unstable	36 Unstable	37 Unstable	42 Unstable	
	23 Unemployed	17 Unemployed	16 Unemployed	22 Unemployed	
Record of drugs (%)	50	69	82	77	Yes
Record of alcohol (%)	8	36	37	63	Yes

Table 11.7 Criminal history of the samples

	Comparison	Unsuitable	Early leavers	Completers	Sig.
Age at first conviction	26	16	15	15	Yes
Age at current conviction	54	30	29	29	Yes
Length of current sentence (months)	124	283	326	135	Yes
Previous sentences served	2	6	5	5	Yes
No. of preconvictions	10	12	19	18	Yes

psychometric tests used in this work, all of which have been described in earlier chapters.

In this cross-sectional comparison between the groups, the Comparison sample tended to have scores reflecting less emotional or interpersonal dysfunction than did the different TC groups. Significant overall differences were observed for most of the scales, and consequently further post-hoc testing was undertaken to pinpoint the sources of these results. Differences

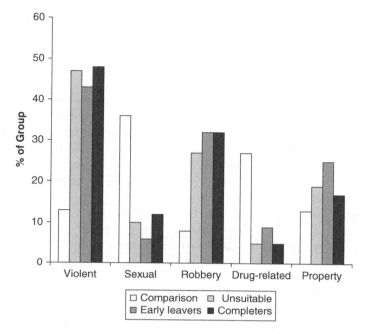

Figure 11.2 Index offence type by prisoner group: Within-group percentages

---

Box 11.5 Battery for group comparisons

- Revised Gudjonsson Blame Attribution Inventory (GBAI-R)
- Culture-Free Self Esteem Inventory 2 (CFSEI-2)
- Hostility and Direction of Hostility Questionnaire (HDHQ)
- Inventory of Altered Self Capacities (IASC)

---

in blame attribution (GBAI-R) were most strong when comparing the Comparison group with the TC Completers, with the latter showing a greater baseline tendency to avoid blame-taking. Self-reported hostility, on the other hand, differed most between the Comparison group and the TC Unsuitable group, with the Comparison group again showing less dysfunction at this baseline point. On the self-esteem measure (CFSEI-2), the Comparison group differed significantly from all of the other groups, reporting a higher level of self-esteem overall. Finally, on the IASC measure, which assessed elements of self-identity and social skills, a similar pattern was again identified, with the Comparison group showing significantly less clinically problematic characteristics than all of the other groups. The full results of these baseline comparisons, of both the demographic characteristics and psychometric responses, have been tabulated and included in the appendix for readers who seek additional detail.

The above exploration has suggested that the TC applicants, whether they were ultimately rejected or admitted, are likely to have more impaired functioning than a sample of offenders drawn from the wider prison population. As this chapter is primarily concerned with outcome, however, it is clear that a cross-sectional assessment of baseline differences is not sufficient to clarify the actual impact of the TC on those who do get admitted and complete time within the intervention. To obtain such an insight, it is important again to adopt a longitudinal perspective. Accordingly, the Comparison sample was reassessed at 18 months, enabling comparison with the progress achieved by the TC Completers.

Wilcoxon signed ranks tests were first performed on the Comparison group data to investigate within-group change, and the group was found to show two principal changes: a decrease in external blame attribution (GBAI-R; $T = 5$, $p < .05$, $r = .24$) and in feelings of guilt (HDHQ; $T = 3$, $p < .05$, $r = .24$). The latter change represented a decrease in inwardly directed hostility and was reflected in the corresponding higher HDHQ scales, Intropunitive and Overall Hostility. No changes were shown by this group on either the CFSEI-2 or IASC measures, suggesting they experienced no meaningful changes in their self-esteem or in clinically relevant aspects of their self-identity during this time. The longitudinal change achieved by the Comparison sample was then compared with that of the TC Completers group. Differences between the groups in terms of their change over the 18-month assessment interval were identified on the IASC, with the TC Completers showing a greater decrease than the Comparison group in their tendency to hold a diffused identity with others ($U = 388.5$, $p < .05$) and in their susceptibility to influence ($U = 350.5$, $p < .05$). Whilst no other scales showed a significant difference, trends did indicate that the Completers sample showed a much more consistent swing towards clinically improved functioning during this time, whilst the Comparison sample remained more static. A more detailed summary of this data is provided in the appendix.

Summary

This chapter has examined the long-term influence of TC residency on the prisoners passing through its doors. In doing so, this examination has employed a number of perspectives, from psychometric testing to reoffending rates. It has established that some improvements in self-esteem, hostility and interpersonal functioning continue to be shown as the TC residents return to mainstream prison and eventually are released back into the community. This testing has likewise shown that there are noteworthy decreases in the feelings of anger and aggression felt by these former residents from when they first entered the

TC. Given the forensic nature of this sample, a particularly positive development was the decrease in the sample's likelihood of expressing thinking styles that supported their previous criminal behaviour. Such changes were also examined in the context of actual propensity to reoffend, and a recidivism rate of 47.8% was observed. The time spent in the TC was, however, a key influence on this rate, with early leavers from the TC intervention having a significantly higher rate than those who successfully completed 18 months. The reconviction results are summarised in Box 11.6.

Box 11.6   Key findings from the reconviction data

- 47.8% reconviction rate amongst those liberated was lower than previously found in other prison treatment programmes.
- The majority of reconvictions (74.5%) were breaches of licence involving absconding.
- There were no reports of serious violent offending and only one report of sexual reoffending.
- Most reoffenders (87.5%) did so within a year of being released into the community.
- Analysis also revealed that 70% of reconvictions were committed by those who had spent less than 18 months in the TC, suggesting a treatment dosage effect.

The importance of time spent in therapy was also reflected in adjudication rates of the former residents who were still within the prison system at the end of the data collection period. These rates captured the former residents' likelihood of violating prison rules, and showed that the prisoners who had spent 18 or more months in the TC had significantly lower rates than those who left prematurely.

The nature of the TC sample in relation to the wider prison population was explored in the concluding sections of this chapter, and this offers a contextualisation for the results here, and indeed in earlier chapters of this book. Whilst the TC at Dovegate appears to comprise and attract prisoners with greater psychological and behavioural dysfunction than other samples drawn from mainstream prison settings, it is clear that those who succeed in completing recommended lengths of stay in the community experience strong and measurable benefits. Overall, this casts a very positive light on the work done at Dovegate TC and highlights the importance of its role in facilitating rehabilitation amongst even the most challenging offenders held within in the UK prison system.

Chapter appendix

Table 11a.1 Post-TC measures: End of therapy vs. six months post-TC

Measure		*n*	Z-score	Significance (*p*)	Corrected cutoff	Significant post-correction?
GBAI-R	Guilt	37	0.27	.784	.050	No
	External	37	0.53	.594	.017	No
	Mental	37	0.44	.661	.025	No
CFSEI-2	CFSEI total	38	2.51	.012	.013	Yes
	General self-esteem	38	2.34	.019	.017	No
	Social self-esteem	35	1.95	.051	.025	No
	Personal self-esteem	38	1.86	.063	.050	No
	Lie scale	*38*	*0.22*	*.826*	*.050*	*No*
CIRCLE	Dominant	27	0.82	.413	.025	No
	Coercive	26	3.98	.000	.006	Yes
	Hostile	27	4.01	.000	.006	Yes
	Withdrawn	27	2.82	.005	.013	Yes
	Submissive	27	0.32	.746	.050	No
	Compliant	27	3.24	.001	.008	Yes
	Nurturant	23	3.06	.002	.020	Yes
	Gregarious	27	1.82	.069	.017	No
HDHQ	Total hostility	31	2.99	.003	.006	Yes
	Intropunitiveness	31	2.63	.009	.010	Yes
	Self-criticism	31	2.22	.026	.013	No
	Guilt	31	1.94	.052	.025	No
	Extrapunitiveness	31	2.77	.006	.008	Yes
	Acting out	31	2.16	.031	.017	No
	Paranoid hostility	31	1.00	.317	.050	No
	Criticism of others	31	2.89	.004	.007	Yes
IASC	Interpersonal conflicts	26	1.95	.052	.008	No
	Idealisation-disillusionment	26	0.80	.422	.025	No
	Abandonment concerns	26	0.55	.583	.050	No
	Identity impairment	26	2.60	.010	.005	No
	Self-awareness	26	2.20	.028	.006	No
	Identity diffusion	26	2.35	.019	.005	No
	Susceptibility to influence	26	1.51	.131	.013	No

	Affect dysregulation	26	2.12	.034	.007	No
	Affect instability	26	1.66	.097	.010	No
	Affect skills deficits	26	2.16	.030	.006	No
	Tension reduction activities	26	1.03	.304	.017	No
URICA	Precontemplation	33	0.22	.828	.050	No
	Contemplation	33	0.95	.343	.017	No
	Action	33	0.69	.491	.025	No
	Maintenance	33	2.16	.030	.013	No

Table 11a.2 Additional post-TC measures: Baseline levels vs. six months post-TC

Scale		n	Z-score	Significance	Corrected cutoff	Significant post-correction?
CES	Total estrangement	32	2.59	.010	.017	Yes
	Existential estrangement	32	2.85	.004	.013	Yes
	Social estrangement	32	0.65	.516	.050	No
	Rule-group	32	1.74	.081	.025	No
CPAI	Passive aggression	38	2.69	.007	.017	Yes
	Resistance to demands	39	2.25	.025	.050	Yes
	Aggressive impulse	38	2.72	.007	.017	Yes
LCB	Total	41	2.21	.027	.050	Yes
PICTS-4	Mollification	28	3.41	.001	.007	Yes
	Cutoff	27	3.11	.002	.008	Yes
	Entitlement	27	2.44	.015	.025	Yes
	Power orientation	28	3.56	.000	.006	Yes
	Sentimental	28	2.73	.006	.017	Yes
	Superoptimism	28	2.33	.020	.050	Yes
	Cognitive indolence	28	3.14	.002	.008	Yes
	Discontinuity	27	3.15	.002	.008	Yes
RAAP	Attitude	32	0.85	.393	.050	No
	Expression	32	2.59	.010	.008	No
	Provocation	32	1.39	.166	.017	No

230

Table 11a.2 (Continued)

Scale		n	Z-score	Significance	Corrected cutoff	Significant post-correction?
	Somatic tension	32	2.61	.009	.007	No
	Duration	32	2.82	.005	.005	Yes
	Sensitivity	32	2.78	.005	.005	Yes
	Victim	32	1.22	.221	.025	No
	Assaultative	32	2.10	.036	.013	No
	Consequence	32	2.20	.028	.010	No
	Control	32	2.71	.007	.007	Yes

Table 11a.3 CFSEI-2 RCI results: From end of therapy to six-month post-TC follow-up

		6–11 Months	12–17 Months	18+ Months
CFSEI	Increase	31% (5)	50% (2)	29% (2)
	Decrease	19% (3)	0% (0)	14% (1)
General	Increase	25% (4)	25% (1)	29% (2)
	Decrease	19% (3)	0% (0)	14% (1)
Social	Increase	8% (1)	25% (1)	29% (2)
	Decrease	15% (2)	0% (0)	14% (1)
Personal	Increase	19% (3)	0% (0)	0% (0)
	Decrease	19% (3)	0% (0)	0% (0)

Table 11a.4 CIRCLE RCI results: From end of therapy to six-month post-TC follow-up

		6–11 Months	12–17 Months	18+ Months
Dominant	Increase	14% (1)	40% (2)	13% (1)
	Decrease	0% (0)	20% (1)	75% (6)
Coercive	Increase	14% (1)	0% (0)	0% (0)
	Decrease	71% (5)	100% (4)	63% (5)
Hostile	Increase	0% (0)	0% (0)	0% (0)
	Decrease	71% (5)	80% (4)	38% (3)
Withdrawn	Increase	0% (0)	0% (0)	50% (4)
	Decrease	71% (5)	60% (3)	25% (2)
Submissive	Increase	14% (1)	0% (0)	38% (3)
	Decrease	29% (2)	20% (1)	0% (0)
Compliant	Increase	57% (4)	100% (5)	63% (5)
	Decrease	0% (0)	0% (0)	13% (1)
Nurturant	Increase	50% (3)	100% (4)	34% (2)
	Decrease	0% (0)	0% (0)	17% (1)
Gregarious	Increase	43% (3)	80% (4)	38% (3)
	Decrease	0% (0)	20% (1)	25% (2)

Table 11a.5   HDHQ RCI results: From end of therapy to six-month post-TC follow-up

		6–11 Months	12–17 Months	18+ Months
Total hostility	Increase	27.2% (3)	0% (0)	0% (0)
	Decrease	36.4% (4)	40% (2)	14.3% (1)
Self-critical	Increase	9.1% (1)	0% (0)	0% (0)
	Decrease	27.3% (3)	0% (0)	14.3% (1)
Hostile guilt	Increase	9.1% (1)	0% (0)	0% (0)
	Decrease	9.1% (1)	40% (2)	14.3% (1)
Acting out	Increase	9.1% (1)	0% (0)	0% (0)
	Decrease	18.2% (2)	20% (1)	28.6% (2)
Paranoid hostility	Increase	27.3% (3)	0% (0)	0% (0)
	Decrease	18.2% (2)	0% (0)	14.3% (1)
Critical of others	Increase	9.1% (1)	0% (0)	0% (0)
	Decrease	36.4% (4)	40 % (2)	14.3% (1)

Table 11a.6   IASC RCI results: From end of therapy to six-month post-TC follow-up

		6–11 Months	12–17 Months	18+ Months
Interpersonal conflicts	Increase	0% (0)	0% (0)	17% (1)
	Decrease	11% (1)	0% (0)	0% (0)
Idealisation-disillusionment	Increase	11% (1)	0% (0)	0% (0)
	Decrease	33% (3)	0% (0)	0% (0)
Abandonment concerns	Increase	0% (0)	0% (0)	0% (0)
	Decrease	11% (1)	0% (0)	0% (0)
Identity impairment	Increase	0% (0)	0% (0)	0% (0)
	Decrease	11% (1)	0% (0)	0% (0)
Self-awareness	Increase	0% (0)	0% (0)	0% (0)
	Decrease	11% (1)	25% (1)	0% (0)
Identity diffusion	Increase	0% (0)	0% (0)	17% (1)
	Decrease	33% (3)	0% (0)	0% (0)
Susceptibility to influence	Increase	0% (0)	0% (0)	0% (0)
	Decrease	0% (0)	25% (1)	0% (0)
Affect dysregulation	Increase	22% (2)	0% (0)	17% (1)
	Decrease	11% (1)	25% (1)	0% (0)
Affect instability	Increase	0% (0)	0% (0)	0% (0)
	Decrease	11% (1)	0% (0)	0% (0)
Affect skill deficits	Increase	22% (2)	0% (0)	17% (1)
	Decrease	11% (1)	25% (1)	0% (0)
Tension reduction activities	Increase	11% (1)	0% (0)	17% (1)
	Decrease	0% (0)	25% (1)	0% (0)

Table 11a.7   GBAI-R RCI results: From end of therapy to six-month post-TC follow-up

		6–11 Months	12–17 Months	18+ Months
Guilt	Increase	0% (0)	0% (0)	0% (0)
	Decrease	0% (0)	0% (0)	0% (0)
External	Increase	0% (0)	0% (0)	0% (0)
	Decrease	14% (2)	0% (0)	0% (0)
Mental	Increase	7% (1)	0% (0)	0% (0)
	Decrease	0% (0)	0% (0)	14% (1)

Table 11a.8   CPAI RCI results: From end of therapy to six-month post-TC follow-up

		6–11 Months	12–17 Months	18+ Months
Passive aggression	Increase	12.5% (2)	33.3% (1)	0% (0)
	Decrease	31.3% (5)	33.3% (1)	55.6% (5)
Resistance to demands	Increase	18.8% (3)	25% (1)	11.1% (1)
	Decrease	43.8% (7)	25% (1)	44.4% (4)
Aggressive impulse	Increase	12.5% (2)	33.3% (1)	0% (0)
	Decrease	31.3% (5)	0% (0)	66.7% (6)

Table 11a.9   RAAP RCI results: From end of therapy to six-month post-TC follow-up

		6–11 Months	12–17 Months	18+ Months
Attitude	Increase	14.3% (2)	20% (1)	25% (2)
	Decrease	21.4% (3)	20% (1)	0% (0)
Expression	Increase	21.4% (3)	0% (0)	0% (0)
	Decrease	21.4% (3)	0% (0)	50% (4)
Provocation	Increase	7.1% (1)	20% (1)	0% (0)
	Decrease	21.4% (3)	0% (0)	50% (4)
Somatic tension	Increase	14.3% (2)	0% (0)	12.5% (1)
	Decrease	28.6% (4)	20% (1)	50% (4)
Duration	Increase	7.1% (1)	0% (0)	0% (0)
	Decrease	35.7% (5)	0% (0)	37.5% (3)
Sensitivity	Increase	28.6% (4)	0% (0)	0% (0)
	Decrease	28.6% (4)	0% (0)	100% (8)
Victim	Increase	42.9% (6)	40% (2)	0% (0)
	Decrease	35.7% (5)	20% (1)	75% (6)
Assaultative	Increase	35.7% (5)	0% (0)	0% (0)
	Decrease	35.7% (5)	40% (2)	62.5% (5)
Consequence	Increase	28.6% (4)	0% (0)	0% (0)
	Decrease	21.4% (3)	40% (2)	37.5% (3)
Control	Increase	40% (4)	0% (0)	62.5% (5)
	Decrease	10% (1)	0% (0)	0% (0)

Table 11a.10   PICTS-4 RCI results: From end of therapy to six-month post-TC follow-up

		6–11 Months	12–17 Months	18+ Months
Mollification	Increase	0% (0)	0% (0)	0% (0)
	Decrease	20% (2)	75% (3)	37.5% (3)
Cutoff	Increase	10% (1)	33.3% (1)	0% (0)
	Decrease	40% (4)	33.3% (1)	50% (4)
Entitlement	Increase	0% (0)	0% (0)	0% (0)
	Decrease	20% (2)	33.3% (1)	50% (4)
Power orientation	Increase	0% (0)	0% (0)	0% (0)
	Decrease	30% (3)	25% (1)	50% (4)
Sentimentality	Increase	10% (1)	25% (1)	0% (0)
	Decrease	20% (2)	25% (1)	50% (4)
Superoptimism	Increase	0% (0)	0% (0)	0% (0)
	Decrease	30% (3)	25% (1)	25% (2)
Cognitive indolence	Increase	10% (1)	25% (1)	0% (0)
	Decrease	30% (3)	25% (1)	50% (4)
Discontinuity	Increase	0% (0)	33.3% (1)	0% (0)
	Decrease	20% (2)	33.3% (1)	75% (6)

Table 11a.11 LCB RCI results: From end of therapy to six-month post-TC follow-up

		6–11 Months	12–17 Months	18+ Months
Locus of control	Increase	25% (4)	0% (0)	20% (2)
	Decrease	0% (0)	0% (0)	0% (0)

Table 11a.12 Group differences for demographics and criminogenic factors

Demographic	Median	Test statistic (H(3))	Significance level (p)
Age at first conviction	16	34.65	<.001
Estimated age at current conviction	29.62	12.8	.005
Length of current sentence (months)	108	24.35	<.001
Previous sentences served	3	20.94	<.001
Number of previous convictions	13.5	19.56	<.001

Table 11a.13 Focused comparisons for demographics and criminogenic factors

Demographic		Comp vs. completers	Comp vs. early leavers	Comp vs. unsuitable
Age at first conviction	U	507.5	1326.5	683.5
	Sig	<.001	<.001	<.001
	r	.48	.42	.41
Estimated age at current conviction	U	1099.5	2187.5	1061
	Sig	.006	.001	.007
	r	.26	.26	.26
Length of current sentence (months)	U	843.5	2174.5	1121.5
	Sig	<.001	<.001	.004
	r	.42	.31	.27
Previous sentences served	U	848.5	1783	777.5
	Sig	.001	<.001	.001
	r	.34	.41	.34
Number of previous convictions	U	1017.5	1953.5	944
	Sig	.003	<.001	.002
	r	.28	.33	.29

Table 11a.14 Significant differences in demographics and criminogenic factors between the four samples

	Chi-square (df = 3)	*p*-value	Contingency coefficient
Reported drug use	3.7	$p < .001$	.34
Reported alcohol use	5.94	$p < .001$	.44
Violent index	2.12	$p < .001$	.26
Sexual index	3.07	$p < .001$	.3
Robbery index	1.17	$p < .01$	.19
Drug index	1.93	$p < .001$	.24
Violent precon	5.79	$p < .001$	.4
Sexual precon	1.02	$p < .05$	.18
Robbery precon	2.8	$p < .001$	.29
Drug precon	1.07	$p < .05$	.18
Property precon	7.27	$p < .001$	.44

Table 11a.15 Median baseline scores on the psychometrics for the four samples

	Comparison (median at base)	Unsuitable (median at base)	Early leavers (median at base)	Completers (median at base)
BA – guilt	10.5	12	12	13
BA – external	2	2	2	2
BA – mental	3	4	4	5
HDHQ – SC	4	7	6	6
HDHQ – G	2	4	3.5	4
HDHQ – AO	4	6	5	5
HDHQ – P	2	3	2	2
HDHQ – CO	4	6	6	5
HDHQ – intp	6	10	10	11
HDHQ – extp	10	14.5	14	11
HDHQ – total	18	26	24	23
CFSEI	25	16	20	17
CFSEI – general	13	8	10	7.5
CFSEI – social	7	5	6	6
CFSEI – personal	6	3	5	3
CFSEI lie	5	6	7	7
IASC – IC	18	20.5	19	19
IASC – ID	15	19	18	16.5
IASC – AC	14	18	16	15
IASC – II	15	23	19	21
IASC – II-S	9	14	12	14
IASC – II-D	5	8	7	7
IASC – SI	13	18.5	18	16.5
IASC – AD	15	21	19	20
IASC – AD-I	7	11	9	10
IASC – AD-S	7.5	11	10	10
IASC – TRA	11	14.5	13	13

Table 11a.16 Group differences for blame attribution

Sub-scale	Median	Test statistic (H(3))	Significance level (*p*)
Guilt	12	6.078	.108
External	2	10.68	<.05
Mental	4	10.35	<.05

Table 11a.17 Focused comparisons for blame attribution

Scales		Comp vs. completers	Comp vs. early leavers	Comp vs. unsuitable
Guilt	U	1155	2716	1319
	Sig	.03	.228	.61
	r	.2		
External	U	1055	2531	1351
	Sig	.009	.09	.891
	r	.25		
Mental	U	1011	2260	1015
	Sig	.003	.006	.02
	r	.28	.21	

Table 11a.18 Group differences for HDHQ

Scale	Median	Test statistic (H(3))	Significance level (p)
Self-critical	6	18.44	<.001
Guilt	3	22.81	<.001
Acting out	5	10.25	<.05
Paranoid	2	6.115	.106
Critical of others	5	11.03	<.05
Intropunitive	10	24.09	<.05
Extrapunitive	13	13.14	<.01
Total hostility	23	18.54	<.05

Table 11a.19 Focused comparisons for HDHQ

Scales		Comp v completers	Comp v early leavers	Comp v unsuitable
Self-critical	U	1129	2057	926.5
	Sig	.003	<.001	.001
	r	.27	.31	.33
Guilt	U	944.5	2184	865.5
	Sig	<.001	<.001	<.001
	r	.37	.28	.36
Acting out	U	1466.5	2589	1010.5
	Sig	.299	.017	.004
	r			.28
Paranoid	U	1545.5	2863.5	1142
	Sig	.552	.132	.035
	r			
Critical of others	U	1588	2654.5	1038.5
	Sig	.727	.031	.007
	r			
Intropunitive	U	975.5	1942	836
	Sig	<.001	<.001	<.001
	r	.35	.35	.38
Extrapunitive	U	1518.5	2518.5	936.5
	Sig	.461	.01	.002
	r			.31
Total	U	1246.5	2175	872
	Sig	.024	<.001	<.001
	r		.28	.36

Table 11a.20 Group differences for CFSEI

Scale	Median	Test statistic (H(3))	Significance level (p)
CFSEI	19	27.31	<.001
SE general	10	30.2	<.001
SE social	6	12.29	<.01
SE personal	4	20.42	<.001
SE lie	7	28.26	<.001

Table 11a.21 Focused comparisons for CFSEI

Scales		Comp vs. completers	Comp vs. early leavers	Comp vs. unsuitable
CFSEI	U	925.5	222.8	764.5
	Sig	<.001	<.001	<.001
	r	.39	.29	.42
SE general	U	819.5	2069	762
	Sig	<.001	<.001	<.001
	r	.44	.32	.42
SE social	U	1341.5	2546.6	909
	Sig	.079	.006	.001
	r		.2	.33
SE personal	U	1049	2851.5	905
	Sig	<.001	.053	.001
	r	.33		.34
SE lie	U	883.5	2165	1268
	Sig	<.001	<.001	.183
	r	.42	.31	

Table 11a.22 Group differences for IASC

Sub-scale	Median	Test statistic (H(3))	Significance level (p)
IPC	19	9.58	<.05
IDD	17	11.15	<.05
ABC	16	3.864	.277
IDI	19	20.16	<.001
SFA	12	21.96	<.001
IDF	7	10.21	<.05
SSI	16	22.28	<.001
AFD	19	17.61	<.01
AFI	9	27.87	<.001
ASD	10	10.53	<.05
TNR	13	11.83	<.01

Table 11a.23   Focused comparisons for IASC

Scales		Comp vs. completers	Comp vs. early leavers	Comp vs. unsuitable
IPC	U	1251	2749.5	1068
	Sig	.036	.041	.004
	r			.26
IDD	U	1443	2672.5	1063.5
	Sig	.314	.023	.003
	r			.27
ABC	U	1605.5	3174	1303
	Sig	.934	.475	.124
	r			
IDI	U	1014.5	2319.5	880.5
	Sig	.001	.001	<.001
	r	.32	.25	.36
SFA	U	960	2321	888.5
	Sig	<.001	.001	<.001
	r	.32	.25	.36
IDF	U	1048	2704	1048
	Sig	<.002	.027	.027
	r	.28		
SSI	U	1005.5	2160.5	834
	Sig	<.001	<.001	<.001
	r	.33	.29	.39
AFD	U	1155	2573	923
	Sig	.008	.01	<.001
	r			.34
AFI	U	905	2353	775
	Sig	<.001	.001	<.001
	r	.38	.25	.42
ASD	U	1338.5	2829.5	1060
	Sig	.106	.06	.003
	r			.27
TNR	U	1289	2799	1007
	Sig	.058	.058	.001
	r			.3

Table 11a.24 Medians on psychometrics at times 1 and 2 for the comparison and completers groups

	Comparison (median at base)	Completers (median at base)	Comparison (median at 18 months)	Completers (median at 18 months)
BA – guilt	10.5	13	10	13
BA – external	2	2	2	2
BA – mental	3	5	3	4
HDHQ – SC	4	6	4	5
HDHQ – G	2	4	1	2
HDHQ – AO	4	5	3	4
HDHQ – P	2	2	2	2
HDHQ – CO	4	5	4	3.5
HDHQ – intp	6	11	5	7.5
HDHQ – extp	10	11	9	10
HDHQ – total	18	23	15	17
CFSEI	25	17	27	24
CFSEI – general	13	7.5	14	11
CFSEI – social	7	6	6	7
CFSEI – personal	6	3	6.5	6
CFSEI lie	5	7	6	7
IASC – IC	18	19	15.5	18
IASC – ID	15	16.5	14	14
IASC – AC	14	15	12	12
IASC – II	15	21	14.5	17
IASC – II-S	9	14	9.5	10
IASC – II-D	5	7	5.5	5.5
IASC – SI	13	16.5	11	13
IASC – AD	15	20	14	15
IASC – AD-I	7	10	7	8
IASC – AD-S	7.5	10	7	6.5
IASC – TRA	11	13	11	10

12
Practice Issues and Research Overview

Introduction

This chapter will offer some final reflections and try to answer the questions raised in the introductory chapter, namely the role played by private prisons, the very existence of TCs within prisons and the means to discover "what works" in a TC prison intervention. In doing we try and identify some of the aspirations discussed by Roland Woodward in his foreword enabling the unlocking of patterns of criminal behaviours through the therapuetic processes that give people their opportunity to change

Richard Shuker opines that "despite their significant role as an intervention, the potential of the TC approach to inform wider forensic practice is perhaps not fully recognised or understood" (Shuker, 2010, p. 50). In part, he says that this is due to the shortage of "good quality evidence" (p. 52). De Leon (2000) suggests that whilst we know something about *whether* the TC works we know less about *why* and *how* (original italics). We hope the evidence presented in this book will make a contribution to fill that gap. We provide a commentary on the research process and the realities of conducting research within a prison TC. Managing longitudinal research in a forensic setting carries with it a number of challenges, not least continuity of the research setting, emotional load on and support for the researchers, and the vagaries of the prison system. In addition, the ethics of conducting research, engaging with a literally "captive" audience, managing disclosures, preserving confidentiality and reporting experiences present live issues which the present authors resolved in a number of ways, as discussed below. We also include here a summary of the TC outcomes and suggest in what ways the findings may impact on policy, implementation and practice.

Should prisons be privatised?

We noted in our Introduction the issue of the private provision of prisons and discussed the relative pros and cons in Chapter 4 with respect to Dovegate TC.

We observed the principled consideration that those involved in setting up Dovegate gave to the potential advantages and disadvantages of prison privatisation. Being able to innovate was a key driver that overcame some lingering sensibilities about commercial companies managing a TC. The editors of a journal special issue devoted to a debate about privatising prisons concluded that the intensity of feelings of those holding opposing views about privatising prisons has cooled somewhat and that the predicted disasters have not transpired (Liebling and Sparks, 2002). Cullen and MacKenzie (2011) are confident that Dovegate was sufficiently protected against commercial pressures whilst noting the "tyranny" of the number 194, the required occupancy rate. Ray Duckworth, the third director of Dovegate TC, said that

> in the summer of 2008 the contract underpinning therapy was radically changed in a bid to rescue the TC from failing miserably. The TC appeared to lose its way for a number of reasons and concerns were raised by HM Chief Inspectorate of Prisons and the Community of Communities (C of C) about the overall performance of the TC in its entirety.
>
> (Duckworth in Cullen and MacKenzie, 2011, p. 250)

The ensuing HM Prison Department Inspection (2012, p. 5) concluded:

> [t]he delivery of therapy had much improved and each community was now appropriately staffed. Good management structures had been put in place to ensure that sentence plans, therapy and parole reports were completed on time...overall it was good to see that significant advances had been made.

This does suggest that contractual adjustments can be made and changes instituted to good effect. We remain agnostic about the concept of privatisation in the provision of prison establishments in general and TCs in particular, and readers wishing to see a lively discussion and articulation of differing perspectives are referred to the Liebling and Sparks special issue.

Can a TC be accommodated within a prison?

We discussed earlier the potential conflicts between the aims of a democratic TC and the security and containment requirements of a prison. A TC within a prison will inevitably face those tensions. David Cooke eloquently describes the demise of the Barlinnie Special Unit (Cooke, 1997), noting how important staff training and morale are in maintaining the integrity of a TC. Ray Duckworth also draws attention to the importance of the relationship between the TC and the mainstream prison, which is brought into particular relief by the proximity of both in the case of Dovegate (Duckworth in Cullen and MacKenzie, 2011, p. 252). Roland Woodward grappled with this tension and uses the concept of symbiosis as an explanatory device to clarify his stance on that relationship (Woodward, 2007). He defines symbiosis thus: "the association of two different organisms living attached to each other or one within the other. It is a living together, and a co-operation of persons, in this case milieu or regimes." With respect to a prison-based TC, Woodward's experience led him to conclude that symbiosis can only be achieved by overcoming and working through the hazards of the host–parasite relationship his analogy implies. If the prison partner is not to be threatened by the TC regime, over-burdened by the "bottom line" or overcome by a TC's falling performance indicators (in which case, as Ray Duckworth warns, a TC could be removed), what is required in Roland's view is resolve, vision, energy and a long-term perspective. Our book has not addressed closely the staffing, training, administrative or contractual matters alluded to in Roland Woodward's essay, as these are very effectively elucidated in the Cullen and MacKenzie book. Rather, we answer our posed question by referring back to the TC residents. Whilst it is true that some residents felt they had made no gains or claimed to be worse off after their TC experience, the majority did positively benefit and showed some significant insights. We discuss the outcomes in more detail later in the chapter, but our answer is an unequivocal yes, TCs can co-exist within the prison establishment if sufficiently and effectively staffed and if constructive relationships are fostered between the mainstream and therapeutic regimes and the community is not compromised by the admission of unsuitable residents.

How can we discover "what works" in prison interventions?

We also raised the issue of the methodological approach to evaluating a TC in our Introduction. Manning (2004) discusses the experimental randomised control trial (RCT) method of evaluation and the difficulties in applying to TCs involving as they do knowledge that is interactively constructed and shared. Shadd Maruna in his paper (Maruna, 2013, p. 18) neatly encapsulates the dilemma when trying to analyse "what works" in therapeutic interventions in prisons. He draws attention to problems in defining the "what" and identifying the processes involved in the "works" bit of what works. On the one hand, there is an over-emphasis on "manual-heavy" programmes following standardised delivery with greater controllability, which are more amenable to RCTs. Critics of TCs argue that "unless obstacles cited against the implementation of randomised control trials (RCT) methods are overcome, support for justifying the use of TCs with this client group [the personality disordered offender] will remain equivocal" (Shuker, 2010, p. 52). On the other hand, this position is countered by Tapp and colleagues (Tapp et al., 2013, p. 1610). They say:

> [w]hilst establishing clinical evidence through controlled trials is intended to circumvent the problems of "soft" boundaries between interventions, which can threaten the validity of findings, these are reductionist and prescriptive.

They go on to point out that there are cumulative and multiple factors to be considered in outcomes, such that other approaches to gathering the evidence should be considered. Eric Cullen and Judith MacKenzie (Cullen and MacKenzie, 2011, p. 243) also discuss "soft" qualitative outcomes that elude quantitative measurement, and they talk about the power of reported experience in understanding risk and its reduction. Tapp and his colleagues agree. In the context of treatment approaches with high-secure patients at Broadmoor, they believe:

> [t]he patient perspective can also offer an in-depth understanding of "what works" in contexts where interventions may contain, or occur alongside, a host of therapeutic "ingredients" that act independently or in concert towards the goal(s) of rehabilitation.

They champion the "experts by experience" approach to inform the "what works" literature.

At the heart of this qualitative vs. quantitative argument in trying to assess what works is prediction vs. explanation. In other words, RCTs are trying to pin down causation in order to justify the intervention, and the experts by experience approach is working towards understanding the process. We are with Maruna, who proposes that not only are the overall aims of both approaches compatible with trying to improve interventions, but also we can, and should, "reimagine" evidence-based policy by changing our research question from what works to how it works and that we should be looking at processes of change. This, in turn, requires a plurality of methods in order to address what is a complex issue, and we adopted what Maruna advises, a mixed-methods approach.

Conducting research in a prison therapeutic community

There are a number of difficulties associated with conducting research within a TC that are exacerbated when the TC is situated within a prison, and a private one to boot. Box 12.1 shows some examples of what we mean.

Box 12.1   Issues when conducting research in a prison

- The complex and volatile nature of the population
- The complexities of the treatment being measured
- The heterogeneity of the clinical population involved
- The diversity of the TC approach
- The need for long-term follow-up and the difficulty of tracing offenders once they have moved on
- The difficulty in identifying appropriate outcome measures
- Establishing and recruiting a suitable control group
- Ethical issues in conducting research with a prison population
- The potential contamination of observations (for example, if participants discuss the research with other participants in the TC this could influence the results).

A prison setting is a complex one, and considerable difficulties are inherent in managing the research tasks alongside the requirements of prisoner needs, the prison regime and staff sensibilities, particularly within a TC. There were several interruptions during the data collection process, particularly days when the prisons were "locked down". There are many reasons why this occurs, including security problems, prisoner punishment, staff training days and/or staff shortages. "Lock down" involved residents being locked in their cells, without the privilege of visitors, for a period of at least a few hours or possibly for the whole day. On occasions when "lock down" occurred, it was impossible to start or complete interviews. Although residents could complete self-report elements of the data gathering whilst locked in their cells, no interview data could be collected on these days. Unfortunately, this aspect of data collection within a prison setting is insurmountable and we just had to live with the interruptions.

Further predicaments affecting data collection within the prison environment were issues to do with record keeping and prisoner tracking. Information was missing from prisoner case files: in particular, PDQ-4 results were absent and some cases could not be traced. These had to be recorded as missing data. The difficulty with prison tracking occurred when our research participants left the TC between baseline and follow-up. When it came to following them up in their new prison establishment, or sometimes in the community, if records had not been updated it was difficult to locate the ex-TC residents. For example, in order to track a prisoner throughout their sentence the Prisoner Location Index (PLI) service had to be contacted and provided with the prisoner's name, date of birth and/or prison number. If any of this information was missing, it was not possible to locate the prisoner in order to complete a follow-up visit, and a number of participants were lost in this way.

One of the most limiting complications facing this research was the recruitment of comparison group participants. We simply failed in our attempt to recruit waiting list controls. So, instead, we enlisted prisoners from two mainstream prisons. They were required to have at least 18 months remaining of their sentence, not to be receiving peer group therapy, to have no history of residence in a TC, and not to be suffering any mental illness. It was extremely difficult to organise access. Once access had been secured, it was still a problem trying to recruit participants. It was not possible to offer any compensation for taking part, and participants were aware of the voluntary nature of their involvement. Many of the prisoners in the normal prison regime were not minded to take part in the research. Prisoners were unhappy about missing out on aspects of their normal routine, such as their prison jobs, education or time in the gym, in order to complete the psychometric tests. This led to the recruitment of a lower number of comparison group participants than was desirable. We had to make a pragmatic decision on whether to use the comparison group as a benchmark, notwithstanding the severe limitations of the data. On balance, we decided that some comparison benchmarking was more helpful than none. The data did establish that, by and large, those volunteering for the TC were psychologically more vulnerable than those in our comparison group who were not interested in participating in a TC.

Prisons and other secure forensic settings can be seen as hostile environments which impede the therapeutic regime and make undertaking research harder. The population housed within prisons is a difficult participant group to engage due to problems in interpersonal styles of relating and suppressed and overt aggression. A further difficulty encountered when conducting research with a prison population is that prisoners can misconstrue the benefits of taking part – they may see engaging in a study as an opportunity to secure early release or as a positive inclusion on their behaviour reports. To this end, some prisoners perhaps saw their participation as an opportunity to "fake good" in order to impress the prison authorities. On the other hand, some participants may view the research as an opportunity to act out and cause disruption in order to gain attention (Lees et al., 2003). It was made clear to all participants in the current research that their participation would have no effect on their prison sentence, treatment in prison or pathway through prison estates.

There were both psychological and physical tolls on the active data gatherers, and a degree of exhaustion. The research team was based in Surrey and the TC was over 160 miles away. It was a long journey and involved overnight stays. Visiting the dispersal prisons involved many miles of travel. It was important to be watchful of each other in terms of stress and fatigue. Being vigilant about boundaries and attentive to what the residents were saying required concentrated effort. We used our clinical colleagues for advice, while also having a very capable and hands-on project manager (SM) and held regular supervisory meetings (with JB).

There are other complications involved when conducting research with offenders. The first problem to affect the research was the voluntary nature of residents' involvement. It was made explicit when gaining participants' informed consent that they were volunteering to take part and were free to leave at any time. A number of participants exercised this right and were, therefore, lost to follow-up. Wherever possible, the team tried to clarify any problems the participant may have had when completing the research and to provide any help that was necessary for them to continue their involvement. For example, some residents declined to take part as they were unhappy with completing the battery of self-report psychometric questionnaires, often due to difficulties with reading or fatigue. In this instance, help was offered, such as reading the questions aloud for the participant to answer, and this often meant that they were able to continue involvement with the project. Some residents simply did not feel like participating on certain days, and these people were asked on the following visit whether they were happy to participate on this occasion, rather than excluding them from the research on their initial refusal.

TCs are deliberately structured so that residents are encouraged to take personal responsibility for their lives and to minimise dependence on professionals. This is very different from the normal prison regime, where prisoners are under lock and key and have no involvement in the decision-making process. The peer group is essential for forming a therapeutic alliance; however, there is a need for strong leadership from staff in order to provide a safe "frame" in which therapeutic work can occur (Association of Therapeutic Communities, 1999). In prison TCs in the UK an important underlying principle is that all involved are encouraged to be curious about themselves, each other, the staff, psychological processes, the group process, the institution and everything else relevant to events and relationships within the community. This is known as the "culture of enquiry". As such, participating in a study conducted by an external party may be seen as interfering with the therapeutic process. Residents engaging in this type of research may be seen as disengaging from the therapeutic process in order to participate in something not directly related to therapy. We tried hard to present the view that the research provided a means to get a handle on therapeutic processes. Providing feedback from the multiple sorting task procedure was one way of illustrating this. We also made strenuous efforts to keep the TC residents and staff informed about the research.

Another important consideration when conducting research within a TC is the possibility that participants may share information with the researcher that they have not shared with community members. This could be considered as undermining one of the principles of the TC. Additionally, the research guarantees anonymity for the participants when reporting results. This may seem to contravene the principle of openness and the "culture of enquiry" – central to the TC approach. It is possible that the therapeutic milieu may be disrupted by divisions forming between those participating in the research and those opting not to. The difficulty here is that sub-groups may form between participants and those opting out of the research, causing fractions within the community and potentially disrupting the therapeutic programme. This was another reason for sharing the results with the community as a whole, maintaining the spirit of openness in so far as confidentiality permitted, and ensuring that the community understood the research, even if some had chosen not to participate. The research was intended to provide a learning experience for all the residents, not just the participants directly involved. However, there is also an issue here about participant disclosure. Disclosures are likely to (and we found that they did) contain information about community processes. We endeavoured to make it clear we would not be a conduit to pass on specific complaints and that such issues should be brought up by residents themselves within community meetings or to TC staff. General themes, such as time available for discussions between residents and staff, were, however, reflected in the feedback in our oral presentations and newsletters.

As a researcher coming into the TC, one may be viewed as an "outsider on the inside" (Lees, Manning, Menzies and Morant, 2004), and it is important to try to establish a rapport with the participants in order to carry out research. This can be difficult with personality disordered offenders, and increasingly so whilst they are immersed in this particular mode of therapy. It was important, as researchers, to be transparent with the research aims whilst maintaining appropriate boundaries with participants. It is vital when conducting research within a TC that the researcher gains an in-depth understanding of principles, practice and daily dynamics of the unit. This understanding informs all stages of the research process (Lees et al., 2003). The participants were invited to give their *informed* consent to participate, which meant that they were fully briefed as to what the research would involve and assured that they could withdraw at any time. There is, of course, an ethical obligation to ensure participants are kept informed as to how the information they provide will be used, but key to the TC is that it has been designed to empower residents. Providing as much information about the research as the participant requires is a component contributing to their sense of empowerment.

Both TC and comparison group participants signed a consent form outlying the particular details and conditions relating to the part of the research programme they might wish to engage in. It contained a reassurance that taking part, or declining, in no way prejudiced their continued therapy at Dovegate or, for comparison participants, life in the normal prison regime. Participants also agreed that researchers could access their case files in order to collect demographic and criminogenic information relevant to the research but that all information collected would be reported anonymously.

Assessing outcomes

In Chapter 4 we set out the broad aims of the research and a series of more specific research objectives. Here we summarise the answers to those questions and then comment on the lessons to be learnt. Before looking at our conclusion, here we pause to reflect on some of the inherent difficulties of measurement, following on from the discussion about methods. Again, we are indebted to Elaine Genders for a steer from her thoughtful and helpful paper, in which she draws attention to problems in developing measures that reflect treatment effects (Genders, 2002). These include the ability to separate the various influences on change. We address her concerns by looking at actual behaviour as well as attitudes, and we compare observer ratings with self-ratings. We also have a comparison group of prisoners not receiving a TC intervention. Our time series data try to address the problem Genders raises about partialling out the TC experience from the totality of a prison sentence.

We accept, as Genders indicates, that direct comparison between prisons is difficult (p. 298), especially as the baseline starting point of those seeking to enter the Dovegate TC was poorer on most of our psychometric measures than the comparison group of prisoners. But, on balance, we felt that some comparison provides us with useful indications. We were able to show that, whilst the comparison group barely changed, we detected sizeable movement in those receiving the TC intervention.

Genders also questions whether the dosage effect is a legitimate measurement by arguing individual differences in responsivity. We used the Reliable Change Index as a way to chart individuals who do change, either progressing or regressing, and, as such, can map change idiographically.

Whilst recognising all these potential pitfalls, we do not subscribe to a counsel of despair that the task is just too difficult, and we have tried to monitor residents' progress by multiple means. We see our research as a contribution to the provision of some markers of therapeutic achievement in a TC.

What is the optimal treatment dosage?

The psychometric measurements provide convincing evidence that 18 months is the optimal period residents should spend in the TC to achieve positive change and for that change to be sustainable. This is evidenced by increases in self-awareness, improvements in emotional regulation and decreases in susceptibility to influence, as compared with baseline scores. This is in accordance with Genders and Player's (1995) findings for Grendon TC residents. Whilst the Dovegate residents who stay for a shorter time, up to about six months, show some change in self-esteem and positive shifts in blame attribution and hostility, periods of this duration do not appear to impact criminogenic needs. For residents spending between 12 and 17 months in therapy, there is a further enhancement of self-esteem, but there is also a marked increase in hostility and evidence of some dysfunctional behaviours. This is a period when there is vulnerability and a risk of dropping out of therapy. This finding fits neatly with those of Jones (1997), who observed a non-linear change process. In other words, change is marked by backward as well as forward movement, as a degree of cognitive dissonance befalls the resident as he confronts and retreats from dealing with criminogenic beliefs. Those staying in therapy for at least 18 months showed decreases in tenseness, levels of distress, blaming, withdrawal and distancing and increases in questioning and arguing (taken as signs of therapeutic engagement) over the course of the residency (Neville et al., 2007). Similarly, behaviourally, more of the 18-month residents showed continued improvement with respect to coercive and hostile behaviours once back in mainstream prison. Residencies of over 18 months do not show appreciably greater improvement.

Who benefits most/least from the TC?

Sex offenders had a more challenging time, both from other members of the group and in their own self-challenges, and they were more susceptible to early drop-out. Tolerating sex offenders seemed to be a breakthrough issue for non-sex offenders. Those who were able to show a degree of understanding and came to realise some aspects of shared histories and who, whilst not condoning, did not condemn sex offenders were more likely to stay in therapy. This demonstrated their progress on other markers of therapeutic gains, such as empathy and patience. Those who could not achieve this acceptance were more likely to drop out. Residents who were able to overcome their barriers to change, who were able to form a strong therapeutic alliance to their therapy group relatively early on, seemed to weather the therapeutic ruptures and personal setbacks better than those whose alliances were weaker. Those who felt rejected and misunderstood (often sex offenders) also found difficulties in completing a full residency. We found that attachment theory helped us to make sense of these findings, as those with dismissive and fearful attachment styles struggled to make the connections needed to benefit from the TC. Our findings chime with Gwen Adshead's (Adshead, 2002) in that a functioning and functional capacity for self-reflection, often disabled by poor attachment, seems key to developing empathy, and care-giving and care-eliciting behaviours develop from this. A dismissive attachment style is associated with a negation or ignoring of affective distress in self and others. Adshead talks of "toxic" attachments, which are dismissive of feelings, with few demonstrations of tenderness, typified by a sense of emptiness. In this state people are used instrumentally and assessed in terms of discrepancies of power and control, on the one hand, and vulnerability for the purposes of exploitation, on the other.

We found few demographic factors or offence histories that demarcated those who completed at least 18 months' residency compared with those who left earlier. A key factor seems to have been personality disorder status. Those with no diagnosis or mild PD (around a quarter of residents) stayed longer in therapy and fared much better than those with more severe PD.

Those who stayed longer were found to bolster their self-awareness and confidence to be able to address more criminogenic factors associated with their offending. Whilst index offence overall did not seem to be a predictive factor, those committing acquisitive crime had a tendency to stay longer and do better than those whose index offence was violent crime or sex offending.

What does the process of change look like?

Our proposed model of change followed Genders and Player (1995) in that we, as they had before us, found some distinct phases. They classify the first phase as entry, followed by acclimatisation, during which traditional prison culture is challenged and the TC establishes new traditions. We found, from our focus groups, the entry phase to be marked by a degree of suspicion, scepticism and doubt, with some cautious exploration. Our more detailed one-to-one interviews revealed that learning to open up feelings and discuss emotions and laying down the foundations of trust to form therapeutic alliances are some of the keys for the resident is to gain the necessary confidence to confront why he offends in order to address his particular issues. Then he draws on his own resilience and the group's support to deal with setbacks and ruptures within therapy. These must interact with positive support from staff and an absence of institutional turbulence, such as staff demoralisation and admission of unsuitable residents. Strong therapeutic alliances were associated with establishing trust and enhancing capacity to access and express feelings. When residents experience a growth in self-confidence and achieve greater awareness not only their own interior lives but also of others, along with tolerance and ability to empathise, they seem more prepared to commit to staying in therapy. This was akin to Genders and Player's resocialisation stage, during which they noted Grendon residents increased their social skills in order to build more positive relationships. Part of this resocialisation was a realigning of attachments. As one resident graphically explained

> "Well I have tried to work this out myself. I didn't like them [prison staff]. I'd been placed on a report a few times for just being abusive . . . for destroying prison property and things like that because I know it's prison property [and]

because I didn't like the staff. But now that...was my own issue, I think is rebellion because I lost my parents when I was young and I couldn't rebel against them anymore, because they weren't there. So my parents were authority figures and the way I am seeing it is...the police, the prison service, all them other authority figures took their place. They became my parents because I came to prison when I was fifteen. And as soon as I was aware of that I just didn't feel like doing it anymore. Its like a process when you are a child and you rebel against your parents, move away from home and then you make up your differences and you get on fine together. And that's what I feel the process is gone with me...but instead of being my parents its been staff and authority."

Thereafter, Genders and Player observed a consolidation stage, which, interestingly, was associated with a detachment from the therapy group as the resident was preparing to leave. By 18 months we noted a greater assertiveness, resilience and self-acceptance. In particular, we found a breakdown of the old criminal hierarchies, especially with respect to sex offenders and the notion of "grassing".

The perpetuation of criminal values, codes and hierarchies through the drug sub-culture, bullying and the presence of instrumentally motivated residents, who "pass" as authentic residents, together with relaxation of admission criteria and staff turnover, all contributed to weakening therapeutic alliances. However, rather than one model of change, we suggest that there are different pathways: (a) plateau, i.e. remaining static with little or no movement; (b) making progress and improving; (c) non-linear improvement marked by periods of regression before further improvement is achieved; (d) deterioration. Plateau and deterioration are associated with prematurely leaving the TC.

What is the process of reintegration into mainstream prison, post-TC?

We detected a number of reintegration strategies adopted by ex-residents on their return to mainstream prison. Reintegration was managed by calling upon previous prison experiences and repertoires on how to handle yourself, and ex-residents resumed the performance of a successful prisoner, even if this did not reflect who they felt themselves to be after their Dovegate experience. Masking was a protective strategy that might be donned in the face of violence or unpredictable prisoners and removed with the more amenable. "Therapeuton" was a label assigned to former residents, whereby there was a level of continued awareness of fellow prisoners' pain and mistakes but an absence of the therapeutic milieu to address this.

Some returning to mainstream prison reflected that it was actually a relief and that the prison, as opposed to the TC, was a familiar and more manageable environment. Others, mostly those de-selected or early leavers, expressed some regret and thought they had left too soon or were angry, feeling disappointment or being let down that they had been voted out of the TC. There was some degree of projection by early leavers blaming other residents, staff or institutional failures for their premature departure, although some of the criticisms were justified (as demonstrated in HM Prison Inspectorate reports and Community of Communities reviews). More than half of the premature leavers did report positive gains, such as being better able to deal with their difficulties, being more tolerant and using more emotionally controlled strategies rather than reverting to violence.

Most did experience a culture shock on re-entry into the mainstream prison system. As one ex-resident put it, it was like returning to a "lunatic asylum". Perhaps most graphically, this was described as returning to a world of "skulduggery, thuggery and buggery". But, rather than the culture shock suggested by the report of the Criminal Justice Joint Inspection of prisons (2013), there was more of a "reverse culture shock", in other words the process of readjusting, reacculturating and reassimilating into a familiar culture after having experienced a different one (Gaw, 1999). Common problems associated with reverse culture shock include disorientation, stress, value conflicts, anger, hostility and feelings of helplessness. Those who had a more firmly established sense of themselves and their changed identity fared better. So perhaps it is unsurprising that we found anger and feelings of rejection most obvious in ex-residents who had had relatively short stays in Dovegate TC and that greater understanding and sustaining strategies were evident in the longer-stay residents.

What personal changes did men attribute to their TC involvement?

Being in Dovegate changed residents' time horizons; they were more likely to think about and plan a (different) future from that of the revolving door of offending and prison, and they reflected on their age and the number of (wasted) years spent in prisons and not wanting another stretch. They became less selfish and egocentric: "I got something from [Dovegate], so why would I want to keep all that to myself...I want to share what I have learnt...and be unselfish to try and pass a little bit on." There was a sense of being able to take a step back and reflect on the kind of characters they were, often not very nice characters. This precipitated building a new identity that was more patient, tolerant and able to empathise: "I'm still getting used to this new me which sometimes I don't recognise and that scares me."

Age was an issue brought up by those who had returned to the outside world, in so far as they felt they were too old to go on serving prison sentences and that their age had been a prime motivation to change. Some wished they had been young enough to have effected greater change in their lives.

Many had been able to discuss their own physical or sexual abuse as a child, some for the first time. Also mentioned were improvements in family relationships, largely by being able to talk issues through and the ex-residents coming to terms with the past and bringing a different perspective to reconcile past conflicts.

Several reflected that they should not return to the location where they had offended, and should also change their associates with whom they had offended. This meant getting a different set of friends and getting away from people "that's on the gear". This might be contrasted with having a sense of attachment to Dovegate TC as possibly one of the first places in adulthood where they had felt accepted and not out of place.

Being able to tackle problems without resorting to violence or reverting to drugs was another key change attributed to their time in Dovegate. Not doing drugs and stopping to think before reacting were put down to their Dovegate experience: "as I wake up I say to myself, today I'm not using drugs." Others commented that through the experience they had "grown up": "Dovegate did that for me and I know it did."

As an element in the resocialisation process was an appreciation that there are conventional social rules that serve to guide behaviour rather than being experienced to frustrate personal inclinations: "The funny thing is, this might sound a bit weird, but I think the [TC] constitution, like not taking drugs and no violence...them things been put into place...if that constitution wasn't there I wouldn't have felt half the things I felt that led me to like...deal with certain issues"

Many ex-residents commented on how hard it was to look at themselves and face the comments from fellow residents. "I think [Dovegate] was the hardest jail I've ever been in." It was hard if a resident had experienced sex abuse when young to have a sex offender in the therapy group. It was hard returning to mainstream prison and it was hard reconstructing a crime-free life once released. For some, the fact that it was so hard meant they gave up; for others, who persevered, it meant a shift in external blame: "for years I used to blame my old man...There's no excuse. That's what I dealt with in Dovegate...so I forgave him in my own way and that's how I can talk to him." Accepting responsibility for the reasons why the individual received a prison sentence meant stopping making excuses and seeing things differently: "when I got my head to thinking in a different way...I wanted to change".

There was an appreciation of the positive learning that came out of their Dovegate experiences and of the staff and residents' support. Counter to this, there was also anger and disappointment that staff turnover, inappropriate selection for the TC, and being stuck in the TC when it was time to move on inhibited progress. Ex-residents attributed their lack of progress to these problems, some of which may have been justified.

Several residents did manage to sustain their Dovegate identity and were recognised as a resource for other prison inmates. The psychometric data demonstrate the maintenance of psychological and behavioural improvements, but these were more likely to be sustained by ex-residents who had achieved at least an 18-month residency.

Does a TC experience result in greater change compared with prisoners not experiencing a TC?

Our control group data suggest that those who opted for or were referred to the TC tended to be in a worse state in terms of most psychometric measures, including self-esteem, hostility, anger and criminal thinking styles, compared with a mainstream, non-TC group. The TC group were more likely to have drink or drug-related problems than the general prison population. The TC residents started their offending younger and were more prolific than the general offending population. Using the Reliable Change Index (RCI) method, a higher percentage of those in our mainstream comparison group stayed the same or deteriorated compared with our Dovegate completers on ratings from the Hostility and Direction of Hostility Questionnaire (HDHQ), which measures guilt and assesses negative, aggressive or punitive cognitions and feelings towards self and others. Overall, the movement, as measured by the psychometric instruments, achieved collectively by the Dovegate sample placed them as being equivalent to scores achieved by the mainstream prisoners.

How effective is the TC in reducing recidivism severity and frequency?

We had reconviction data on 94 of our Dovegate residents who had been released into the community. Notwithstanding the limitations of this as an outcome measure, 48% were reconvicted, and all but one of these served new prison sentences. This was not directly associated with length of residency, and there was no difference between those directly released into the community and those released after returning to mainstream prison. Most were reconvicted within a year of release. These rates should take into account that 22 of those reconvicted failed the Assessment and Relocation Unit (ARU) assessment, so in reality 72 were actually ex-residents in the sense that they had participated in at least some therapy. We might suppose that the 22 were at least predisposed to changing, but they tended to reoffend more quickly than the therapy group. When we considered two broad groupings of ex-residents, those spending less than 18 months in Dovegate and those residing at least 18 months, 70% reoffended compared with 29% of the former. The nature of the offences largely involved absconding and breaches of licence. Where a criminal offence was committed this was most likely to be acquisitive crime: drug possession, burglary, breaking and entering, or theft.

How effective is the TC in reducing adjudication severity and frequency?

We managed to obtain adjudication data one year prior to entering the TC and one year after a residency. We were able to show a marked decrease in adjudications after a residency, with the greatest improvement associated with longer periods of residency. The average number of prior adjudications directly matched the length of stay in the TC, with the shortest stay being associated with the greatest number of prior adjudications.

Practice implications

Our findings point clearly to 18 months as the length of residency which is most likely to effect sustainable change in a prisoner entering into a TC. Creating a strong therapeutic alliance is essential in sustaining a resident through personal challenges and setbacks caused by inevitable ruptures in the therapy group. Establishing the groundwork for such an alliance is best undertaken early on, and requires the building of trust between TC staff and residents and amongst the residents. We acknowledge that this is a complex undertaking, given likely insecure attachment styles, and support the idea of using attachment to inform practice interventions. Assessing attachment style in new residents would be a useful diagnostic and the sorting task described in Chapter 8 provides one tool for doing this. Strengthened thereapuetic alliances would be assisted by continuity of staff, who themselves are well trained and supported, and also maintaining the eligibility criteria for new residents. We identify breakpoints where residents feel misunderstood, are struggling or giving up, and these struggles are community-wide. Our interviews with premature leavers suggest a degree of regret that they left when the going got tough. This implies being watchful and supportive at the point in therapy for wavering residents and intervening to discuss with the resident the implications of staying or leaving.

We did detect some experiences of racism from the relatively few non-white TC residents. The lack of diversity in the TC population was also commented upon by HM Prison Inspectorate. Clearly, the recruitment into the TC and the community's non-tolerance of racial discrimination are issues that need attention.

The presence of sex offenders in the TC presents something of a conundrum. On the one hand, they themselves experience a particularly hard time, and there may be a conflict between entering the TC and accepting a Sex Offender Treatment Programme (SOTP) that may coincide. These challenges and bureaucratic conflicts can mean they exit prematurely from the TC. On the other hand, being confronted with their offending and also being exposed to the victims of sexual abuse presents a challenge to sex offenders that is qualitatively different from the environment in which they participate in an SOTP that involves only sex offenders. Non-sex offenders in the TC do find it diffi-cult to overcome the criminal hierarchy that places sex offenders at the bottom, thereby enabling a certain complacency about the consequences of their own wrongdoing. Overcoming this and discovering a common past history as pre-cursors to offending is often a breakthrough point for the non-sex-offending resident and permits development of greater tolerance and empathy. So, the presence of sex offenders can both hinder and help the therapeutic process. On balance, it would seem that being confronted by non-sex-offending peers happens from the outset, and sex offenders may need some additional support if they are to survive this type of challenge early on before trusting relation-ships can be built. Perhaps making sex offending a more explicit issue would bring this out into the open and it could be presented as material for the group to work on.

Returning to mainstream prison is also a challenge. The Criminal Justice Joint Inspection (2013) generally, as well as HM Prison Inspectorate comments on Dovegate, particularly suggested that relocation and resettlement planning is not always sufficient. If returning to mainstream prison is conceptualised as reverse culture shock, this may help in preparing residents to develop con-structive strategies to manage their exit from the TC and their re-entry into the realities of mainstream prisons, giving them tactics to preserve their TC gains. Greater attention to permitting the resident to achieve a positive separa-tion from his therapy group and anticipating the relative "lunacy" of ordinary prison life may require explicit discussion within the group about relapse prevention.

There are outcomes that clearly will satisfy the Home Office and prison authorities, in so far as a TC experience does appear to positively affect reoffending rates and also attracts greater compliance to prison life, as mea-sured by the number of adjudications following return to prison. However, it is important not to underplay the personal changes that the TC demonstrably brings about in individuals. The residents are asking for continuity of well-trained staff together with clarity of therapy direction, the absence of which demonstrably de-stabilises the TC. Holding the line with regard to the eligibil-ity criteria and resisting pressures to admit unsuitable potential members to the community may be hard in the commercial climate and in the face of pressure on prison places. Failing to resist and filling places regardless of suitability is a rather Pyrrhic victory. Contractual obligations may be met, but at the cost of the therapeutic process. Returning men who are no longer in therapy to main-stream prisons as quickly as possible is highly desirable, but may not be entirely within the gift of the TC. Finding better ways to manage this within the prison may be the least worst option.

Whilst a number of interventions have been employed for the alleviation of personality disorder symptoms, the TC is the only *offender model* which specifically targets personality disorder. A systematic review of the effectiveness of TCs in treating personality disorders (Lees et al., 1999) found that the TC model was efficient in treating difficult prisoners, leading to a reduction in violent incidences. Clearly it is possible to treat the more difficult symptoms related to personality disorder, such as violence, within a TC framework, but what is the nature of this change? Are some personality disorders more amenable to this particular treatment than others?

Earlier research had shown that offenders with paranoid personality disorder are the most prone to drop out of therapy (Miller et al., 2004). Subsequently, we found that those with paranoid personality disorder who entered the therapeutic community were able to tolerate the treatment and made positive therapeutic gains over the course of a year. Furthermore, those who were unable to remain in the TC for the full course of treatment (usually considered to be at least 18 months) and returned to mainstream prison early (most likely due to de-selection, according to our results) still made clinically significant improvements in the symptoms of avoidant personality disorder.

Unfortunately, in support of the claims published by Rice and colleagues (1992), the TC can offer antisocial participants the opportunity to develop manipulative and deceitful traits, and this particular personality disorder appears to get worse. An increase in anti-social personality trait behaviour is supported by the finding of an increase in number of adjudications recorded on return to mainstream prison for those who left therapy after between 6 and 18 months of treatment. This finding highlights the need for staff who are trained in dealing with personality disordered offenders to prevent the TC from becoming a challenging and unsafe environment.

For the work focusing particularly on personality disorder within TCs, the measures of self-esteem, anger and interpersonal relating were the psychometrics most closely considered. Problems with these three elements (anger, self-esteem and relationships) can be part of the presenting problem of personality disorder and be risk factors for offending. It was found that treatment in a TC led to slightly increased levels of self-esteem; improvements in expression, duration, sensitivity and control of anger; and reductions in dominant and coercive styles of interpersonal relating. Blackburn (1998) asserts that the dominant and coercive styles are most closely related to persistent criminality, and this is an encouraging result for the reduction of risk of reoffending for personality disordered offenders. However, rule-breaking and challenging behaviour (as measured by the number of adjudications post-TC) only improves after a minimum of 18 months in therapy. For those who stay in the TC for between 6 and 18 months, there is an increase in the number of adjudications recorded after return to mainstream prison.

Tyrer and colleagues' (2010) paper on the treatment of dangerous and severe personality disorder states that risk can be independent of personality disorder and treating the disorder may not necessarily reduce risk of serious reoffending. This certainly seems to be the case in the medium term (12 months' follow-up); however, the case for treatment of personality disordered offenders in the TC seems positive over the longer term (18 months plus), supporting the research carried out at HMP Grendon previously (Genders and Player, 1995; Marshall, 1997; Taylor, 2000).

The primary practical implication from SN's research on measuring personality disorder is that the current tool being used for the assessment of personality disorder is unsuitable due to its inaccuracy. The prisons taking part in the current research (HMPs Dovegate, Woodhill and Blundeston) used the self-report Personality Disorder Questionnaire-4 (Hyler, 1994). The PDQ-4 only correctly identified half of the participants with antisocial personality disorder, which is unsurprising for a self-report measure assessing individuals who are prone to exaggeration. i.e. dissembling. This result is of concern, as those with this disorder tend to be amongst the most dangerous and persistent offenders. Furthermore, antisocial personality disorder has been found to be the most prevalent amongst the general prison population (Singleton et al., 1998), and it is important to gain an accurate understanding of how these offenders respond to treatment, which begins with an accurate assessment on admission.

PDQ-4 data for antisocial personality disorder were missing for 65% of $n=250$ residents. It was unclear why these data were missing, as this is part of the initial assessment for suitability for admission on to the TC proper (conducted on the Assessment and Resettlement Unit). One of the practical recommendations from this research is that this is improved upon by the introduction of a structured clinical interview-based assessment of personality disorder for all prisoners admitted for assessment at the TC.

The PDQ-4 was also found to under-diagnose paranoid personality disorder, identified as the second most prevalent personality disorder within the general prison population (Singleton et al., 1998). Results showed that offenders with paranoid personality disorder made the most significant improvement in symptoms over the course of 12 months in therapy. It would, therefore, seem particularly important to accurately diagnose PD so as to maximise responsivity to therapy and allow future researchers to clarify who benefits most from therapy. It would also allow the therapists to tailor the structure of the therapeutic programme accordingly.

The PD results also showed that offenders with antisocial personality disorder can get worse during time spent in a TC. A practical implication of this result is that the therapeutic programme should be developed to specifically address this issue. Special training in working with offenders with antisocial personality disorder could be introduced to enable staff to deal more effectively with the more manipulative and deceitful residents. Working with this type of personality disorder is particularly difficult and can quickly lead to staff burn-out – the introduction of regular staff supervision and reflective practice could also address this issue. Roland Woodward in his foreword, asked whether research observation killed or saved Schrödinger's cat. He mused that for some residents, immersion in the TC did help them change, for others it was less successful and for yet others change was sustained. We as the researchers were not untouched by our involvement in this project. We were privy to the struggles and challenges of residents, staff and the three directors. As the residents kept telling us, 'change is hard.' Tom Main in his essay 'knowledge, learning and freedom from thought' says that mastery of new knowledge, concepts, facts and skills gives pleasure, power and hope. Pleasure because the learning replaces feelings of helplessness, power because new competencies have been acquired and hope because these can be applied as useful tools for the future (Main, 1990, p. 59). We certainly learnt a great deal from conducting the research, we observed change in the TC residents, and we hope our findings will assist in the further development of the prison based therapeutic communities.

Concluding reflections from the residents

We would like to end our book with some reflections by the residents in Dovegate from a focus group convened by Amelie Bobsien. Amelie asked the residents what was a good outcome as far as they were concerned. This is a selection of their responses.

> To have a much better awareness of myself, to be able to have faith in myself and my abilities. To be able to deal with my guilt, be able to deal with bereavements and things that happened in my life ... to make sure that what I've done never happens to me again.

> To not come back to jail again. To take responsibility for my kids, to be a benefit to society. A little bit of redemption in there.

> Just to lead a so called normal life and stop hurting people that I love and stop creating victims.

> I want to gain an understanding of how I came to be doing what I did, get some tools to cope with guilt and remorse.

> Not to have the self destruct button anymore.

> To stop creating victims, I mean I am really ashamed of my offences and I don't want to deal with any new bad stuff again.

Appendices

Appendix one census summary

	2004*	2006**	2008***	2011****
Sentence length				
2 to <4 years		3% (6)	2% (3)	–
4 but <10 years	62% (222)	59% (114)	21% (41)	9% (17)
10 years or more but not life		39% (78)	29% (49)	6% (12)
Life	40% (138)	–	42% (82)	40% (77)
Indeterminate Sentence for Public Protection (ISPP)				44% (84)
Main offence				
Violence	43% (152)	43% (85)	45% (90)	59% (112)
Sexual	6.5% (23)	9% (17)	6% (11)	7% (13)
Burglary	8.5% (30)	11% (22)	7% (14)	4% (7)
Robbery	28% (98)	19% (38)	26% (50)	21% (41)
Drug	7% (25)	4% (8)	9% (17)	2% (4)
Age				
21–29	40% (93)	29% (57)	28% (55)	31% (59)
30–39	36% (87)	38% (75)	38% (73)	41% (78)
40–49	16% (39)	22% (44)	25% (48)	18% (35)
50–59	6% (15)	10% (20)	8% (15)	8% (15)
60+	2% (4)	1% (2)	2% (3)	2% (4)
Ethnicity				
White	81% (232)	85% (166)	83% (160)	84% (84)

Note: *Data collected by Louise Harnet for the Dovegate project.
**HM Inspectorate of Prisons (2006) *Report of an Unannounced Short Follow-Up Inspection of HMP Dovegate Therapeutic Community 29–31 August by HM Chief Inspector of Prisons*. London: HM Chief Inspectorate of Prisons.
***HM Inspectorate of Prisons (2008) *Report of an Announced Short Inspection of HMP Dovegate Therapeutic Community 16–20 June 2008 by HM Chief Inspector of Prisons*. London: HM Chief Inspectorate of Prisons.
****HM Inspectorate of Prisons (2012) *Report of an Unannounced Short Follow-Up Inspection of HMP Dovegate Therapeutic Community 11–13 October 2011 by HM Chief Inspector of Prisons*. London: HM Chief Inspectorate of Prisons.

Notes

4 The Data

1. The census was undertaken by Louise Harsent.
2. This survey was carried out by Amelie Bobsien as part of her research dossier for her practitioner doctorate in counselling and psychotherapeutic psychology (Bobsien, 2004).
3. These interviews were conducted by Rosemary Simmonds.
4. The post-release case studies were constructed by Emily Cahalane for her master's dissertation in forensic psychology.
5. Co-occurrence between variables is referred to as the "principle of continuity" (Lingoes, 1979).
6. Sensitivity refers to the way in which partitioning is able to enclose target items within a zone as a function of the overall number of target items; selectivity refers to the exclusivity of target items being in a particular partitioned zone as a function of all items in that zone (Brown & Barnett, 2000).
7. Includes tariffs in the case of residents serving life sentences.
8. Where inmates had multiple index offences recorded, the most serious was selected for purposes of comparison.
9. Includes all offence types for each participant.
10. Where inmates had multiple index offences recorded, the most serious was selected for purposes of comparison.

5 Personality Disorder

1. DSM-V still under revision at time of writing.

6 Changes over Time: The Psychometric Data

1. This includes tariffs in the case of residents serving life sentences.
2. The censored and drop-out groups were not mutually exclusive.
3. Where inmates had multiple index offences recorded, the most serious was selected for purposes of comparison.
4. Includes all offence types for each participant.

9 After the TC: Post-Residency Questionnaire, Interviews and Psychometrics

1. Amelie Bobsien undertook the survey of leavers as part of her practitioner doctorate research portfolio and further details can be found in Bobsien (2004).
2. Rosemary Simmonds carried out the post-Dovegate interviews and the present chapter draws on the work she did in synthesising the material she collected and analysed.

Her original contribution was included in our final report (Brown et al., 2008) and we have undertaken some further analytic work to develop her findings as presented in this chapter. Additional analyses can be found in (Simmonds, 2008).

10 Back in the Outside World: Case Studies of Former Residents on Release

1. Emily Cahalane was at the time studying for her master's in forensic psychology at the University of Surrey. She explained to potential volunteers that, although part of the Dovegate evaluation, she would also be using the data she collected for her dissertation. Six of those approached and agreeing to participate on this understanding are reported in this chapter. Emily gained ethical approval for her research from the University of Surrey ethics committee.

11 Getting It: A Quantification of Long-Term Outcomes

1. A complete summary of the results is provided in the appendix. It should be noted that these results, and those reported in chapters 6 and 9 do not make reference to IVE (Impulsivity, Venturesomeness and Empathy); EPQr (Eysenck's Personality Questionnaire); MSI (Multi-phasic Sex Inventory); and MAS (Masculinity Scale).

Bibliography

Adshead, G. (2002). Three degrees of security; attachment and forensic institutions. *Criminal Behaviour and Mental Health*, 12 (2 suppl) s31–45.

Alwin, N., Blackburn, R., Davidson, K., Hilton, M., Logan, C., & Shine, J. (2006). *Understanding Personality Disorder: A Report by the British Psychological Society.* Leicester: BPS.

American Psychiatric Association. (1987). *Diagnostic and Statistical Manual of Mental Disorders*, 3rd Edn. Revised. Washington, DC: APA.

American Psychiatric Association. (1994). *Diagnostic and Statistical Manual of Mental Disorders*, 4th Edn. Washington, DC: APA.

American Psychiatric Association. (2000). *Diagnostic and Statistical Manual of Mental Disorders*, 4th Edn. Revised. Washington, DC: APA.

Andrews, D.A., Bonta, J., & Hoge, R.D. (1990). Classification for effective rehabilitation: Rediscovering psychology. *Criminal Justice and Behavior*, 17(1), 19–52.

Association of Therapeutic Communities. (1999). *The Need for an NHS Policy on Developing the Role of Therapeutic Communities in the Treatment of "Personality Disorder".* London: ATC.

Atkinson, D., Worthington, R., Dana, D., & Good, G. (1991). Etiology beliefs, preferences for counseling orientations, and counseling effectiveness. *Journal of Counseling Psychology*, 38, 258–264.

Bachelor, A. (1995). Clients' perceptions of the therapeutic alliance: A qualitative analysis. *Journal of Counselling Psychology*, 42(3), 323–337.

Baker, E., & Beech, A.R. (2004). Dissociation and variability of adult attachment dimensions and early maladaptive schemas in sexual and violent offenders. *Journal of Interpersonal Violence*, 19, 1119–1136.

Barnes, E., Griffiths, P., Old, J., & Wells, D. (1997). *Face-to-Face with Distress.* London: Butterworth-Heinemann.

Barrett, B., Byford, S., Seivewright, H., Cooper, S., Duggan, C., & Tyrer, P. (2009). The assessment of dangerous and severe personality disorder: Service use, cost, and consequences. *The Journal of Forensic Psychiatry and Psychology*, 20(1), 120–131.

Bartholomew, K., & Horowitz, L.M. (1991). Attachment styles among young adults: A test of a four-category model. *Journal of Personality and Social Psychology*, 61, 226–244.

Bateman, A.W., & Fonagy, P. (2000). Effectiveness of psychotherapeutic treatment on personality disorder. *British Journal of Psychiatry*, 177, 138–143.

Battle, J. (1992). *Culture Free Self-Esteem Inventories*, 2nd Edn. Austin, TX: Pro-ed.

Beck, A.T., & Freeman, A. (1990). *Cognitive Therapy of Personality Disorders.* New York: Guilford.

Becker, D., Grilo, C., Edell, W., & McGlashan, T. (2000). Comorbidity of borderline personality disorder with other personality disorders in hospitalized adolescents and adults. *American Journal of Psychiatry*, 157, 2011–2016.

Benjamin, L.S. (1993). Dimensional, categorical, or hybrid analyses of personality: A response to Widiger's proposal. *Psychological Inquiries*, 4, 91–95.

Birgden, A. (2004). Therapeutic jurisprudence and responsivity: Finding the will and the way in offender rehabilitation. *Psychology, Crime and the Law*, 10(3), 283–295.

Birtchnell, J., Hammond, S., Horn, E., & DeJong, C. A. J. (2007). A shorter version of the Person's Relating to Others Questionnaire (The PROQ3). Unpublished Article.

Blackburn, R. (1998). Psychopathy and the contribution of personality to violence. In T. Millon, E. Simonsen, M. Birket-Smith, & R.D. Davis (Eds.), *Psychopathy: Antisocial, Criminal and Violent Behaviour* (pp. 50–68). London: Guilford Press.

Blackburn, R. (1998). Psychopathy and personality disorder; implications of interpersonal theory. In D.J. Cooke, S.J. Hart, & A.E. Forth (Eds.), *Psychopathy Theory, Research and Implications for Society* (pp. 269–301). Amsterdam: Kluwer.

Blackburn, R. (1999). *The Psychology of Criminal Conduct: Theory, Research and Practice.* Chichester: Wiley.

Blackburn, R., & Renwick, S.J. (1996). Rating scales for measuring the interpersonal circle in forensic psychiatric patients. *Psychological Assessment,* 8(1), 76–84.

Bobsien, A. (2004). *A Portfolio of Academic, Therapeutic Practice and Research.* Practitioner Doctorate Portfolio submitted to the University of Surrey.

Bodlund, O., Grann, M., Ottoman, H., & Svanborg, C. (1998). Validation of the self-report questionnaire DIP-Q in diagnosing DSM-IV personality disorders: A comparison of three psychiatric samples. *Acta Psychiatrica Scandinavica,* 97, 433–439.

Bogaerts, S., Vanheule, S., & Desmet, M. (2006). Personality disorders and romantic adult attachment: A comparison of secure and insecure child molesters. *International Journal of Offender Therapy and Comparative Criminology,* 50(2), 139–147.

Bordin, E.S. (1979). The generalisability of the psychoanalytic concept of the working alliance. *Psychotherapy: Theory, Research and Practice,* 16, 252–260.

Borg, J.C., & Lingoes, I. (1983). A quasi-statistical model for choosing between alternative configurations derived from ordinally constrained data. *British Journal of Mathematical and Statistical Psychology,* 36, 36–53.

Bower, P., & King, M. (2000). Randomised controlled trials and the evaluation of psychological therapy. In N. Rowland & S. Goss (Eds.), *Evidence-Based Counselling and Psychological Therapies.* London: Routledge.

Bowlby, J. (1980). *Attachment and Loss: Volume 3. Loss, Sadness and Depression.* New York: Basic Books.

Bowlby, J. (1988). *A Secure Base.* New York: Basic Books.

Bradley, L.K. (2009). *The Bradley Report: Review of People with Mental Health Problems or Learning Disabilities in the Criminal Justice System.* London: COI for the Department of Health.

Brewin, C.R., & Bradley, C. (1989). Patient preferences and randomised clinical trials. *British Medical Journal,* 299, 313–315.

Briere, J. (2000). *Inventory of Altered Self-Capacities Professional Manual.* Odessa, FL: Psychological Assessment Resources.

Briere, J., & Runtz, M. (2002). The inventory of altered self capacities: A standardized measure of identity, affect regulation, and relationship disturbance. *Assessment,* 9, 230–239.

Brown, J., & Barnett, J. (2000). Facet theory: An approach to research. In G. Breakwell, S. Hammond, & C. Fife-Schaw (Eds.), *Research Methods in Psychology,* 2nd Edn. London: Sage Publications.

Brown, J., Miller, S., O'Neill, D., Philpen, C., Sees, C., Simmonds, R., Bobsien, A., Burdett, S., Cahalane, E., Frith, S., Neville, L., Northey, S., & Vallice, N. (2008). *HMP Dovegate Therapeutic Community Longitudinal Evaluation.* Guilford: Forensic Psychology Research Group, University of Surrey. Unpublished report.

Cahalane, E. (2006). *Life after a Prison-based TC.* Master's dissertation submitted to the University of Surrey.

Caine, T., Foulds, G., & Hope, K. (1967). *Manual of the Hostility and Direction of Hostility Questionnaire*. London: London University Press.

Campbell, S. (2003). *The Feasibility of Conducting an RCT at HMP Grendon*. London: Home Office.

Campling, P. (1992). Audit of premature departure in a therapeutic community – A preliminary report. *Therapeutic Communities*, 13(1), 45–53.

Campling, P., & Haigh, R. (1999). *Therapeutic Communities: Past, Present and Future. Therapeutic Communities 2*. London and Philadelphia: Jessica Kingsley Publishers Ltd.

Cann, J., Falshaw, L., Nugent, F., & Friendship, C. (2003). *Understanding What Works: Accredited Cognitive Skills Programmes for Adult Men and Young Offenders*. Home Office Research Findings (No. 226). London: HMSO.

Canter, D. (1982). Family correlates of male and female delinquency. *Criminology*, 20, 149–167.

Canter, D., Brown, J.M., & Groat, L. (1985). A multiple sorting procedure for studying conceptual systems. In M. Brenner, J.M. Brown, & D. Canter (Eds.), *The Research Interview; Uses and Methods* (pp. 79–114). London: Academic Press.

Carter, L.P. (2007). *Securing the Future: Prospects for the Efficient and Sustainable Use of Custody in England and Wales*. London: House of Lords.

Caverley, A., & Farrall, S. (2011). The sensual dynamics of processes of personal reform: Desistance from crime and the role of emotions. In S. Karstedt, I. Loader, & H. Strang (Eds.), *Emotions, Crime and Justice*. Oxford: Hart Publishing.

Chiesa, M. (2000). Hospital adjustment in personality disorder patients admitted to a therapeutic community milieu. *British Journal of Medical Psychology, 73 (Part 2)*, 259–267.

Chiesa, M., Drahorad, C., & Longo, S. (2000). Early termination of treatment in personality disorder treated in psychotherapy hospital. Quantitative and qualitative study. *British Journal of Psychiatry*, 177, 107–111.

Clarke, A., Simmonds, R., & Wydall, S. (2004). *Delivering Cognitive Skills Programmes in Prison: A Qualitative Study*. Home Office Research Findings (No. 242). London: Home Office.

Clarkson, P. (1995). *The Therapeutic Relationship in Psychoanalysis, Counselling Psychology and Psychotherapy*. London: Whurr.

Cohen, C. (1960). A coefficient of agreement for nominal scales. *Educational and Psychological Measurement*, 20, 37–46.

Coid, J., Yang, M., Tyrer, P., Roberts, A., & Ullrich, S. (2006). Prevalence and correlates of personality disorder in Great Britain. *British Journal of Psychiatry*, May, 188, 423–431.

Conrad, P. (1987). The experience of illness: Recent and new directions. In J.A. Roth & P. Conrad (Eds.), *Research in the Sociology of Health Care* (Vol. 6, pp. 1–31). London: JAI Press Inc.

Cooke, D.J. (1997). The Barlinnie special unit: The rise and fall of a therapeutic experiment. In E. Cullen, L. Jones, & R. Woodward (Eds.), *Therapeutic Communities for Offenders*. Chichester: Wiley.

Copas, J., & Marshall, P. (1998). The offender group reconviction scale: The Statistical Reconviction Score for use by probation officers. *Journal of the Royal Statistical Society*, Series C, 47, 159–171.

Cordess, C. (2001). Forensic psychotherapy. In C. Hollin (Ed.), *Handbook of Offender Assessment and Treatment* (pp. 309–329). Chichester: Wiley.

Corston, B.J. (2007). *The Corston Report: A Review of Women with Particular Vulnerabilities in the Criminal Justice System*. London: Home Office.

Craig, A.R., Franklin, J.A., & Andrews, G. (1984). A scale to measure locus of control of behaviour. *British Journal of Medical Psychology*, 57, 173–180.

Craissati, J., Horne, L., & Taylor, R. (2002). Effective treatment models for personality disordered offenders. http://normanmark.net/trainers_resources/Resources/Offenders/ Treatment%20personality%20disorders%20offenders%20DOH%20-%20Copy.pdf (accessed 21 October 2013).

Creswell, J.W. (2003). *Research Design: Qualitative, Quantitative and Mixed Methods Approaches*, 2nd Edn. Thousand Oaks, CA: Sage.

Criminal Justice Joint Inspection (2013). *A Joint Inspection of Life Sentence Prisoners*. London: CJJI.

Cullen, E. (1992). The Grendon reconviction study: Part 1. *Prison Service Journal*, 99, 35–37.

Cullen, E. (1993). The Grendon reconviction study: Part 1. *Prison Service Journal*, 90, 35–37.

Cullen, E. (1994). Grendon: The therapeutic prison that works. *Therapeutic Communities*, 15(4), 307–311.

Cullen, E. (1997). Can a prison be a therapeutic community? The Grendon template. In E. Cullen, L. Jones, & R. Woodward (Eds.), *Therapeutic Communities for Offenders* (pp. 75–100). Chichester: Wiley.

Cullen, E., Jones, L., & Woodward, R. (Eds.), (1997a). *Therapeutic Communities for Offenders*. Chichester: Wiley.

Cullen, E., & MacKenzie, J. (2011). *Dovegate: A Therapeutic Community in a Private Prison and Developments in Therapeutic Work with Personality Disordered Offenders*. Hook: Waterside Press.

Cullen, E., & Miller, A. (2010). Dovegate therapeutic community: Bid, birth, growth and survival. In R. Shuker & E. Sullivan (Eds.), *Grendon and the Emergence of Forensic Therapeutic Communities: Developments in Research and Practice*. Chichester: Wiley.

Cullen, E., Newell, T., & Woodward, R. (1997b). Key issues for the future. In E. Cullen, L. Jones, & R. Woodward (Eds.), *Therapeutic Communities for Offenders* (pp. 252–267). New York: Wiley.

Custodial Review (2012). Dovegate therapeutic prison. http://www.custodialreview.co. uk/Dovegate_Therapeutic_Prison-a-124.html (accessed 21 October 2013).

Cuppleditch, L. and Evans, W. (2005). 'Re-offending of adults: results from the 2002 cohort, Home Office Statistical Bulletin 25/05, London: Home Office.

Day, A., Bryan, J., Davey, L., & Casey, S. (2006). The process of change in offender rehabilitation programmes. *Psychology, Crime & Law*, 12(5), 473–487.

De Leon, G. (2000). *The Thereapuetic Community; Theory, Model and Method*. New York: Springer.

Department of Health. (1998). *A First Class Service. Quality in the New NHS*. Wetherby: NHS. Executive.

Department of Health. (2003). *Policy Implementation Guidance for the Development of Services for People with Personality Disorder*. London: Stationery Office.

Department of Health (2006). Mental health policy implementation guide: Community mental health teams. Department of Health. http://www.rcn.org.uk/downloads/ professional_development/mental_health_virtual_ward/treatments_and_therapies/ cmhtguidancepdf.pdf (accessed March 2006).

Doctor, R. (2001). Psychotherapy and the prisoner – Impasse or progress? In J. Williams Saunders (Ed.), *Life within Hidden Worlds* (pp. 55–67). London: Karnac Books.

Dolan, B. (Ed.) (1996). *Perspectives on Henderson Hospital*. Sutton: Henderson Hospital.

Dolan, B. (1998). Therapeutic community treatment for severe personality disorders. In T. Millon, E. Simonsen, M. Birket-Smith, and R. Davis (Eds.), *Psychopathy: Antisocial, Criminal, and Violent Behaviour* (pp. 407–430). New York: The Guildford Press.

Dolan, B., & Coid, J. (1993). *Psychopathic and Antisocial Personality Disorders: Treatment and Research Issues.* London: Gaskell.

Dolan, B., & Coid, J. (1994). *Psychopathetic and Antisocial Personality Disorders, Treatment and Research Issues.* London: Gaskell/Royal College of Psychiatrists.

Donald, I.J. (1995), Facet theory: Defining research domains. In G. Breakwell, S. Hammond, & C. Five-Schaw (Eds.), *Research Methods in Psychology*, 2nd Edn. London: Sage Publications.

Drahorad, C. (1999). Reflections on being a patient in a therapeutic community. *Therapeutic Communities*, 20(3), 195–215.

Duckworth, R. (2011). Next steps for Dovegate. In E. Cullen, & J. MacKenzie (Eds.), *Dovegate: A Therapeutic Community in a Private Prison and Developments in Therapeutic Work with Personality Disordered Offenders.* Hook: Waterside Press.

Duggan, C. (2004). Does personality change and, if so, what changes? *Criminal Behaviour and Mental Health*, 14, 5–16.

Duncan, B.L., & Moynihan, D. (1994). Applying outcome research: Intentional utilization of the client's frame of reference. *Psychotherapy*, 31, 294–301.

Dutton, D.G., Saunders, K., Starzomski, A., & Bartholomew, K. (1994). Intimacy-anger and insecure attachment as precursors of abuse in intimate relationships. *Journal of Applied Social Psychology*, 24, 1367–1386.

Egan, V. (2010). Personality theories and offending. In J. Brown & E. Campbell (Eds.), *Cambridge Handbook of Forensic Psychology*. Cambridge: CUP.

Elliott, R., Fischer, C., & Rennie, D. (1999). Evolving guidelines for publication of qualitative research studies in psychology and related fields. *British Journal of Clinical Psychology*, 38, 215–229

Emery, R.E., & O'Leary, K.D. (1982). Children's perceptions of marital discord and behavior problems of boys and girls. *Journal of Abnormal Child Psychology*, 10, 11–24.

Falshaw, L., Friendship, C., Travers, L., & Nugent, F. (2003). *Searching for What Works: An Evaluation of Cognitive Skills Programmes.* Home Office Research Findings (No. 206). London: HMSO.

Fallon, P., Bluglass, R., Edwards, B., and Daniels, G. (1999). *Report of the commission of inquiry into the personality disorder unit, Ashworth Special Hospital*, Volume 1. Cm 4194.11. London: Stationery Office.

Farrall, S., Bottoms, A., & Shapland, J. (2010). Social structures and desistance from crime. *European Journal of Criminology*, 7(6), 546–570.

Farrington, D.P. (2002). Criminology. *Criminal Behaviour and Mental Health*, 12, s10–s16.

Farrington, D.P., Ohlin, L.E. and Wilson, J.Q. (1986). *Understanding and Controlling Crime: Toward a New Research Strategy.* New York: Springer-Verlag.

First, M.B., Gibbon, M., Spitzer, R.L., Williams, J.B.W., & Benjamin, L.S. (1997). *Structured Clinical Interview for DSM-IV Axis II Personality Disorders (SCID II).* Washington, DC: American Psychiatric Publishing Inc.

Fonagy, P., Leigh, T., Steele, M., Steele, H., Kennedy, R., Matton, G., Target, M., & Gerber, A. (1996). The relationship of attachment status, psychiatric classification and response to psychotherapy. *Journal of Consulting and Clinical Psychology*, 64 (1) 22–31.

Fonagy, P. (1999). Attachment, the development of self, and its pathology in personality disorders. In J. Derksen, & C. Maffei (Eds.), *Treatment of Personality Disorders* (pp. 53–68). New York: Kluwer Academic/Plenum.

Fonagy, P., Leigh, T., Steele, M., Steele, H., Kennedy, R., Mattoon, G., Target, M., & Gerber, A. (1996). The relation of attachment status, psychiatric classification, and response to psychotherapy. *Journal of Consulting and Clinical Psychology*, 64(1), 22–31.

Foss, C., & Ellefsen, B. (2002). The value of combining qualitative and quantitative approaches in nursing research by means of method triangulation. *Journal of Advanced Nursing*, 40(2), 242–248.

Friendship, C., Blud, L., Erikson, M., & Travers, R. (2002). *An Evaluation of Cognitive Behavioural Treatment for Prisoners.* Home Office Research Findings (No. 161). London: HMSO.

Frodi, A., Dernevik, M., Sepa, A., Philipson, J., & Bragesjo, M. (2001). Current attachment representations of incarcerated offenders varying in degree of psychopathy. *Attachment & Human Development*, 3, 269–283.

Furnham, A., & Bochner, S. (1986). *Culture Shock. Psychological Reactions to Unfamiliar Environments.* London: Routledge.

Gaw, K.F. (2000). Reverse culture shock in students returning from overseas. *International Journal of Intercultural Relations*, 24, 83–104.

Genders, E. (2002). Legitimacy, accountability and private prisons. *Punishment and Society*, 4(3), 285–303.

Genders, E. (2003). Privatisation and innovation – Rhetoric and reality: The development of a therapeutic community prison. *The Harvard Journal*, 42(2), 137–157.

Genders, E. (2007). The commercial context of criminal justice and the perversion of purpose. *Criminal Review*, July, 513–529.

Genders, E., & Player, E. (1995). *Grendon: A Study of a Therapeutic Prison.* Oxford: Clarendon Press.

Genders, E., & Player, E. (2004). Grendon: A therapeutic community in prison. In J. Lees (Ed.), *A Culture of Enquiry: Research Evidence and the Therapeutic Community.* London and New York: Jessica Kingsley Publishers.

Gendreau, P., & Ross, R. (1987). Revivification of rehabilitation: Evidence from the 1980s. *Justice Quarterly*, 4, 349–408.

Gendreau, P., & Ross, R. (1979). Effective correctional treatment: Bibliotherapy for cynics. *Crime and Delinquency*, 25, 463–489.

Gendreau, P., & Ross, R.R. (1980). Effective correctional treatment: Bibliotherapy for cynics. In R.R. Ross, & P. Grendreau (Eds.), *Effective Correctional Treatment.* Toronto: Butterworths.

Gibson, H.B. (1969). Early delinquency in relation to broken homes. *Journal of Child Psychology and Psychiatry*, 10, 195–204.

Giuliani, M. V. (2003). Theory of attachment and place attachment. In M. Bonnes., T. Lee, & M. Bonaiuto (Eds.), *Psychological Theories for Environmental Issues* (pp. 137–170). Aldershot: Ashgate

Glasby, J., Lester, H., Briscoe, J., Clark, M., Rose, S., & England, L. (2003). *Cases for Change: User Involvement.* London: Department of Health/National Institute for Mental Health.

Glider, P., Mullen, R., Herbst, D., Davis, C., & Fleishman, B. (1997). Substance abuse treatment in a jail setting: A therapeutic community model, In De Leon G. (Ed.), *Community as Method; Therapeutic Communities for Special Populations and Special Settings.* (Chapter 7, pp. 97–114). Westport, CT. Praeger.

Gocke, B. (1991). *Tackling Denial in Sex Offenders.* Social work monographs, monograph 98, Norwich.

Griffiths, P., & Hinshelwood, R.D. (1997). Actions speak louder than words. In P. Griffiths, & P. Pringle (Eds.), *Psychosocial Practice within a Residential Setting.* Cassel Monograph No. 1. London: Karnac.

Griffiths, P.J., & Hemmings, M. (2006). *Reintegrating offenders back into main stream prison: A review of HMP Dovegate TC's three day intensive program.* Unpublished report paper.

Grossman, J., & Mackenzie, F.J. (2005). The randomized controlled trial: Gold standard, or merely standard? *Perspectives in Biology and Medicine*, 48(4), 516–534.

Gudjonsson, G. H. (1990). Cognitive distortions and blame attributions among paedophiles. *Sexual and Marital Therapy*, 5(2), 183–185.

Gudjonsson, G.H., & Singh, K. (1988). Attribution of blame for criminal acts and its relationship with type of offence. *Medicine Science and the Law*, 28, 301–303.

Gudjonsson, G.H., & Sigurdsson, J.F. (2004). Motivation for offending and personality. *Legal and Criminological Psychology*, 9, 69–81.

Gudjonsson, G.H., & Singh, K.K. (1989). The revised Gudjonsson blame attribution inventory. *Personality and Individual Differences*, 10, 67–70.

Gunn, J., & Robertson, G. (1987). A ten-year follow-up of men discharged from Grendon prison. *The British Journal of Psychiatry*, 151, 674–678.

Gunn, J., Robertson, G., Dell, S., & Way, C. (1978). *Psychiatric Aspects of Imprisonment.* London: Academic Press.

Gustafson, P.E.R. (2001). Meanings of place, everyday experience and theoretical conceptualisations. *Journal of Environmental Psychology*, 21(1), 5–16.

Haigh, R. (1999). The quintessence of a therapeutic environment: Five universal qualities. In P. Campling & R. Haigh (Eds.), *Therapeutic Communities: Past, Present and Future* (pp. 246–257). London: Jessica Kingsley.

Haigh, R. (2002). Therapeutic community research: Past, present and future. *Psychiatric Bulletin*, 26, 65–68.

Haigh, R. (2013). The quintessence of a therapeutic environment: Therapuetic communities. *International Journal of Therapeutic Communities*, 34, 6–15.

Hammond, S. (1988). *The Meaning and Measurement of Adolescent Estrangement.* PhD thesis, University of Surrey.

Hammond, S. (2000). Using psychometric tests. In Breakwell, G., Hammond, S., & Fife-Schaw, C. (Eds.), *Research Methods in Psychology*, 2nd Edn. (pp. 175–193). London: Sage.

Hammond, S.M., O'Rourke, M.M., O'Sullivan, D., & Horgan, J. (2006). Passive aggression: A psychometric tool. *Assessment*, Submitted.

Hammond, S.M. (2010). *The passive aggression index; professional manual*, London: RAMAS Foundation.

Hansard Debates House of Commons (2001). 7th February column 294WH to 302WH.

Hare, R. (1998). Psychopaths and their nature: Implications for the mental health and Criminal Justice System. In T. Millon, E. Simonsen, R.D. Davis, & M. Birket-Smith (Eds.), *Psychopathy: Antisocial, Criminal, and Violent Behavior.* New York: Guildford Press.

Hare, R.D. (1991). *The Hare Psychopathy Checklist – Revised.* Toronto: Multi-Health Systems.

Hare, R.D. (1999). *Without Conscience: The Disturbing World of the Psychopaths Among Us.* New York: Guilford Press.

Hare, R.D. (2003). *Hare Psychopathy Checklist, PCL-R*, 2nd Edn. Revised. North Tonawanda, NY: Multi-Health Systems.

Hare, R.D., Cooke, D., & Hart, S.D. (1999). Psychopathy and sadistic personality disorder. In T. Millon, P. Blaney, & R. Davis (Eds.), *Oxford Textbook of Psychopathology* (pp. 555–584). New York: Oxford University Press.

Hare, R.D., & McPherson, L.M. (1984). Violent and aggressive behaviour by criminal psychopaths. *International Journal of Law and Psychiatry*, 7, 35–50.

Harris, G., Rice, M., & Cormier, C. (1994). Is the therapeutic community therapeutic? *Therapeutic Communities*, 15(4), 283–299.

Hazan, C., & Shaver, P. (1987). Romantic love conceptualized as an attachment process. *Journal of Personality and Social Psychology*, 52, 511–524.

Hazan, C., & Shaver, P. R. (1994). Attachment as an Organizational Framework for Research on Close Relationships. *Psychological Inquiry: An International Journal for the Advancement of Psychological Theory*, 5(1), 1–22.

Healy, D. (2012). *The Dynamics of Desistance: Charting Pathways through Change*. Abingdon: Routledge.

Herpertz, S., Wreth, U., Lukas, G., Qunaibi, M., Schuerkens, A., Kunert,H., Freeze, R., Flesch, H., Mueller-Iskem, R., Osterhelder, M., & Henning Sass, M. (2001). Emotion in criminal offenders with psychopathy and borderline personality disorder. *Arch Gen Psychiatry*, 58(8), 737–745.

Hinshelwood, R.D. (2001). *Thinking about Institutions*. London: Jessica Kingsley.

HM Inspectorate of Prisons (2003). *A Full Announced Inspection of HM Prison Dovegate. 31 March-4 April 2003 by HM Chief Inspector of Prisons*. London: HM Chief Inspectorate of Prisons.

HM Inspectorate of Prisons (2004). *A Full Announced Inspection of HM Prison Dovegate. 29 March-2 April 2004 by HM Chief Inspector of Prisons*. London: HM Chief Inspectorate of Prisons.

HM Inspectorate of Prisons (2006). *Report of an Unannounced Short Follow-Up Inspection of HMP Dovegate Therapeutic Community. 29–31 August by HM Chief Inspector of Prisons*. London: HM Chief Inspectorate of Prisons.

HM Inspectorate of Prisons (2008). *Report of an Announced Short Inspection of HMP Dovegate Therapeutic Community. 16–20 June 2008 by HM Chief Inspector of Prisons*. London: HM Chief Inspectorate of Prisons.

HM Inspectorate of Prisons (2012). *Report of an Unannounced Short Follow-Up Inspection of HMP Dovegate Therapeutic Community. 11–13 October 2011 by HM Chief Inspector of Prisons*. London: HM Chief Inspectorate of Prisons.

HM Prison Service Order (2005). PSO, Democratic therapeutic communities. January 2005. https://www.Justice.gov,UK/offender/psos (accessed January 2006).

Hoch, P. (1955). Aims and limitations of psychotherapy. *American Journal of Psychiatry*, 112, 321–327.

Hodkin, G., & Woodward, R. (1996). Another British first: Gartree's therapeutic community for lifers. *Prison Service Journal*, 103, 47–50.

Hoffman, M.L. (1971). Father absence and conscience development. *Developmental Psychology*, 4, 400–406.

Hollin, C. (1990). Social skills training with delinquents: A look at the evidence and some recommendations for practice. *British Journal of Social Work*, 20, 483–493.

Hollin, C. (1999). Treatment programs for offenders: Meta-analysis, "What Works," and beyond. *International Journal of Law and Psychiatry*, 22(3–4), 361–372.

Hollin, C. (2001). The role of consultant in developing effective Correctional Programmes. In G. Bernfeld, D. Farrington & A. Leschied (Eds.), *Offender Rehabilitation in Practise: Implementing and Evaluating Effective Programs* (pp. 269–281). Chichester: John Wiley & Sons.

Hollin, C., McGuire, J., Hounsome, J., Hatcher, R., Bilby, C., & Palmer, E. (2008). Cognitive skills behavior programs for offenders in the community: A reconviction analysis. *Criminal Justice and Behavior*, 35, 269–283.

Hollin, C., Palmer, E., McGuire, J., Hounsome, J., Hatcher, J., Bilby, C., & Clark, C. (2004). *Pathfinder Programmes in the Probation Service: A Retrospective Analysis*. Home Office Online Report 66/04.

Holm, S. (1979). A simple sequentially rejective multiple test procedure. *Scandinavian Journal of Statistics*, 6(2), 65–70.

Home Office (1987). Prison department circular instruction, 21. In E. Genders, & E. Players, *Grendon. A Study of Therapeutic Prison.* Oxford: Clarendon Press, 1995.

Horvath, H.O., & Luborsky, L. (1993). The role of the therapeutic alliance in psychotherapy. *Journal of Counselling and Clinical Psychology,* 61(4), 561–573.

House of Commons Home Affairs Select Committee. (2005). Rehabilitation of prisoners. First report of session 2004/5. Volume 1 Report. London: The Stationery Office.

Houston, J. (1998). *Making Sense with Offenders. Personal Constructs, Therapy and Change.* Chichester: Wiley.

Howells, K., & Day, A. (1999). *The Rehabilitation of Offenders: International Perspectives Applied to Australian Correctional Systems.* Trends and Issues in Crime and Criminal Justice, 112. Canberra: Australian Institute of Criminology.

Hubble, M.A., Duncan, B.L., & Miller, S.D. (1999). *The Heart and Soul of Change: What Works in Therapy.* Washington, DC: American Psychological Association Books.

Hyler, S.E. (1994). *Personality Diagnostic Questionnaire – 4.* New York: New York State Psychiatric Institute.

Hyler, S.E., Skodol, A.E., Kellman, H.D., Oldham, J., & Rosnick, L. (1990). The validity of the Personality Diagnostic Questionnaire: A comparison with two structured interviews. *American Journal of Psychiatry,* 147, 1043–1048.

Incardi, J.A., Martin, S.S., Butzin, C.A., Hooper, R.M., & Harrison, L.D. (1997). An effective model of prison-based treatment for drug-involved offenders. *Journal of Drug Issues,* 27(2), 261–278.

Ireland, J. L., & Power, C. L. (2004). Attachment, emotional loneliness, and bullying behaviour: A study of adult and young offenders. *Aggressive Behavior,* 30(4), 298–312.

Jacobson, N.S., & Truax, P. (1991). Clinical significance: A statistical approach to defining meaningful change in psychotherapy research. *Journal of Consulting and Clinical Psychology,* 59, 12–19.

Jadad, A. (1998). *Randomised Controlled Trials: A User's Guide.* London: BMJ Books.

Johnson, J.E., Burlingame, G.M., Olsen, J.A., Davies, D.R., & Gleave, R.L. (2005). Group climate, cohesion, alliance and empathy in group psychotherapy: Multilevel: structural equation models. *Journal of Counselling Psychology,* 52(3), 310–321.

Jones, L. (1997). Developing models for managing treatment integrity and efficacy in a prison-based TC: The Max Glatt Centre. In E. Cullen, L. Jones, & R. Woodward (Eds.), *Therapeutic Communities for Offenders.* London: Wiley.

Jones, M. (1968). *Beyond the Therapeutic Community.* New Haven and London: Yale University Press.

Jones, P.R. (1996). Risk prediction in criminal justice. In A.T. Harland (Ed.), *Choosing Correctional Options that Work: Defining the Demand and Evaluating the Supply.* Thousand Oaks, Calif: Sage.271/

Kelly, G. (1955). *The Psychology of Personal Constructs.* Oxford: W. W. Norton.

Kennard, D. (1983). *An Introduction to Therapeutic Communities.* London: Routledge.

Kershaw, C., Goodman, J., & White, S. (1999). *Reconvictions of Offenders Sentenced or Discharged from Prison in 1995, England and Wales.* Research Development and Statistics Directorate, Research Findings (No. 101). London: HMSO.

Landis, J.R., & Koch, G.G. (1977). The measurement of observer agreement for categorical data. *Biometrics,* 33(1), 159–174.

Larkin, K., & Paget, S. (2008). *Democratic Therapeutic Communities in Prison: National Joint Review Report 2007–2008.* London: Association of Therapeutic Communities (CETU Publication: CRTU58).

Lawson, D.M., Barnes, A.D., Madkins, J.P., & Francios-Lamonte, B.M. (2006). Changes in male partner abuser attachment styles in group treatment. *Psychotherapy: Theory, Research, Practice, Training,* 43(2), 232–237.

Lees, J., & Kennard, D. (1999). *Association of Therapeutic Communities' Response to: Managing Dangerous People with Severe Personality Disorder.* Proposals for policy development: Association of Therapeutic Communities.

Lees, J., Manning, N., & Rawlings, B. (1999). Therapeutic Community Effectiveness. A systematic international review of therapeutic community treatment for people with personality disorders and mentally disordered offenders. http://www.therapeuticcommunities.org/briefingpaper.htm (accessed 17 April 2008).

Lees, J., Manning, N., & Rawlings, B. (2003). A culture of enquiry: Research evidence and the therapeutic community. *Psychiatric Quarterly*, 75(3), 279–294.

Lees, J., Manning, N., Menzies, D., & Morant, N. (Eds.) (2004). *A Culture of Enquiry; Research Evidence and the Therapeutic Community.* London: Jessica Kingsley.

Lees, J., Manning, N., & Rawlings, B. (2004). Therapeutic community research: An overview and meta-analysis. In J. Lees, N. Manning, D. Menzies, & N. Morant (Eds.), *A Culture of Enquiry* (pp. 36–54). London: Jessica Kingsley.

Leibrich, J. (1993). *Straight to the Point: Angles On Giving Up Crime.* Otago, New Zealand: University of Otago Press.

Leiper, R., & Kent, R. (2001). *Working through Setbacks in Psychotherapy: Crisis, Impasse & Relapse.* London: Sage Publications.

Lenzenweger, M.F. (2006). The longitudinal study of personality disorders: History, design, considerations and initial findings. *Journal of Personality Disorders*, 20(6), 645–670.

Liebling, A., & Sparks, R. (2002). Editors preface. *Punishment & Society*, 4, 283–284.

Linehan, M.M. (1993). *Cognitive Behavioural Treatment of Personality Disorder.* New York: Guilford.

Lingoes, J.C. (1979). The multivariate analysis of qualitative data. In J.C. Lingoes, E.E. Roskam, & I. Borg (Eds.), *Geometric Representations of Relational Data.* Ann Arbor, MI: Mathesis Press.

Lingoes, J.C., & Guttman, L. (1973). *The Guttman-Lingoes Non-Metric Program Series.* Ann Arbor, MI: Mathesis Press.

Lipsey, M.W. (1992). Juvenile delinquency treatment: A meta-analysis inquiry into the variability of effects. In T.D. Cook, H. Cooper, D.S. Cordray, H. Hartmann, L.V. Hedges, R. Light, T. Louis, & F. Mosteller (Eds.), *Meta-Analysis for Explanation: A Casebook* (pp. 83–127). New York: Russell Sage.

Lykken, D.T. (1995). *The Antisocial Personalities.* Hillsdale, NJ: Lawrence Erlbaum Associates, Inc.

Lyn, T.S., & Burton, D.L. (2004). Adult attachment and sexual offender status. *American Journal of Orthopsychiatry*, 74, 150–159.

Lyn, T., & Burton, D. (2005). Attachment, anger, and anxiety of male sexual offenders. *Journal of Sexual Aggression*, 11, 127–137.

MacLean Committee (2000). *Report on Serious Violent and Sexual Offenders.* Scottish Executive.

Maffei, C., Fossati, A., Agostoni, I., Barraco, A., Bagnato, M., Deborah, D., Namia, C., Novella, L., & Petrachi, M. (1997). Interrater reliability and internal consistency of the structured clinical interview for DSM-IV axis II personality disorders (SCID II), version 2.0. *Journal of Personality Disorder*, 11(3), 279–284.

Main, T. (1983). The concept of the therapeutic community: Variations and vicissitudes. In M. Pines (Ed.), *The Evolution of Group Analysis.* London: Routledge and Kegan.

Main, T. (1990). Knowledge, learning, and freedom from thought. *Psychoanalytic Psychotherapy*, 5(1), 59–78.

Main, M. (1991). Metacognitive knowledge, metacognitive monitoring, and singular (coherent) vs. multiple (incoherent) models of attachment: Findings and directions for future work. In C.M. Murray-Parkes, J. Stevenson-Hinde, & P. Morris (Eds.), *Attachment across the Life Cycle* (pp. 127–159). London: Routledge.

Main, T. (1993). The concept of the therapeutic community; varieties and vicissitudes. In M. Pine (Ed.), *The Evolution of Group Analyst*. London: Routledge and Kegan.

Main, T., Kaplan, N., & Cassidy, J. (1985). Security in infancy childhood and adulthood: A move to the level of representation. *Monographs of the Society for Research in Child Development*, 50(1–2), 66–104.

Manning, N. (1991). *The Therapeutic Community Movement: Charisma and Routinization.* Worcester: Routledge.

Manning, N. (2004). The gold standard; what are RCTs and where did they come from? In J. Lees, N. Manning, D. Menzies, & N.Morant. (Eds.), *A Culture of Enquiry: Research Evidence and the Therapeutic Community* (pp. 109–119). London: Jessica Kingsley.

Manning, N., & Morant, N. (2004). Principles and practices in therapeutic community research. In J. Lees, N. Manning, D. Menzies, & N. Morant (Eds.), *A Culture of Enquiry: Research Evidence and the Therapeutic Community* (Vol. 6, pp. 21–35). London: Jessica Kingsley.

Marshall, P. (1997). *A Reconviction Study of HMP Grendon Therapeutic Community*. Research Findings, London: Home Office Research and Statistics Directorate (No. 53).

Martinson, R. (1974). What works? Questions and answers about prison reform. *The Public Interest*, 35, 22–54.

Martinson, R. (1979). New findings, new views: A note of caution regarding sentencing reform. *Hofstra Law Review*, 7, 243–258.

Maruna, S. (2001). *Making Good: How Ex-Convicts Reform and Rebuild their Lives.* Washington, DC: American Psychological Association Books.

Maruna, S. (2013). *"What works" and Desistence from Crime: Merging Two Approaches to Research: A Discussion Paper Prepared for the Correctional Services Accreditation and Advice Panel*. Belfast: Queens University.

McConnaughy, E.A., DiClemente, C.C., Prochaska, J.O., & Velicer, W.F. (1989). Stages of change in psychotherapy: A follow-up report. *Psychotherapy*, 26(4), 494–503.

McConnaughy, E.A., Prochaska, J.O., & Velicer, W.F. (1983). Stages of change in psychotherapy: Measurement and sample profiles. *Psychotherapy: Theory, Research and Practice*, 20(3), 368.

McCord, J. (1979). Some child-rearing antecedents of criminal behaviour in adult men. *Journal of Personality and Social Psychology*, 37, 1477–1486.

McCord, J. (1983). A forty year perspective on effects of child abuse and neglect. *Child Abuse and Neglect*, 7, 265–270.

McGuire, J. (1995). *What Works: Reducing Re-offending, Guidelines from Research and Practice.* Chichester: Wiley.

McGuire, J. (2002). Integrating findings from research reviews. In J. McGuire (Ed.), *Offender Rehabilitation and Treatment: Effective Programmes and Policies to Reduce Re-offending* (pp. 3–38). Chichester: Wiley.

McMurran, M. (2010). Theories of change. In J. Brown & E. Campbell (Eds.), *Cambridge Handbook of Forensic Psychology* (pp. 118–125). Cambridge: CUP.

McMurran, M., & Ward, T. (2010). Treatment readiness, treatment engagement and behaviour change. *Criminal Behaviour and Mental Health*, 20, 75–85.

Melnick, G., De Leon, G., Thomas, G., Kressel, D., & Wexler, H.K. (2001). Treatment process in prison therapeutic communities: Motivation, participation and outcome. *American Journal of Drug and Alcohol Abuse*, 27(4), 633–650.

Messina, N., Wish, E., & Nemes, S. (2000). Predictors of treatment outcomes in men and women admitted to a therapeutic community. *American Journal of Drug and Alcohol Abuse*, 26, 207–227.

Mikulincer, M., & Nachshon, O. (1991). Attachment styles and patterns of self-disclosure. *Journal of Personality and Social Psychology*, 61(2), 321–331.

Miller, F.G. (2000). Placebo-controlled trials in psychiatric research: An ethical perspective. *Biological Psychiatry*, 47(8), 707–716.

Miller, Q.J. (1982). Preliminary considerations of psychological test/retest scores and their bearing on criminal reconviction. *Grendon Psychology Unit Series D*, Report 13.

Miller, S., Brown, J., & Sees, C. (2004). A preliminary study identifying risk factors in drop-out from a prison therapeutic community. *Journal of Clinical Forensic Medicine*, 11, 189–197.

Miller, S., Brown, J., & Sees, C. (2006). Key aspects of therapeutic change amongst residents of a prison therapeutic community. *Howard Journal of Criminal Justice*, 45(2), 116–128.

Miller, W.R., & Rollnick, S. (2002). *Motivational Interviewing: Preparing People for Change*, 2nd Edn. London: The Guildford Press.

Millward, L.J. (2000). Focus groups. In G.M. Breakwell, S. Hammond, & C. Fife-Schaw (Eds.), *Research Methods in Psychology*, 2nd Edn. (pp. 303–324). London: Sage.

Ministry of Justice. (2008). *Re-offending of Adults; New Measures of Re-offending 2000–2005 England and Wales*. Ministry of Justice Statistical Bulletin. London: Ministry of Justice.

Moffitt, T.E. (2003). Life-course persistent and adolescence-limited antisocial behaviour: A 10-year research review and a research agenda. In B.B. Lahey, T.E. Moffitt, & A. Caspi (Eds.), *The Causes of Conduct Disorder and Serious Juvenile Delinquency* (pp. 49–75). New York: Guilford Press.

Moran, P. (2002). The epidemiology of personality disorders. *Psychiatry*, 1(1), 8–11.

Moran, P., Leese, M., Lee, T., Walters, P., Thornicroft, G., & Mann, A. (2003). Standardised Assessment of Personality – Abbreviated Scale (SAPAS): Preliminary validation of a brief screen for personality disorder. *British Journal of Psychiatry*, 183, 228–232.

Mulder, M.J., Joyce, P.R., & Frampton, C. (2003). Relationships among measures of treatment outcome in depressed patients. *Journal of Affective Disorders*, 76, 127–135.

National Institute for Health and Clinical Excellence (NICE) (n.d.). Guidelines of good practice. http://www.nice.org.uk/ (accessed December 2005).

Neale, B., & Flowerdew, J. (2003). Time, texture and childhood: The contours of longitudinal qualitative research. *International Journal of Social Research Methodologies*, 6(3), 189–199.

Neville, L., Miller, S., & Fritzon, K. (2007). Understanding change in a therapeutic community: An action systems approach. *The Journal of Forensic Psychiatry & Psychology*, 18(2), 181–203.

Newman, C.F. (2002). A cognitive perspective on resistance in psychotherapy. *Psychotherapy in Practice*, 58, 165–174.

Newton, M. (1971). Reconviction after treatment at Grendon. *Chief Psychologist Report Series* B, 1. Prison Department Home Office. (Abridged version in J.H. Shine, (Ed.) (2000) *A compilation of Grendon research* (pp. 205–219). Leyhill Press. Available from Psychology Unit HMP Grendon, Grendon Underwood, Aylesbury, HP18 OTL).

Newton, M. (1973). *Progress of Follow-Up Studies and Comparison with Non-Patients Carried out at HMP Oxford*. Grendon Psychology Unit Report, Series A, no. 15. Aylesbury: HMP Grendon Underwood.

Newton, M. (1998). Changes in measures of personality, hostility and locus of control during residence in a prison therapeutic community. *Legal & Criminal Psychology*, 3, 209–223.

Norcross, J.C., & Beutler, L. (1997). Determining the relationship of choice in brief therapy. In J.N. Butcher (Ed.), *Personality Assessment in Managed Health Care*. Oxford: Oxford University Press.

Norcross, J.C. (2001). Purposes, processes, and products of the task force on empirically supported therapy relationships. *Psychotherapy*, 38(4), 345–365.

Norton, K., & Dolan, B. (1995). Acting out and the institutional response. *The Journal of Forensic Psychiatry*, 6(2), 317–332.

Ogles, B., Lunnen, K., & Bonesteel, K. (2001). Clinical significance: History, application and current practice. *Clinical Psychology Review*, 21(3), 421–446.

O'Neill, D. (2010). Reliable change and clinical significance. In J. Brown, & E. Campbell (Eds.), *Cambridge Handbook of Forensic Psychology*. Cambridge: CUP.

O'Rourke, M., & Hammond, S. (2001). *The RAAP Anger Assessment Profile Psychometric Norms and Professional Manual*. London.

O'Rourke, M., & Hammond, S. (2001). *An Introduction to Personality Disorder: Definitions, Treatment Issues and Government Proposals*. London: Mental Health Foundation.

Paget, S., & Turner, K. (2010). Democratic therapeutic communities in prisons: Joint-review handbook. http://www.rcpsych.ac.uk/pdf/HMP%20Integrated%20Audit%20Handbook.pdf (accessed 21 October 2013).

Paget, S., & Turner, K. (n.d.) (Eds.) *Democratic Therapeutic Communities in Prisons Joint-review Handbook*. Community of Communities.

Paris, J. (1997). Childhood trauma as an etiological factor in the personality disorders. *Journal of Personality Disorders*, 11(1), 34–49.

Paris, J., Brown, R., & Nowlis, D. (1987). Long-term follow-up of borderline patients in a general hospital. *Comprehensive Psychiatry*, 28, 530–535.

Petrucci, C., Winick, B., & Wexler, D. (2003). Therapeutic jurisprudence: An invitation to social scientists. In D. Carson, & R. Bull (Eds.), *Handbook of Psychology in Legal Contexts*, 2nd Edn. (pp. 579–601) Chichester: Wiley.

Porter, R.F.C., Frampton, C., Joyce, P.R., & Mulder, R.T. (2003). Randomized controlled trials in psychiatry. Part I: Methodology and critical evaluation. *Australian and New Zealand Journal of Psychiatry*, 37, 257–264.

Prochaska, J., & DiClemente, C. (1983). Stages and processes of self-change of smoking: Towards an integrative model of change. *Journal of Consulting and Clinical Psychology*, 51, 390–395.

Prochaska, J.O., DiClemente, C.C., & Norcross, J.C. (1992). In search of how people change: Applications to addictive behaviours. *American Psychologist*, 47, 1102–1114.

Proshaska, J.O., & Velior, W.F. (1997). The transtheoretical model of health behavior change. *American Journal of Health Promotion*, September/October 12(1), 38–48.

Raine, A. (1993). *The Psychopathology of Crime*. San Diego: Academic Press.

Rapkin, B.D., & Trickett, E.J. (2005). Comprehensive dynamic trial designs for behavioral prevention research with communities: Overcoming inadequacies of the randomized controlled trial paradigm. In E.J. Trickett (Ed.), *Community Interventions and Aids: Targeting the Community Context*. Cary, NC: Oxford University Press.

Rapoport, R. (1960). *Community as Doctor: New Perspectives on a Therapeutic Community*. London: Tavistock Publications.

Rawlings, B. (1998). The therapeutic community in the prison: Problems in maintaining therapeutic integrity. *Therapeutic Communities*, 19(4), 281–294.

Rawlings, B. (1999). Therapeutic communities in prisons: A research review. *Therapeutic Communities*, 20(3), 177–193.

Rawlings, B. (2001). Life and therapy in a prison therapeutic community: The experience of researcher, staff and inmates. *Therapeutic Communities*, 22(4), 319–333.

Raymond, C.M., Brown, G., & Weber, P. (2010). The measurement of place attachment: Personal, community and environmental connections. *Journal of Environmental Psychology*, 30, 422–434.

Rice, M.E., Harris, G.T., & Cormier, C.A. (1992). An evaluation of a maximum security therapeutic community for psychopaths and other mentally disordered offenders. *Law and Human Behaviour*, 16(4), 399–412.

Roberts, J. (1999). History of the therapeutic community. In E. Cullen, L. Jones, & R. Woodward (Eds.), *Therapeutic Communities for Offenders* (pp. 3–22). Chichester: Wiley.

Robertson, G., & Gunn, J. (1987). A ten-year follow-up of men discharged from Grendon prison. *The British Journal of Psychiatry*, 151, 674–678.

Robinson, J., & Smith, G. (1971). The effectiveness of correctional programs. *Crime and Delinquency*, 17, 67–80.

Ross, T., & Pfäfflin, F. (2007). Attachment and interpersonal problems in a prison environment. *Journal of Forensic Psychiatry and Psychology*, 18(1), 90–98.

Royal College of Psychiatrists (1999). *Offenders with Personality Disorder*. London: Royal College of Psychiatrists (CR71).

Rutter, D., & Crawford, M. (2005). The efficacy of therapeutic communities in the treatment of personality disorders. *Psychiatry*, 4(3), 19–22.

Rutter, M. (1971). Parent-child separation: Psychological effects on the children. *Journal of Child Psychology and Psychiatry*, 12, 233–260.

Ryle, A. (1997). *Cognitive Analytic Therapy and Borderline Personality Disorder: The Model and Method*. Chichester: Wiley.

Sapouna, M., Bisset, C., & Conlon, A.M. (2011). *What Works to Reduce Reoffending: A Summary of the Evidence*. Justice Analytical Service: The Scottish Government.

Shine, J., & Morris, M. (2000). Addressing criminogenic needs in a prison therapeutic community. *Therapeutic Communities*, 21(3), 197–220.

Shuker, R. (2010). The contribution of therapeutic communities as a forensic intervention: Recent developments and challenges over the past 25 years. Forensic Update Special 100th, 50–53.

Shuker, R., & Newton, M. (2008). Treatment outcome following intervention in a prison-based therapeutic community: A study of the relationship between reduction in criminogenic risk and improved psychological well-being. *The British Journal of Forensic Practice*, 10(3), 33–44.

Shuker, R., & Newberry, M. (2010). Changes in interpersonal relating following therapeutic community treatment at HMP Grendon. In E. Sullivan & R. Shuker (Eds.), *Grendon and the Emergence of Forensic Therapeutic Communities: Developments in research and practice* (pp. 293–304). Chichester: Wiley-Blackwell.

Shuker, R., & Sullivan, E. (Eds.) (2010). *Grendon and the Emergence of Forensic Therapeutic Communities: Developments in Research and Practice*. Chichester: Wiley.

Shumaker, S.A., & Taylor, R.B. (1983). Toward a clarification of people-place relationships: A model of attachment to place. In N.R. Feimer, & E.S. Geller (Eds.), *Environmental Psychology. Directions and Perspectives* (pp. 219–251). New York: Praeger.

Silk, K.R. (2000). Borderline personality disorder: Overview of biological factors. *Psychiatric Clinics of North America*, 23, 61–75.

Simkins, M. (2003). *What's My Motivation*. London: Ebury Press.

Simons, D.A., Wurtele, S.K., & Durham, R.L. (2008). Developmental experiences of child sexual abusers and rapists. *Child Abuse and Neglect*, 32, 549–560.

Simmonds, R. (2008). *Back to the Future? Accounts of Men Who Left a Prison Based Therapeutic Community and Returned to Mainstream Prisons; A Qualitative Study*. Guilford: Forensic Psychology Research Group, University of Surrey. Unpublished report.

Singleton, N., Meltzer, H., Gatward, R., Coid, J., & Deasy, D. (1998). *Psychiatric Morbidity among Prisoners in England and Wales*. London: Stationery Office.

Skeem, J.L., & Cooke, D.J. (2010). Is criminal behavior a central component of psychopathy? Conceptual directions for resolving the debate. *Psychological Assessment*, 22(2), 433–445.

Skett, S. (1995). What works in the reduction of offending behaviour. *Forensic Update*, 42, 20–27.

Smallbone, S.W., & Dadds, M.R. (1998). Childhood attachment and adult attachment in incarcerated adult male sex offenders. *Journal of Interpersonal Violence*, 13(5), 555–573.

Smartt, U. (2001). *Grendon Tales: Stories from a Therapeutic Community*. Hook: Waterside Press.

Smith, J.A. (1996a). Beyond the divide between cognition and discourse; using interpretative phenomenological analysis in health psychology. *Health Psychology*, 11(2), 261–271.

Smith, J. A. (1996b). Evolving issues for qualitative psychology. In J. Richardson (Ed.), *Handbook of Qualitative Research Methods* (pp. 189–202). Leicester: BPS.

Smith, J.A., Jarman, M., & Osborn, M. (1999). Doing interpretative phenomenological analysis. In M. Murray, & M.M.K. Chamberlain (Eds.), *Qualitative Health Psychology: Theories and Methods*. London: Sage.

Stephenson, R.M., & Scarpitti, F.R. (1968). Argot in a therapeutic correctional milieu. *Social Problems*, 15(3), 384–395.

Stewart, D.W., & Shamdasani, P.N. (1990). *Focus Groups: Theory and Practise*. Newbury Park, CA: Sage Publications.

Stewart-Ong, G., Harsent, L., Roberts, L., Burnett, R., & Al-Attar, Z. (2004). *Think First Prospective Research Study: Effectiveness and Reducing Attrition*. National Probation Service Programme Evaluation Findings. London: National Probation Service.

Stirpe, T., Abracen, J., Stermac, L., & Wilson, R. (2006). Sexual offenders' state-of-mind regarding childhood attachment: A controlled investigation. *Sexual Abuse: A Journal of Research and Treatment*, 18, 289–302.

Sullivan, E. (2011). Reflections on Grendon: interviews with men who are about the leave. In E. Shuker, & E. Sullivan (Eds.), *Grendon and the Emergence of Forensic Therapeutic Communities; Developments in Research and Practice* (pp. 185–202). Chichester: Wiley-Blackwell.

Tan, L. & Grace, R.C. (2008). Social desirability and sexual offenders: a review. *Sex Abuse*, 2(1), 61–87.

Tapp, J., Warren, F., Fife-Schaw, C., Perkins, D., & Moore, E. (2013). What do the experts by experience tell us about "what works" in high secure forensic inpatient hospital service? *The Journal of Forensic Psychiatry*, 24, 160–178.

Taylor, R. (2000). *A Seven Year Reconviction Study of HMP Grendon Therapeutic Community*. Home Office Research Findings (No. 115). London: Home Office.

Teddlie, C., & Tashakkori, A. (2003). Major issues and controversies in the use of mixed methods in the social and behavioural sciences. In A. Tashakkori & C. Teddlie (Eds.), *Handbook of Mixed Methods in Social and Behavioural Research*. Thousand Oaks: Sage.

Thompson, P. (2004). *The Transferability and Sustainability of Progress Made in a Prison Based Therapeutic Community: Three Case Studies*. Master's dissertation presented to the University of Surrey.

Thorne, J., & Paget, S. (Eds.) (2012). *Democratic Communities in Prisons: National Audit Report 2011–2012*. London: Association of Therapeutic Communities (Publication number CCQI126).

Thornton, D. (1987). Treatment effects on recidivism: A reappraisal of the "nothing works" doctrine. In B.J. McGurk, D. Thornton, & M. Williams (Eds.), *Applying Psychology to Imprisonment: Theory and Practice* (pp. 181–189). London: HMSO.

Torgerson, D., & Sibbald, B. (1998). Understanding controlled trials: What is a patient preference trial? *British Medical Journal*, 316(7128), 360.

Twigger-Ross, C., & Uzzell, D. (1996). Place and place identity process. *Journal of Environmental Psychology*, 16(3), 205–220.

Tyrer, P. (2001). Personality disorder. *British Journal of Psychiatry*, 179, 81–84.

Tyrer, P., Duggan, C., Cooper, S., Crawford, M., Seivewright, H., Rutter, D., Maden, T., Byford, S., & Barrett, B. (2010). The successes and failures of the DSPD experiment: The assessment and management of severe personality disorder. *Medicine, Science and the Law*, 50, 95–99.

Van Ijzendoorn, M.H., Feldbrugge, J.T.T.M., Derks, F.C.H., deRuiter, C., Verhagen, M.F.M., Philipse, M.A., Van der Staak, C., & Riksen-Walraven, J. (1997). Attachment representations of personality disordered criminal offenders. *American Journal of Orthopsychiatry*, 67, 449–459.

Vitaro, F., Brendgen, M., & Tremblay, R.E. (2000). Influence of deviant friends on delinquency: Searching for moderator variables. *Journal of Abnormal Child Psychology*, 28, 313–325.

Wakeling, H., & Travers, R. (2010). Evaluating offending behaviour programmes in prison. In J. Brown & E. Campbell (Eds.), *Cambridge Handbook of Forensic Psychology*. (pp. 820–829). Cambridge: CUP.

Walters, G.D. (2002). The Psychological Inventory of Criminal Thinking Styles (PICTS): A review and meta-analysis. *Assessment*, 9, 278–291.

Ward, T., Hudson, S.M., & Marshall, W.L. (1996). Attachment style in sex offenders: A preliminary study. *The Journal of Sex Research*, 33, 17–26.

Ward, T., Hudson, S. M., Marshall, W. L., & Siegert, R. J. (1995). Attachment style and intimacy deficits in sexual offenders: A theoretical framework. *Sexual Abuse: A Journal of Research and Treatment*, 7, 317–335.

Warren, F. (1994). What do we mean by therapeutic community for offenders? *International Journal of Therapeutic Communities*, 15(4), 312–318.

Warren, F., McGauley, G., Norton, K., Dolan, B., Preedy-Fayers, K., Pickering, A., & Geddes, J.R. (2003). *Review of Treatments for Severe Personality Disorder*. London: Home Office Report 30/03. http://www.homeoffice.gov.uk/rds/onlinepubs1.html. (accessed 20th May 2014).

Warren, F., Zaman, S., Dolan, B., Norton, K., & Evans, C. (2006). Eating disturbance and severe personality disorder: Outcome of specialist treatment for severe personality disorder. *European Eating Disorders Review*, 14, 69–78.

Warwick, L. (1991). *Probation Work with Sex Offenders*. Social work monographs, monograph 104, Norwich.

Waszak, C., & Sines, M.C. (2003). Mixed methods in psychological research. In A. Tashakkori & C. Teddlie (Eds.), *Handbook of Mixed Methods in Social and Behavioural Research* (pp. 557–576). Thousand Oaks, CA: Sage.

West, M., & George, C. (1999). Abuse and violence in intimate adult relationships: New perspectives from attachment theory. *Attachment and Human Development*, 1(2), 137–156.

Westen, D., Novotny, C.M., & Thompson-Brenner, K. (2004). The empirical status of empirically supported psychotherapies: Assumptions, findings, and reporting in controlled clinical trials. *Psychological Bulletin*, 130(4), 631–663.

Wexler, H.K. (2003). The promise of prison-based treatment for dually diagnosed inmates. *Journal of Substance Abuse Treatment*, 25, 223–231.

Wexler, H.K., Melnick, G., Lowe, L., & Peters, J. (1999). Three-year reincarceration outcomes for amity in-prison therapeutic community and aftercare in California. *The Prison Journal*, 79, 321–336

Whiteley, J.S. (1980). The Henderson Hospital: A community Study. *International Journal of Therapeutic Communities*, 1, 38–58.

Whiteley, S.J. (1997). Ethical issues in the therapeutic community. *Israel Journal of Psychiatry and Related Sciences*, 34(1), 18–25.

Widom, C.S. (1989). The cycle of violence. *Science*, 244, 160–166.

Wile, D. (1977). Ideological conflicts between clients and psychotherapists. *American Journal of Psychotherapy*, 37, 437–449.

Willig, C. (2001). *Introducing Qualitative Research in Psychology: Adventures in Theory and Method*. Berkshire: Open University Press.

Wilson, D., & McCabe, S. (2002). How HMP Grendon "Works" in the words of those undergoing therapy. *Howard Journal of Criminal Justice*, 41, 229–291.

Wilson, M., & Hammond, S. (2000). Structuring qualitative data using a scaling procedure. In G. Breakwell, S. Hammond, & C. Five-Schaw (Eds.), *Research Methods in Psychology*, 2nd Edn. (pp. 281–293). London: Sage Publications.

Wolff, N. (2000). Using randomized controlled trials to evaluate socially complex services: Problems, challenges and recommendations. *The Journal of Mental Health Policy and Economics*, 3, 97–109.

Wood, P. (2000). Meta-analysis. In G. Breakwell, S. Hammond, & C. Five-Schaw (Eds.), *Research Methods in Psychology*, 2nd Edn. (pp. 414–425). London: Sage Publications.

Woodward, R. (1999). The prison communities; therapy within a custodial setting. In P. Campling & R. Haigh (Eds.), *Therapeutic Communities: Past, Present and Future. Therapeutic Communities 2*. (pp. 162–173) London and Philadelphia: Jessica Kingsley Publishers Ltd.

Woodward, R. (2007). Symbiosis: Therapeutic communities in non therapeutic community organisations. In M. Parker (Ed.), *Dynamic Security: The Democratic Therapeutic Community in Prisons*. (pp. 222–231). London/New York: Jessica Kingsley Publishers.

Woodward, R. (2011). The director's tale: A search engine for meaning. In E. Cullen & J. MacKenzie, *Dovegate: A Therapeutic Community in a Private Prison and Developments in Therapeutic Work with Personality Disordered Offenders*. (pp. 127–154). Hook: Waterside Press.

Woodward, R., Cullen, C., Hemmings, M., Moore, C., Chekwas, E., Angeli, G., & Jameson, A. (2000). *Dovegate Therapeutic Community: Staff Training Manual*. London: Home Office

World Health Organization (1992). *The ICD-10 Classification of Mental and Behavioural Disorders*. Geneva: World Health Organization.

Worthington, R., & Atkinson, D. (1996). Effects of perceived etiology attribution similarity on clients ratings of counsellor credibility. *Journal of Counseling Psychology*, 43, 423–429.

Yalom, I.D. (1995). *Theory and Practice of Group Psychotherapy*. New York: Basic Books.

Zimmerman, M., Rothschild, L., & Chelminski, I. (2005). The prevalence of DSM-IV personality disorders in psychiatric outpatients. *American Journal of Psychiatry*, 162(10), 1911–1918.

Index

Note: Figures, Tables and Blocks in **bold**.

CPSIA information can be obtained
at www.ICGtesting.com
Printed in the USA
FSOW03n1241080416
18990FS

9 781137 306203